# Education *for a* Civil Society

## HOW GUIDANCE TEACHES YOUNG CHILDREN DEMOCRATIC LIFE SKILLS

**Dan Gartrell**

**National Association for the Education of Young Children, Washington DC**

National Association for the
Education of Young Children
1313 L Street NW, Suite 500
Washington, DC 20005-4101
202-232-8777 • 800-424-2460
www.naeyc.org

**NAEYC Books**

**Chief Publishing Officer**
*Derry Koralek*

**Editor-in-Chief**
*Kathy Charner*

**Director of Creative Services**
*Edwin C. Malstrom*

**Managing Editor**
*Mary Jaffe*

**Senior Editor**
*Holly Bohart*

**Design and Production**
*Malini Dominey*

**Assistant Editor**
*Elizabeth Wegner*

**Editorial Assistant**
*Ryan Smith*

Through its publications program, the National Association
for the Education of Young Children (NAEYC) provides a forum
for discussion of major issues
and ideas in the early childhood
field, with the hope of provoking
thought and promoting professional growth. The views expressed or implied in this book
are not necessarily those of the
Association or its members.

**Text Permissions and Credits**

Portions of text on pages 79–82, 83–84, 88–89, 103, 104, 105, and 106 and anecdotes on
pages 83–84, 85–86, 89, 92–93, 94, 131–132, and 140–141 are from D. Gartrell, *A Guidance
Approach for the Encouraging Classroom,* 5th ed., © 2011 Wadsworth, a part of Cengage
Learning, Inc. Reproduced by permission. www.cengage.com/permissions.

Portions of text on pages 107–108 are from D. Gartrell, *The Power of Guidance: Teaching
Social-Emotional Skills in Early Childhood Classrooms,* 1st ed., © 2004 Wadsworth, a part
of Cengage Learning, Inc. Reproduced by permission. www.cengage.com/permissions.

Portions of text on pages 78, 79, and 83 are adapted from *Exchange* magazine, July/
August 2010; www.ChildCareExchange.com.

Portions of text on pages 114–115, 129–130, and 137–138 are adapted from D. Gartrell,
*What the Kids Said Today: Using Classroom Conversations to Become a Better Teacher,*
© 2000 Daniel Gartrell. Published by Redleaf Press.

**Photo Credits**
Copyright © by: Bob Ebbesen: 36, 41, 96, 113; Julia Luckenbill: 64; Karen Phillips: 49, 70,
131; Ellen B. Senisi: cover (right), 9, 18, 23, 31, 38, 42, 53, 58, 60, 62, 65, 75, 79, 82, 85, 88,
90, 97, 100, 102, 109, 111, 115, 118, 120, 123, 124, 135, 136, 139, 140, 143, 145, 147, 150;
Thinkstock: 47, 51, 68.
Copyright © NAEYC: Peg Callaghan: cover (left and middle), 1, 3, 31, 45, 127; Rich
Graessle: 54, 77; Susan Woog Wagner: 106.

Cover design: J. Michael Myers

Editorial assistance: Stacey Reid

Library of Congress Control Number: 2012944235
ISBN: 978-1-928896-87-6
NAEYC Item #356

# About the Author

**Dan Gartrell** started his career in education as a teacher at an inner-city elementary school in Ohio and later taught in the Head Start program of the Red Lake Band of Ojibwe in Minnesota. He holds a doctorate in teacher education/early childhood and is Professor Emeritus of Early Childhood and Foundations Education at Bemidji State University in Minnesota. As former director of Bemidji's Child Development Training Program, a CDA trainer, and a student teaching supervisor, he has helped scores of students start their journey to becoming excellent educators.

Once introduced at a conference as "the guidance guy," Dan has spoken extensively on using guidance with young children and related topics. He writes the Guidance Matters column in NAEYC's journal, *Young Children,* and has contributed several additional articles to the journal. The sixth edition of his textbook on guidance, *A Guidance Approach for the Encouraging Classroom*, will be forthcoming in 2013. Dan has also written *The Power of Guidance: Teaching Social-Emotional Skills to Young Children* and *What the Kids Said Today.*

Dan and his wife, Dr. Julie Jochum, live in Minnesota. The 11 grandchildren in their blended family know Dan as the grandpa who tells friendly jokes and makes pretty good "papadanpancakes" (the secret is strawberry yogurt in the batter). He enjoys nature photography and being outdoors in the north woods and on the lake near Bemidji, Minnesota.

## Acknowledgments

First, I would like to thank the staff, children, and families of Mahube Head Start, centered in Detroit Lakes, northwest Minnesota. Serving as a staff coach, I benefitted greatly from the grounding and support they gave me over the two years this book was in writing and editing. Three Mahube staff members provided model teaching for the enhanced ebook that is based on Part Three of this book, and the collegiality and professionalism shown by all is reflected, I hope, in these pages. For the anecdotes that occur throughout the book, I greatly thank the Mahube staff along with scores of former students, most of whom are now successful teachers in Minnesota and many other states.

Also, I would like to thank the editorial staff at NAEYC who stayed the marathon and worked with me to turn my original, folksy magnum opus (including, I must say, more humor) into a leaner and cleaner exposition of the democratic life skills. In particular, I would like to thank Senior Editor Holly Bohart, Assistant Editor Elizabeth Wegner, Chief Publishing Officer Derry Koralek, Editor-in-Chief Kathy Charner, Managing Editor Mary Jaffe, Editorial Assistant Ryan Smith, and former Editorial Director Bry Pollack. Thanks also go to Akimi Gibson, former Editor-in-Chief, for her initial receptiveness to the idea.

My wife, for her unwavering support and acceptance of my endless writing, and our 11 grandkids for who they are and will be, also deserve my unconditional acknowledgment for their inspiration and love. And to young children, past, present, and future, this book is for you.

## Dedication

To the spirit of the early childhood community at
Bemidji State University

**Contents**

# Foundations

# 1

# A New Education for Civility

I write this book at a time when the need for civility, for mutually respectful communication, and for ethical interactions between and among groups has never been more acute. To sustain a promising future for our children and grandchildren, individuals and groups need to find ways to work cooperatively and respectfully. Hope for improved civility and dialogue, in my view, lies as much in the hearts and minds of the young as it does with us adults. The questions for me have become these: What kind of education fosters the nascent capacities in young children to reach out and listen to those different from themselves? What will lead them to work together to address problems with solutions that are both intelligent and ethical?

To answer these questions for myself, I have looked to the democratic traditions in education and to individual social, behavioral, and developmental psychologists. These experts hold a shared belief that we are just beginning to understand the miracle of human potential. The path for the future lies in learning how the development of human potential unfolds and nurturing that development as respectfully as possible. My hope is that readers as well will find this shared meaning from these sources, as discussed in the book.

**DLS 1: Finding acceptance as a member of the group and as a worthy individual**

**DLS 2: Expressing strong emotions in non-hurting ways**

**DLS 3: Solving problems creatively—independently and in cooperation with others**

**DLS 4: Accepting unique human qualities in others**

**DLS 5: Thinking intelligently and ethically**

Those familiar with my writing know that my usual focus is classroom **guidance.** By guidance I mean a way of teaching that nurtures each child's potential through consistently positive (sometimes firm, but always friendly) interactions. Over the years, partial expressions of the ideas in this book have appeared in my textbook, *A Guidance Approach for the Encouraging Classroom* (sixth edition, forthcoming), and in Guidance Matters, my column in the National Association for the Education of Young Children (NAEYC) journal, *Young*

**guidance:** a way of teaching that nurtures each child's potential through consistently positive (sometimes firm, but always friendly) interactions; classroom management that teaches rather than punishes

*Children.* For the first time, the ideas are linked together in a coordinated thesis that civility, through the development of the five democratic life skills (I'll discuss these in a bit), can and should be taught and learned.

In the past, writers have referred to education that takes this viewpoint as *teaching for the whole child.* More recently, descriptions of this education reflect findings from neuroscience—*education for the healthy formation of executive function*—and the understanding that intelligence is multifaceted: *education for multiple intelligences* (Gardner 2006). Such an approach to education balances support for cognitive development with emotional, social, and physical development. Thus, teachers educate not just so children can acquire knowledge that can be measured by tests, but also so children can build the skills needed for intelligent and ethical functioning in modern democratic society. This kind of education happens in classrooms in which teachers implement developmentally appropriate practices.

## Where the Author Comes From

Almost 50 years ago, after graduating from university, my first teaching assignment was in the sixth grade of an inner-city school in Ohio. On the first day of orientation, the principal issued paddles to every teacher. I didn't take one. Corporal punishment was the way of that school, however, and I worked with sixth-graders who had known paddling for years. I made it through the year, but I could not be the teacher I wanted to be in that school and moved on.

**progressive education:** forward-looking education that respects diversity and educates the whole child; that balances the needs of the developing child with academics; and that focuses on development that advances children's ability to learn in the context of a democratic community

For the next few years I taught preschoolers enrolled in the Head Start program of the Red Lake Band of Ojibwe in northern Minnesota. Red Lake is one of very few closed Native American reservations, meaning the tribe holds all land in trust for its members and the land cannot be bought or sold. With the assistance of my colleagues, I learned about the culture of the families we served and what life was like in the untamed nature of the north woods. As best we could, we incorporated this knowledge into the education program.

Together, these two formative teaching experiences gave rise to my long-term commitment to the practice of guidance and to the field of early childhood education. Later, I consolidated that commitment as I taught adults who teach young children. First as a trainer of Child Development Associate (CDA) candidates, then when I was supervising student teachers, and recently while serving as a staff coach for a Head Start program, I have kept my experience with young children, their teachers, and their families fresh. My respect for the learning potential of every child has been ever renewed.

> I will always remember the children in my Head Start class, and in particular Virgil and Karen. On a breezy summer day Virgil patiently explained to me that the wind happens because the "trees push the air. The leaves are fans, of course." The following winter Karen drew Rudolph the red-nosed reindeer with a yellow nose "so Santa can see better." This 4-year-old improved on the whole Rudolph concept.

A long career in teaching and writing has given me an enduring perspective on the connection of **progressive education**—education of the whole child, with academics kept in appropriate balance—to social reform. That still-developing perspective has led to this book.

## The Democratic Life Skills

For a long-lasting solution to the issue of incivility in modern life, it is time to look anew at the social and cultural purposes of schooling. Education that prepares the whole child for modern, democratic society incorporates the best practices of early childhood education. Under the umbrella term popularized by NAEYC, **developmentally appropriate**

**practice** (see Copple & Bredekamp 2009), three aspects essential in meeting the needs of all children are particularly relevant to promoting the democratic life skills:

- Reciprocal and respectful family-teacher partnerships
- Curriculum and teaching methods aligned with principles of child (and brain) development
- Teacher-child interactions and relationships that guide children toward prosocial behaviors (the practice of guidance as opposed to discipline)

The goals of progressive education constitute five social-emotional skills that together illustrate a comprehensive, contemporary concept of civility. These **democratic life skills** (DLS) are the emotional and social capacities individuals need to function civilly in our modern, diverse, and complex democratic society. The skills are:

1. Finding acceptance as a member of the group and as a worthy individual

2. Expressing strong emotions in non-hurting ways

3. Solving problems creatively—independently and in cooperation with others

4. Accepting unique human qualities in others

5. Thinking intelligently and ethically

The highest of the skills, the ability to think intelligently and ethically, defines the core of civility.

The strength of the early childhood education field is that it is widely researched and its best practices are continually vetted (see Part Two). Teachers support young children's acquisition of developmentally appropriate emerging academic skills—as well as the social-emotional capacities that constitute the development of the democratic life skills. An education that teaches the ability *and* a willingness to engage in literacy, numeracy, scientific inquiry, artistic expression, and physical activity—in concert with the five social-emotional skills—has much to offer. Further, as shown in Part Two, early childhood education's best practices have documented, unmatched promise as an approach for what education at all levels should be.

## Toward Civil Democracy

One way of looking at our diverse society is as the continual interaction of independently functioning groups of every kind: families; classroom and school communities; civic, religious, and recreational clusters; business, service, and professional structures; political entities; and cultural and ethnic groups. Education that teaches children the skills they need to be contributing members of a civil society begins with classroom communities that embrace inclusive—mutually respectful—communication.

Of course, I do not suggest a blind equality among all members of any given group, including in the classroom. Families have parents or parent surrogates. Businesses have managers. Corporations have executives. Unions have presidents. Organizations have directors. Classrooms have teachers. Civility means that intelligent and ethical communication occurs vertically within groups, a prerequisite for cooperation and collaboration across memberships in groups to come. When the members of differing social groups find common ground they are able to cooperate and to create and implement sustainable solutions to the vexing problems of the day.

Education for a civil society models these principles for straightforward but friendly communication both within and across the diverse groups of society. We progressive early childhood educators view the role of schools as preparing citizens for the only form of political society in which all individuals have equal opportunity to actualize their

**developmentally appropriate practice (DAP):** an approach to teaching that is grounded in how young children develop and learn and in what is known about effective early education

**democratic life skills (DLS):** the emotional and social capacities individuals need to function civilly in modern, diverse, and complex democratic society

**civility:** intelligent and ethical communication among individuals within and across groups

potential: one that has a rich mix of diverse, democratic communities. Through modeling as well as other teaching strategies, teachers can educate young children to connect with and extend these communities in civil but responsive ways.

Now, to think that society can be transformed by a new education for a civil democracy in my lifetime or even yours would be . . . you supply the adjective. I write this book to make the case for democratic (thus prosocial and developmentally appropriate) education for learners of all ages, which will, over time, lead to a more civil democracy.

## In Three Parts

The book has three parts: Foundations, The Early Childhood Lead, and Teaching for the Democratic Life Skills. The democratic life skills are introduced in Part One, expanded on in Part Two, and form the entirety of Part Three. Each of the chapter-essays explores a topic relating to the need to educate for civility.

### Part One: Foundations

Part One establishes the educational and psychological foundations for an education to promote civility. Chapter 2 documents the progressive tradition in education, with profiles of Johan Comenius, Friedrich Froebel, Maria Montessori, and John Dewey. Chapter 3 explores the psychology of the democratic life skills with profiles of interesting, visionary, courageous intellects who have furthered our understanding about the connection between humane education in childhood and civil living by adults.

The final chapter in Part One addresses the neuroscience of nurturing relationships. This material is essential to the new education for civility because it highlights the importance of children's early relationships, including those with teachers. Nurturing relationships help children manage stress levels, kindle mastery motivation (interest in learning for its own sake), and support executive function skills.

### Part Two: The Early Childhood Lead

Part Two presents conditions necessary for teaching the democratic life skills. The theme developed in Part Two is that guidance (and thus teaching for the democratic life skills) is possible only through the use of developmentally appropriate practice.

Chapter 5 makes the case that best practices in early childhood education point the way for what education at all levels should be. Chapter 6 discusses why family-school partnerships are at the heart of education for a civil democracy. Chapter 7 explores the meaning of developmentally appropriate practice for progressive education. When developmentally appropriate practices are in place, curriculum tends to emerge from the interests and life experiences of the classroom community, with the teacher serving as mediator between children's life experiences and the educational standards for the program.

Chapters 8 and 9 address the practice of guidance with the group and with the individual child. The final chapter in Part Two discusses including every child, particularly active boys and children vulnerable for stigma.

### Part Three: Teaching for the Democratic Life Skills

Chapter 11 provides an overview of the democratic life skills and addresses the hierarchical order of learning the skills. (Gaining the safety-needs skills, 1 and 2, must precede attainment of the growth-needs skills, 3, 4, and 5.)

The next five chapters focus on the democratic life skills. Each chapter explains one of the democratic life skills, provides behavioral indicators that document progress toward gaining the skill, includes a composite case study of young children in the process of learning the skill, and concludes with a list of teaching practices that promote each skill's development. I make the case that adults should teach *for* the democratic life skills rather than try to directly teach them. The skills are developmental capacities within a child's developing mind and can be nurtured and fostered, but not directly taught.

**Chapter 12: Democratic Life Skill 1: Finding Acceptance as a Member of the Group and as a Worthy Individual.** DLS 1 has to do with the ability of the child to develop secure attachments with significant adults, the foundational emotional acceptance that each child needs in the home and classroom for progress with the other skills.

**Chapter 13: Democratic Life Skill 2: Expressing Strong Emotions in Non-Hurting Ways.** This capacity is both foundational to the child's ability to transition toward the three remaining democratic life skills and fundamental to the individual's ability to sustain all five skills through life.

**Chapter 14: Democratic Life Skill 3: Solving Problems Creatively—Independently and in Cooperation with Others.** The chapter explores how meeting the early democratic life skills, DLS 1 and DLS 2, enables children to develop both *individual* and *cooperative* problem-solving skills.

**Chapter 15: Democratic Life Skill 4: Accepting Unique Human Qualities in Others.** DLS 4 builds upon creative problem solving but is a more generalized capacity of the developing mind. Moving past feeling "this person is not like me" to relating in friendly ways to individuals of whatever human qualities is a capacity most of us adults still work on.

**Chapter 16: Democratic Life Skill 5: Thinking Intelligently and Ethically.** Some readers might reasonably argue that young children, due to limitations in life experience and brain development, cannot rise to DLS 5. But Piaget argued that although young children cannot reason about prosocial actions, they can act prosocially (Piaget [1932] 1960). In his theory of multiple intelligences (discussed in Chapter 3), Howard Gardner also makes the case that intrapersonal and interpersonal intelligences can and should be cultivated in young children—and can be seen in their behaviors.

**Chapter 17: Education for a Civil Society.** Chapter 17 provides a recommendation for bringing the democratic life skills into American educational practice. This concluding chapter suggests what can result when more citizens understand the need to intentionally educate the young to apply civil action—intelligent and ethical decision making—in their daily lives.

## Anecdotes . . . and a Sprinkling of Humor

Many readers know that I begin each Guidance Matters column with an anecdote, a brief account of something that took place in an early childhood classroom. Similarly, anecdotes also appear throughout this book. The following classic involves a child who swears, and his befuddled teacher.

Early in my first year of teaching Head Start, whenever 4-year-old Joey got upset he said, "Damnit to hell." I found a quiet moment with Joey and we discussed the situation. I explained that we all get upset sometimes and that is okay, but the words he was using bothered people at Head Start. I gave him a significant nod and told him whenever he got upset, he could say "Ding-dong it" instead. Those would be all-right words to use.

The next day Joey came into the classroom, got upset about something, and declared, "Ding-dong it. Damnit to hell!" I had just increased his vocabulary! My assistant almost fell off her chair laughing, and I did some re-teaching with Joey, trying to contain my grin.

Over the years, from experiences like this, I have learned at least three lessons. First, it is important to have a friendly sense of humor, whether dealing with people big or small. Situations in early childhood classrooms rarely go exactly as we expect, and, whenever we can, we should try to enjoy the moment.

Second, we teachers at any level learn even as we teach (an absolute necessity when we are teaching for the democratic life skills).

Third, never underestimate the abilities of young learners, especially their ability to increase their vocabularies!

I hope readers find these three lessons helpful as we make our way together through the ideas in the book.

# Education for Democracy: The Progressive Tradition

G oing back to the early 1600s, there have been educators who challenged widely held views of their times that worked against children's best interests. These progressive educators put their reputations and sometimes their lives on the line to contest child labor practices that prevented children from attending school as well as beliefs that entire groups of children (because of gender, social class, or ethnicity) did not need school, that it was unnecessary for all but a privileged few.

In this chapter we look at four farsighted reformers who, in the face of social forces largely unsympathetic to the very idea of childhood as a distinct stage of human development, saw education as a way to implement democratic ideals. I've selected these educators not so much for the specific practices they advocated, but for the integrity with which they actualized their visions. The educators are Johan Comenius, Friedrich Froebel, Maria Montessori, and John Dewey.

Through fundamentally progressive education, these individuals sought to build democratic traditions in their countries that would lead to an equalizing of long-standing inequities. The view that every child, given an appropriate education, can benefit from and contribute to democratic society is their legacy.

## Johan Comenius: Early Proponent of Humane Education

During the seventeenth century, the time in which he lived, Johan Comenius was greatly influenced by Bacon in the field of science, Descartes in philosophy, and Luther in religion. Like these giants, Comenius brought seminal ideas to his field of education, influencing thought and practice to this day. Comenius was a classic man for all seasons—a Protestant cleric, scholar, philosopher, educator, and linguist.

## An Arduous Childhood

Born in 1592 in Moravia, a region in the east of what is now the Czech Republic, Comenius was raised in the Protestant faith of the Moravian Brotherhood. Comenius became an orphan when his father died in 1602 and his mother a short time later. Young Comenius survived poverty, strict religious schooling, and severe headmasters to become ordained as a minister and recognized as an educator and a scholar.

Even among Protestants, Comenius was persecuted for the views of his particular sect. Comenius was a religious refugee of the Thirty Years' War between Catholics and Protestants for much of his adult life, moving with his family among several European countries.

## An Educator for All Seasons

As Froebel did 200 years later, Comenius turned difficult life circumstances into an approach to education that was humane and progressive. His lasting contributions were both to everyday practice and the theory of education. As to practice, Comenius served as a rector to schools in at least three communities where he was a religious leader between 1614 (at the age of 22) and 1638. In 1638 he began a new phase of his career, advising governments in Sweden and England on his innovative ideas about coordinated education systems. He believed that boys and girls from all walks of life deserved an education.

Comenius was an early proponent of the view that humans develop in stages, to which education at different age levels should respond. In 1628 he wrote *Informatory of the Mother's School,* which emphasized informal teaching in the home, right from the cradle, through conversation, stories, and songs. He also authored *Orbis Pictus* (1658), the first illustrated children's book, which remained in use for more than 200 years—along with many other textbooks for children. An accomplished linguist, Comenius translated his books into several different languages.

As to theory, in *The Great Didactic* ([1638] 1896) Comenius set out a complete approach to an education that was the first directed to the whole, naturally developing child. He wrote other philosophical works as well, including an attempt at an organized collection of all human knowledge. This was destroyed along with most of his library when the Thirty Years' War reached his home in Lissa, Poland, in 1657.

## A Rediscovered Legacy

The major educational contributions of Comenius help us to chart the tradition of progressive education and frame its essential ideas. With *The Great Didactic* (Comenius [1638] 1896) as my chief reference, I outline these contributions and their lasting impact on democratic traditions in education.

- ◆ **Nature of the child.** In the seventeenth century students were seen as basically wayward, and were expected to show acquiescence and obedience to schoolmasters. Students who showed any sign of disagreement or defiance had "the devil beaten out of them" through various forms of corporal punishment, the most extreme being flogging.

    Comenius, in contrast, considered children to be good, like all things created by God, or to at least have the potential to become good through the redemption of a humane education. He likened the brain of the child to still-warm wax that needed to be impressed with care (215). (He emphasized that older wax could not be so worked.) Of the mother's work as first teacher, Comenius wrote: "The greatest care must be taken of children, God's most precious gift" (5). Comenius's appreciation of every child as having a natural ability to grow and learn (with adult nurturing) remains a tenet of progressive education today.

◆ **Nature of the learning process.** Comenius saw a natural learning process flowing from the development of the child that should follow four 6-year periods or stages: early childhood, middle childhood, adolescence, and young adult. He regarded the inability of a child to learn at any stage as a failure of the teacher, whose job it was to relate curriculum to children in ways they could understand (290). Comenius stressed that all learning, including that which takes place outdoors, happens through the senses, and that the natural state of childhood is busy-ness, to be encouraged through play as well as work. Books were to illustrate ideas that children could relate to in their everyday lives—like the books that Comenius himself created.

◆ **Who can be educated.** Comenius argued that "Not the boys of the rich or the powerful only, but of all alike, both boys and girls, both noble and ignoble, rich and poor, in cities and towns, villages and hamlets, should be sent to school" (218). Chapter 9 of *The Great Didactic,* titled "All the Young of Both Sexes Should Be Sent to School," develops this argument. The time was not right for Comenius to fully implement this principle in the schools for which he was rector, but he was the first to bring public attention to this tenet of universal education.

◆ **The use of discipline.** In Comenius's day, discipline was strict and what Keatinge, in his introduction to Comenius's work, described as widely abusive of the boys in attendance. Comenius advocated for a far different type of education; "This education will be conducted without blows, [undue] rigour, or compulsion, as gently and pleasantly as possible, and in the most natural manner (233). . . . In a word, if [teachers] treat their pupils kindly, they will easily win their affections, and will bring it about that they prefer going to school than remaining at home (283)." The schools of Comenius were not completely free of punishment, but he brought forward the discussion, consistent in progressive education ever since, that there are better ways to teach and to manage behaviors than to rely on punishment. Comenius clearly stated that goodness as a virtue is taught principally through adult example.

The educational practices advocated by Comenius were centuries before his time. In his introduction to Comenius's monumental work ([1635] 1896), Keatinge lamented that education reformers in the nineteenth century would have benefitted greatly from more access to the work of Comenius.

Comenius, like Froebel and Montessori after him, was devoutly religious. All three saw the being (soul) of the child in a dynamic, spiritual state of development, a transcendental interpretation of Judeo-Christian theology. This essentially optimistic religious philosophy merged with the psychology of human development early in the twentieth century—a line of thought that follows through to progressive education today.

## Friedrich Froebel: How the Kindergarten Came to Be

During the nineteenth century, Friedrich Froebel renewed the vision of Comenius that schooling, including early education, could be a progressive social force. While his kindergarten movement proved too democratic for authoritarian Prussian governments during the first half of the century, kindergarten became a worldwide trend in the second half.

## Froebel's Beginnings

Born in Oberweissbach, Germany, in 1782, Froebel excelled at academics despite difficult family circumstances. His mother died while he was young. His father, a minister already distant from his son, married a woman who never accepted Friedrich into the new family. During his childhood Friedrich educated himself through a combination of attending an informal community school, reading on his own, and continually studying nature.

Despite his trying childhood, Froebel's intelligent character came through. On his own, the young man gained admission to the University of Jena. His immersion in the intellectual culture there affirmed his continued development toward *transcendental idealism*. This view, shared by other social reformers of the time, held that individuals learn through their senses and grow in mind toward individual self-consciousness and a universal truth of spiritual unity with God (Blow 1908). Transcendental idealism provided a basis for Froebel's forward social thinking and guided his ideas about education.

After his program at Jena, Froebel found a position in one of Pestalozzi's progressive schools in Switzerland. Pestalozzi, an Italian educator, was greatly influenced by naturalistic (child-centered) developmental views popular among intellects of the time. Froebel's autobiography (1889) includes this telling comment about his vision of himself as an educator, made during this period:

> It seemed I found something I had never known, but always longed for, always missed; as if my life had at last discovered its native element. I felt happy as the fish in water, the bird in the air. (58)

## The Kindergarten

Beginning in 1817, Froebel founded an educational institute that continued for several years. Although it proved popular, from the beginning officials persecuted Froebel's program for being too liberal. Despite political oppression that followed him throughout his life, Froebel's genius was that he was able to link his deeply held philosophy with the operation of educational institutions that adapted to the ways young children learn.

Froebel established the first *kindergarten* ("children's garden") in Bäd Blankenburg in eastern Germany. Intended for children ages 3 to 6, the kindergarten quickly became popular with German middle-class families in the region and surrounding German states (Shapiro 1983). The kindergarten, a stand-alone preprimary school (now often called an *infant school* in Europe), tied together Froebel's transcendental Christian philosophy, his keen observations about the developing child, and materials and activities that accommodated young children's learning characteristics (Weber 1969).

Children in the kindergarten used materials Froebel himself invented, called *gifts* and *occupations*. Even infants could begin to use the first gifts, and children as old as 6 engaged with the advanced occupations. Froebel's innovations extended to the daily program; he initiated time blocks for hands-on learning activities, outdoor play, and circle time. During circle time children sang songs, heard stories, and did finger plays. Although children and teachers have enjoyed circle time as a predictable period of pleasant, social learning activities within the context of the group for more than 170 years (Weber 1969), it was a radical departure from schooling practices of the time.

Froebel saw the kindergarten as a program that would allow for a transition between learning at the mother's knee and the demanding nature of the German primary school (Froebel [1826] 1887). Rote learning from textbooks, the basis of the typical elementary school curriculum at the time, was not part of Froebel's program. Instead, Froebel saw structured play, what today we might call focused engagement with manipulatives, as central to the kindergarten philosophy.

About play, Froebel writes: "Play is the purest, most spiritual activity of man at this stage, and, at the same time, typical of human life as a whole....It gives joy, freedom, contentment, inner and outer rest, peace with the world" (Froebel [1826] 1887, 55). Froebel envisioned that through play, children could transcend the immediacy of childhood and grasp an awareness of what they might become.

Through his unique perspective on hands-on learning, Froebel added to our understanding about developmental sequences in learning. In his words, "The A, B, C of things must precede the A, B, C of words, and give to the words (abstractions) their true foundations" (Froebel [1826] 1887, 30). In current times, with instructional experiences in many schools reduced to the two-dimensional—abstractions on paper and computer screens—many educators can still learn from the philosopher's vision.

## The Goodness of Children

Froebel saw a God-given spiritual dynamic within children as the prime source of motivation to learn. Like Pestalozzi, Froebel considered children as essentially good, though vulnerable to negative influence by others (Blow 1908). Froebel ([1826] 1887) discusses this idea:

> It is certainly a great truth that it generally is some other human being, not unfrequently the educator himself, that first makes the child bad. This is accomplished by attributing evil—or at least wrong—motives to all that the child does from ignorance, social participation, or even from a keen and praiseworthy sense of right or wrong. . . . Punishment very often teaches children, or at least brings to their notice, faults of which they were wholly free. (106–107)

Froebel decried the then-common use of corporal punishment and public shaming in schools (Froebel [1826] 1887). His rejection of forced compliance to a rote, academic curriculum is echoed in today's educational reformers, those who speak out against a continued reliance in some American schools on corporal punishment, suspensions, and the push-out phenomenon—in which students who feel educators have rejected them as failures drop out of school (Children's Defense Fund 2011; Khadaroo 2010). Froebel maintained that if methods and curriculum were responsive to the development of the individual learner, most discipline problems would be prevented. Froebel clearly provided foundations for the guidance techniques used since by progressive educators.

## Froebel's Vision

Acknowledging persistent Prussian repression of his programs, Froebel wrote in 1826 that America might be a more hospitable climate for the kindergarten. By 1851, kindergartens throughout Germany, as well as Froebel's fledgling teacher-training institute, were forced to close. In 1856, four years after Froebel's death, Carl and Margarethe Schurz started the first American kindergarten in their home in Watertown, Wisconsin. While the first kindergartens in the United States were German speaking, run by German immigrants for their children, the idea of the kindergarten caught on. By the mid-1870s kindergartens were becoming part of public school systems in the Midwest. By 1890, 5,000 kindergartens flourished across the United States (Osborn 1991).

By the end of World War I the kindergarten had become largely Americanized—less spiritual and more geared to children's everyday lives (Ross 1976). Although still subject to opposing viewpoints by those who advocate a more academic program, on the one hand, and those who support a more developmentally appropriate curriculum on the other, kindergartens remain perhaps the most widespread example of the advance of progressive education in American schools (Ross 1976; Shapiro 1983). The effect of the kindergarten's coming to America has been progressive reform at all levels of schooling.

Osborn (1991) reported that in 1871 Superintendent William Harris accepted Susan Blow's offer to begin a kindergarten program in the St. Louis, Missouri, school system. Blow volunteered to do so without pay. After studying Froebel's kindergarten approach in New York, the "kindergarten crusader" returned to St. Louis where she recruited, trained, and directed several new teachers. The kindergartens Blow implemented in St. Louis were the first reported public school kindergartens in the country. When Harris resigned in 1874, the new superintendent reassigned the kindergarten program under the elementary education supervisors. Fearing the program would become overly academic, Blow and her followers resigned. The academic-versus-whole-child debate around kindergarten continues to this day.

Froebel envisioned an education process in accord with what he considered to be the natural pattern of human development beginning in the young child. In his vision, from an inclusive classroom community come enlightened citizens who invigorate democratic society. Froebel's vision, in harmony with that of Comenius 200 years earlier, provides a direction for progressive education to this day.

## Maria Montessori: Educating for Self-Discipline

Maria Montessori was born in 1870, 88 years after Froebel, and just as the struggle to unify the Italian states ended and Italy as we know it came to be. Unlike Comenius and Froebel, whose mothers died while they were young, Maria had a strong and lasting relationship with her mother, Renilde. Kramer (1988) recounts that the relationship no doubt contributed to Maria's self-confidence, inner strength, and indomitable will. She needed these qualities. Comenius and Froebel before her had faced political turmoil; Montessori dealt with the lifelong challenge of being a modern woman in male-dominated, tradition-bound Italian culture (Standing [1959] 1988).

### Montessori the Physician

When Maria was 12 her family moved from a small town to Rome. There she enrolled in public school and then continued her studies at a technological institute, unheard of for a female at the time. Studying the biological sciences convinced Montessori that she wanted to become a doctor. Her father, however, opposed her going to medical school, which was the unquestioned domain of male students (Kramer 1988; Standing [1959] 1988). A retired military officer, her father instead encouraged her to pursue teaching. Both Standing and Kramer indicate that "candid" family discussion occurred around this issue; with Maria's mother supporting her, the vote was two to one.

In 1890 the director of the University of Rome Medical School turned down Montessori's initial application to enroll (Kramer 1988). Undeterred, Montessori gained entry to another University of Rome program in math and the sciences. Obtaining her degree in this program with honors two years later, she again applied to the medical school. On the basis of having earned the earlier degree, along with the probable (though not verified) intercession of Pope Leo XIII, she was accepted, becoming the country's first female medical student (Kramer 1988).

As part of the lore about Montessori in medical school, Standing ([1959] 1988) tells of an elderly professor who related that during a freak Rome snowstorm, Montessori was the only student to make it to campus for his lecture (which the professor nonetheless gave). Another story is that Montessori had to wait until the 99 male medical students entered the lecture hall of a particular professor before she was allowed to take her seat. Overcoming gender bias, Montessori won awards and scholarships, paid her tuition by tutoring, astounded a ten-physician panel with her capstone dissertation, and graduated with almost perfect scores on the final examinations (Kramer 1988; Standing [1959] 1988).

## From Physician to Educator

The Montessori Australia Foundation (2011) recounts how Maria found her calling in the two years after medical school:

> Montessori's involvement with the National League for the Education of Retarded Children led to her appointment as co-director, with Guisseppe Montesano, of a new institution called the Orthophrenic School. The school took children with a broad spectrum of disorders and proved to be a turning point in Montessori's life, marking a shift in her professional identity from physician to educator. (Montessori Australia 2011)

Over the next decade, Montessori refined her educational philosophy through study and clinical work that included inventing her well-known materials for supporting children's independently guided learning. In 1907, when developers in Rome renovated a housing complex for low-income families, they approached Montessori to develop a program for the children who were left to themselves while their parents were working (Kramer 1988).

Montessori accepted the proposal and started the first *Casa dei Bambini,* or "Children's House," which later would be replicated not only in Italy but in many other European countries (Kramer 1988; Standing [1959] 1988). As the Montessori Australia Foundation (2011) reports,

> By the autumn of 1908 there were five Case dei Bambini operating, four in Rome and one in Milan. Children in a Casa dei Bambini made extraordinary progress, and soon 5-year-olds were writing and reading. News of Montessori's new approach spread rapidly, and visitors arrived to see for themselves how she was achieving such results. Within a year the Italian-speaking part of Switzerland began transforming its kindergartens into Case dei Bambini, and the spread of the new educational approach began. (Montessori Australia 2010)

## The Montessori Method Spreads in Europe

For a few years before World War I, the Montessori Method swept the United States, and Maria's book of that title became a national bestseller. As war loomed, however, policy makers came to disparage Montessori's approach as foreign and therefore un-American (Standing [1959] 1988). Some American psychologists regarded as outdated and naïve her theory that intelligence could be nurtured by rich teaching during the sensitive periods of early childhood (Kramer 1988). Perhaps Montessori's approach was just too forward looking for the America of the time. Only a few years after the introduction of the Montessori Method in the United States, most American educators turned against the approach and remained so until the 1960s (Kramer 1988). It would be 50 years before the Montessori Method again gained popularity in the United States, with the rise of Head Start and growing acceptance of early childhood education (Lillard 1998).

During the 1930s, before World War II, emerging Fascist governments in Germany, Italy, and Spain found Montessori programs too progressive and shut them down (Kramer 1988). Montessori was burned in effigy in Germany and expelled from both Italy and Spain. After being mistakenly arrested in India and then released, Montessori and her son, Mario, trained thousands of teachers there in her method until the war ended.

Montessori's books and approach remained popular in Europe, however (Standing [1959] 1988). In 1917, with her son, Mario, and his family, she moved to Barcelona, where the city established a center for the study of child development (Seminari-Laboratori de Pedagogia) for her. With the move, Montessori switched her base of operations from Italy to Spain. By 1924, Montessori schools and societies (advocacy groups) existed in most European countries and on six continents (Kramer 1988).

## Montessori's Legacy

After World War II, Montessori broadened her vision to advocate for peace education and received three nominations for the Nobel Peace Prize for her efforts. The greatness of Montessori's vision is the transition she accomplished from a spiritual to a scientific conception of an education that is responsive to children's development. She used her physician's skill of observation to chart child development more systematically than had been done in the past by educators like Froebel and Pestalozzi. She was also able to balance her strong Catholic faith with the characteristics of a social scientist in forming her education system. Summarized here are some of her contributions.

- **Developmental stages.** Montessori recognized three distinct sensitive periods in childhood, what are termed *stages* today. She saw these periods—birth to 6 years, 6–12 years, and 12–18 years—as corresponding to patterns of physical development (Montessori [1912] 1964). Children's modes of learning in these sensitive periods differ as they move from pre-conventional to conventional thought (Montessori [1949] 2007).

- **Prepared environment.** Montessori stressed the importance of a prepared learning environment, organized and ready for the child's self-directed learning activities. This environment—including materials, equipment, furniture, and layout—is to be responsive (appropriate for each child) throughout the stages of development represented in the group (Montessori [1912] 1964).

- **Guided learning activity.** Montessori considered the naturally developing mind to be a miracle (which suggests the spiritual dimension in her psychology). This meant to her that instruction could not consist of drill and recitation using a preset curriculum (Montessori [1912] 1964). Instead, as "directress," the teacher guides the child through his own learning sequence and maintains a classroom decorum that respects the self-directed learning of each child. The effort by the teacher is epitomized in Montessori's famous quote: "Our work is not to teach but to help the absorbent mind in its work of development" (Montessori [1949] 2007, 24).

During the late 1950s, long-term studies on child development provided the research basis for the Kiddie Corps, renamed in 1965 as Head Start. As part of a new understanding of the importance of early childhood education at this time, the public rekindled an interest in the Montessori Method—with the Montessori programs generally serving a much different, more affluent population than in the original programs in Rome.

- **Practical life skills.** Although best known as an approach to early childhood education, the Montessori Method has been adapted to levels of education through high school (NNDB 2012). Montessori stressed academic learning (as in the areas of literacy and mathematics) but *through the use of practical life skills.* Food preparation is an example, studied with increasing degrees of intellectual complexity at different developmental levels. In so doing she popularized another educational trend, advocated in the United States by John Dewey. Dewey emphasized the use of practical life experiences, through projects, as a method for teaching academic skills. (See the discussion on Dewey later in this chapter.)

- **Teaching for self-discipline.** When the curriculum is relevant to children's experiences, interests, and developmental stages, the teacher can guide children toward civil, socially responsive behaviors. Without having to force student compliance to an imposed curriculum through rewards and punishments, adults can authentically model and teach the skills of thinking intelligently and ethically. Building this sense of ethical independence was for Montessori the key not just to smoothly running schools but also to creating better functioning societies (Montessori [1949] 2007). As she states concerning what some would view as the naughtiness of a child,

> What a change there would be in society if the "evildoer" evoked compassion and we made an effort to console him. It would mean compassion for him as we have when he has a physical illness. Wrongdoing is often a psychological illness due to an unfavorable environment or the condition of birth or some such misfortune. It ought to evoke compassion and help, not merely punishment. This understanding would change our social structure for the better. (Montessori [1949] 2007, 194)

Montessori aspired to balance high expectations of herself and others with a sense of deep human compassion throughout her life.

## John Dewey: Democracy in Learning and Life

John Dewey was born in 1859, 77 years after the death of Froebel and 11 years before the birth of Montessori. His birth occurred in the same year as the publishing of Darwin's *Origin of the Species* and just a few years before the founding of the Massachusetts Institute of Technology. The timing is significant: A new, empirical age was dawning, and throughout his life Dewey accommodated his thinking to this new era.

Much as Montessori had done in Europe, the American Dewey helped effect a transition in thought about education from a field dependent on Christian philosophy, which dominated educational thinking of the day, to a field defined by *pedagogy* (education as a subject of study). This new view built upon the accumulating facts of the fledgling social sciences (Baker 1966).

John came from New England stock. His father, Archibald Dewey was known as a good-natured man with a sense of humor. A sign in his store window in Burlington, Vermont, once read: *Ham and Tobacco—Smoked and Unsmoked.* His mother, Lucina Rich Dewey was zealous in her Calvinist Protestant beliefs, her foremost concern being that John and his older brother, Davis, make something of their lives to justify their "heavenly worth."

Throughout his youth, Dewey felt torn between the external pressures of Calvinist Protestantism and an internal need for spiritual growth. His eventual rejection of organized religion characterized a pattern of intellectual independence in the face of authority that Dewey continued—and suffered because of—throughout his life (Westbrook 1995).

### Education of an Intellect

In 1875, John, aged 16, and Davis enrolled in the University of Vermont, the first members of the Dewey family to pursue higher education. "They were able to attend college due to its nearness, low tuition, and some scholarship help" (Brickman & Lehrer 1959, 15). A senior-year course in moral philosophy—"which included instruction in political economy, law, history, psychology, ethics, philosophy of religion, and logic"—particularly stimulated John's intellect (Westbrook 1995, 5). His out-of-class reading of contemporary American works and of British periodicals on evolutionary biology added to his education.

After a year as a secondary teacher in rugged Oil City, Pennsylvania, Dewey found his life direction as a scholar and professor rather than a classroom teacher (Westbrook 1995). We get a sense of this direction by a series of articles on metaphysics that appeared in *The Journal of Speculative Philosophy* during this time—the first two written while he was still teaching. Based on the success of his articles, in 1882 Dewey applied to and was accepted into doctoral study at the new Johns Hopkins University in Baltimore, Maryland. Undeterred by the lack of an offer of financial assistance by the university, this storekeeper's son "borrowed $500 from an aunt and headed south to join a new breed of academic professionals" (Westbrook 1995, 8).

Johns Hopkins University apparently lost all copies of Dewey's doctoral dissertation on Kant, written by one of its most illustrious graduates (Westbrook 1995). The dissertation remains Dewey's only major work never to be published, perhaps—this is conjecture—due to his preference for philosophy over the scientific study urged upon him by the university president.

Dewey gravitated to one professor in particular, George Morris, taking all of Morris's classes, studying on an individual basis with the professor, and completing his dissertation on Kant under Morris's supervision. After his graduation in 1884, Dewey followed Morris to the University of Michigan, where he took a position as assistant professor in philosophy. There he met and in 1886 married Alice Chipman, who had been a student of Dewey's.

## From Academic to Social Reformer

Alice and her sister had been raised to be independent and self-sufficient by their pioneer grandparents in the wilds of Michigan. Alice's influence on her husband was, in Dewey's words, to put "guts and stuffing" into his life and work (Westbrook 1995). His writing during this time, including "Education and the Health of Women" (1885) and "The Ethics of Democracy" (1888), took on a new egalitarian focus. In academic circles across the nation, Dewey gained acclaim as an intellect on the rise.

In 1894, John and Alice relocated to Chicago, where Dewey became chairman of the Department of Philosophy, Psychology, and Pedagogy at the University of Chicago (Brickman & Lehrer 1959). There, Dewey felt he could actively integrate his philosophical, psychological, and sociological principles in a coordinated educational approach with children (Westbrook 1995). After two years of negotiation with university officials, Dewey and Alice established the University Elementary School in 1896 with 16 children

and 2 teachers. The "Dewey School," as some knew it, soon grew to 143 children, most from families in the university community, and 16 teachers. ("Laboratory School" and "Experimental School" were other names used.)

In 1904, apparently concerned with what they considered its radical nature, university officials undermined John and Alice's leadership in the school, and Dewey resigned from the university. Dewey's supporters at Columbia University, the prestigious educational research institution in New York City, stepped forward with the offer of a faculty position. Dewey immediately accepted. He remained at Columbia for the rest of his long and esteemed career.

Accounts of Dewey's life as educational philosopher often neglect Dewey's monumental activism for progressive causes during the first half of the twentieth century. Even before his experience at the University of Chicago, Dewey had begun a lifelong dramatic shift from academic to committed activist on behalf of democracy. Beginning in 1899, he was an instrumental, sometimes founding, member of associations including the National Association for the Advancement of Colored People, the American Civil Liberties Association, and America's first teacher's union in New York City.

A measure of his foresight and activism was his persistent warning of the dangers of the rise of Fascism in Europe. Dewey began expressing his concern in the first half of the 1930s, before most social commentators had begun to recognize the danger (Westbrook 1995).

## A Philosopher of Democracy

In his five decades at Columbia, Dewey enjoyed fame and, in the face of criticism, a secure base of operation for his lecturing and writing. After retiring from active university teaching in 1930, Dewey spent his remaining 22 years as emeritus professor, continuing his work as a preeminent educator and social reformer. In total he authored or coauthored 350 works, including as coauthors former students and colleagues as well as his daughter Evelyn. He spoke on education and democracy at universities in Japan and China (1919–20), Turkey (1924), Mexico (1926), Soviet Russia (1928), and France (1930). While he addressed many social issues on the world stage, Dewey's integrating vision remained the role of education in sustaining democracy across the diverse communities of modern society.

Dewey was at heart a social philosopher who emphasized the parts of democracy relating to "of the people, by the people" (Westbrook 1995). While critics painted Dewey as leftist for his political views, Dewey viewed with alarm the ruthless power of authoritarian governments in the Soviet Union as well in Germany and Japan. He assailed political practices of whatever leaning they might be that diminished the worth and civic power of individual citizens.

The democratic vision of progressives like Dewey is that citizens who are educated to fully participate in their everyday communities also contribute to society as a whole. Civility increases as community members feel they have a valid say in the governing of the communities of which they are a part. He believed that democratic social relations within the context of the classroom are the best preparation for the extension of participatory democracy in businesses and civic life, making the ethics embedded in democracy more integral to society.

## Dewey's "New" Education

As an intellectual giant of the twentieth century, John Dewey is a name known to nearly all contemporary educators. His writing is difficult to read, however, which has allowed writers to lionize his name while giving discretionary levels of attention to his views. In this section I discuss selected quotes from three of Dewey's main works that address the roles of the child, learning, teaching, and the school and society.

### The School and Society, 1897

His first major works on education, *The School and Society* ([1897] 2010) and *The Child and the Curriculum* ([1902] 2010), were written during the Deweys' operation of the experimental school in Chicago. Collected from reports and presentations in 1897, *The School and Society* was the more developed work of the two and the first to be released. By reporting on practices of the school, Dewey sought to illustrate his premise that schools should be a microcosm of the democratic society he envisioned. At the opening of *The School and Society*, Dewey states,

> What the best and wisest parent wants for his own child, that must be what the community wants for all of its children. Any other ideal for our schools is narrow and unlovely; acted upon it destroys our democracy. All that society has accomplished for itself is put, through the agency of the school, at the disposal of its future members. . . . Only by being true to the full growth of all individuals who make it up can society by any chance be true to itself. (6)

Dewey decried the prevailing focus on rote academic instruction. For the new education, he borrowed from Froebel the term "occupations" as the basic element of the curriculum. By occupations, Dewey meant small-group activities based on real-life matters, such as garment making. Dewey saw the occupations not as manual training or busy work, but as intrinsically motivating experiences through which students could live cooperatively in the present and also learn skills and concepts that would be of direct benefit in the future. Dewey states,

> The great thing to keep in mind, then, regarding the introduction into the school of various forms of occupation, is that through them the entire spirit of the school is renewed. It has a chance to affiliate itself with life, to become the child's habitat, where he learns through di-

rected living; instead of only being a place to learn lessons having an abstract and remote reference to some possible living to be done in the future. [The school] gets a chance to be a miniature community, an embryonic society. (10)

Dewey also protested the strict discipline used to ensure students' compliance with a curriculum he declared of little relevance to them. In *The School and Society* he provides the basis for modern guidance through his description of a curriculum of relevance to the child. He reflects,

> If you have the end in view of [a classroom of] children learning certain set lessons, to be recited to a teacher, your discipline must be devoted to securing that result. But if the end in view is the development of a spirit of social cooperation and community life, discipline must grow out of and be relative to this. There is a certain disorder in any busy workshop; there is not silence; persons are not engaged in maintaining certain fixed physical postures; . . . they are not holding their books thus and so. They are doing a variety of things, and there is the confusion, the bustle that results from activity. But of occupation, out of doing things that are to produce results, and out of doing these in a social and cooperate way, there is born a discipline of its own kind and type. Our whole conception of school discipline changes when we get this point of view. (9–10)

In so stating, Dewey marks the transition from discipline to guidance, a paradigm shift instigated by this educator's insight more than 100 years ago that progressive educators today can look to with admiration.

### Democracy and Education, 1916

*Democracy and Education* represents Dewey's most comprehensive presentation on the subject of education; in this book he attempted to incorporate his entire philosophy. Dewey never moved far from his initial outline for experimental education, but in *Democracy and Education,* he attempted to refine, further develop, and cogently express his ideas.

Education for an industrial age must, Dewey believed, prepare workers and professionals alike to bring scientific inquiry to their callings, that is, the capacity to continue an effective learning process after the conclusion of formal education. He saw an education that taught *how to learn* as the greatest contribution education could make to the diverse communities of family, work, and civic life in which educated citizens would find themselves.

A philosophical premise of Dewey's work is that citizens educated to function in democracy further that democracy. He articulated an observation echoed by later education reformers that schools in all societies build in social controls—they serve a socializing function. Schools fostering democratic values need to create social controls consistent with democratic life. This idea, which critics interpret as calling for a dogmatic equality between students and teacher, has sparked controversy over the years.

In one section of *Democracy and Education* Dewey makes the connection between democracy and education this way:

> The devotion of democracy to education is a familiar fact. Since a democratic society repudiates the principle of external authority, it must find a substitute in voluntary disposition and interest; these can be created only by education. A democracy is more than a form of government; it is primarily a mode of associated living, of conjoint communicated experience. (87)

> Such a society must have a type of education which gives individuals a personal interest in social relationships and [shared] control, and the habits of mind which cure social changes without introducing disorder. (99)

### Experience and Education, 1938

This "little volume," as Dewey termed it, represented his attempt at age 79 to crystallize his educational philosophy in clear and concise terms (Westbrook 1995). At 81 pages,

*Experience and Education* is probably the most widely read of Dewey's works.

In the monograph Dewey revisited his argument for an educational approach that involves neither the suppression of children's motivation found in many educational approaches nor the excessive freedom of child-centered education ([1938] 1997). He argued for a new education that is teacher centered, in which the teacher's job is to actively assist the student in finding purpose and continuing motivation in classroom activity relevant to the child's experience.

The teacher's strategy is to assist the child to move past the impulse of the moment to find meaning in a sustained learning experience (Dewey [1938] 1997). Dewey maintained that when the child finds purpose in planning activity and implementing the plan, she progresses toward the ultimate goal of the new education: learning how to learn.

Knowing Dewey's emphasis on the social context of learning, it is not surprising that he concludes his statement on the educational meaning of purpose and planning this way:

> The plan, in other words, is a co-operative enterprise, not a dictation. The teacher's suggestion is not a mold for a cast-iron result but is a starting point to be developed into a plan through contributions from the experience of all engaged in the learning process. The development occurs through reciprocal give-and-take, the teacher taking [listening] but not being afraid also to give [to guide]. The essential point is that the purpose grow and take shape through the process of [shared social experience]. (72)

Dewey referred to his system as *new education* or *experimental education* and shunned the term *progressive education* ([1938] 1997). Through much of the twentieth century, progressive education was used to describe very permissive, child-centered education. This was the approach of G. Stanley Hall and the child study movement in the first half of the century—and later of A.S. Neill's Summerhill, a famous residential free school, so called because the curriculum became entirely what the resident students made it (Neill 1995). Dewey chafed that his own approach of learning by purposeful experience was being lumped in with child-centered education, an education that Dewey called "progressive."

In these times, and certainly in this book, the term *progressive education* means something else. Close to the heart of Dewey's work, progressive education here means a forward-looking schooling approach that seeks to optimize students' learning in the context of a democratic community. As noted by the Progressive Education Network (2012), it has been challenging to arrive at a single definition for progressive education. The Network defines it through the following principles:

- Education must prepare students for active participation in a democratic society.

- Education must focus on students' social, emotional, academic, cognitive and physical development.

- Education must nurture and support students' natural curiosity and innate desire to learn. Education must foster internal motivation in students.

- Education must be responsive to the developmental needs of students.

- Education must foster respectful relationships between teachers and students.

- Education must encourage the active participation of students in their learning, which arises from previous experience.

- Progressive educators must play an active role in guiding the educational vision of our society.

Dewey's timeless argument is for teachers to rise above the role of technicians who compliantly implement curricula of little relevance or meaning to the lives of the children in their classrooms. Instead, he would have teachers use their professional skills to guide learners in the grand problem-solving process of education, in classrooms that are laboratories for democracy. He would grant to teachers the professional status of doctors and lawyers in this regard, consistent in his conviction that teachers can learn the skills, understandings, and dispositions necessary to be true professionals. The political and educational questions posed by Dewey's ideas remain dauntingly large. As we continue into the twenty-first century, they deserve to be asked, studied, and civilly discussed.

It seems to me that Dewey's goal for the new education in this age would be two-fold: 1) to close the education gap caused by social and cultural disparities (that he so long worked to reduce) and perpetuated by politics (that he for so long contended with), and 2) to educate all students for intelligent and ethical (civil) participation in the many communities of a modern, diverse society—family, school, work, civic, religious, social, and political. Dewey well earned the title "philosopher of democracy." That some today still regard his ideas as radical indicates to me the profundity of his vision.

# Healthy Self, Healthy Society: Psychology of the Democratic Life Skills

The legacy of pioneers in progressive education—particularly the four profiled in the previous chapter—is the focus on children in the schooling process. The pioneers realized that if individual learners experienced a humane education that furthered the skills of civil living, society fundamentally would benefit. Progressive educators today sustain this view and look especially to a psychology that holds that when the healthy development and well-being of the child are nurtured in the classroom, society progresses toward its democratic ideals.

Emerging neuroscience (discussed in Chapter 4) and developmentally appropriate practice (discussed in Part Two) substantiate the case that cognitive gains can be achieved using an educational approach that directly teaches for the democratic life skills. This chapter explores and summarizes the thinking of a sampling of psychologists and educators of the last 50 years who have furthered this view. Let's begin the discussion of a *psychology for the democratic life skills* by reasserting the need to foster the growth of the individual child in the classroom.

Reports on U.S. trends in high school graduation indicate that since 1969, national graduation rates have not significantly changed, from about 77 percent (Khadaroo 2010). In particular, students who lack resources and are stressed by the effects of poverty are not staying in school. Less than half of male students of color are graduating from high school, and the average graduation rate from large urban high schools is 54 percent (Khadaroo 2010). Although many factors are at play here, too many students are finding schools to be unfriendly places. To help remedy this situation—which I and others consider a national failing—we need to advocate for an educational psychology that fosters self-respect together with mutual respect, the worthy child contributing to the well-being of the classroom group. Such a psychology has a history and, in fact, exists today.

## The Individual in Society

During the 1920s in Austria, the psychiatrist Alfred Adler maintained that healthy personal development happens as young individuals have their basic needs for physical and emotional security met, and that the product of healthy personal development is creative and productive human behavior (Ansbacher & Ansbacher 1956). Adler saw that social injustice, as in sexism and ethnic prejudice, directly impacts mental health by inducing "inferiority complexes" in individuals, resulting in dysfunctional behaviors.

Originally a rising star in Sigmund Freud's circle of Vienna psychiatrists, Adler split from the group when his concepts were found to be "too positive" (Ansbacher & Ansbacher 1956). After the Nazis closed Adler's clinics in the 1930s due to his Jewish heritage—as they did Freud's—Adler immigrated to the United States. He became affiliated with universities around New York City, including Columbia, Dewey's home base. Adler died in 1937, but he influenced a generation of American psychologists, who have developed constructs compatible with Adler's seminal idea: Mental health in individuals leads to socially productive behaviors, making more possible a society responsive to the needs and rights of individual citizens (Ansbacher & Ansbacher 1956).

This psychology of *healthy self, healthy society* has been developed by social scientists into current times. Together, neo-Adlerian psychologists provide a map for the healthy development of individuals, empowering a capacity to function intelligently and ethically—civilly—in modern society.

## Conceptions of the Self

The **self** can be thought of as the sum of the feelings and thoughts one has about who one is (self-identity), along with the mental processes—conscious, preconscious, and unconscious—that together write, direct, and produce those feelings and thoughts. Components of self are the self-concept (the ideas one has about oneself) and the self-image (the feelings one has about oneself) (Gartrell, forthcoming). Self-identity tends toward constancy throughout life, even while self-concept and self-esteem evolve, especially in early life, due to individuals' perceptions of their ongoing experiences.

For example, Mathilde, a toddler, summons the courage to go down a slide for the first time and excitedly repeats the feat for 16 more turns, while adults look on and give acknowledgment—at least for the first 10 turns. (Mathilde's attention span here exceeds the adults'—often true with developmentally appropriate learning experiences.) From mastering the slide and gaining acknowledgment for doing so, the toddler internalizes perceptions about herself as a capable person, able to engage in learning. She also stores as emotional memories positive feelings about herself mastering the sliding experience.

Historically, most early childhood educators have been comfortable with a view of the self as having positive potential and being in an ongoing process of development—continuously taking big and little steps like Mathilde did (Copple & Bredekamp 2009; Froebel [1826] 1887; Montessori [1949] 2007). But this is not the only conception of the self that arose during the twentieth century. During that time, three differing conceptions of the developing self emerged. Each is significant for its influence on American education practice.

**self:** the sum of the feelings and thoughts one has about who one is (self-identity), along with the mental processes that together write, direct, and produce those feelings and thoughts

- *The genetic self*—the view, crystallized at the beginning of the twentieth century, that personality is a function of heredity and can only be slightly altered, if at all, by experience. Edward Thorndike is a prominent psychologist linked to this construct (Hofstater [1944] 1992). An artifact of genetic-self theory has been the rationale for intelligence tests and other standardized measures of human abilities. Practices such as ability grouping and beliefs about relative superiority and inferiority of differing social groups have also been linked to the construct.

- *The behavioral self*—the view that formation of the self is not due to particular genetics ("nature") but to the individual's environment ("nurture"), through reinforcement of select experiences. B.F. Skinner is credited with popularizing this construct across the mid-twentieth century. Effective learning occurs when the individual receives strategic rewards for desired behaviors from significant adults. Behavioral reinforcement, behavioral objectives, learning outcomes, targeted instruction, and focused assessments to measure progress toward preset standards are educational products of the behavioral view. The construct implies institutionalized differences between those who shape others' behaviors and those whose behaviors are being shaped.

- *The integrated self*—the view that the self is due neither to *only* genetics nor to *only* the shaping effects of the environment, but to the interaction of both. The making of an integrated self begins with a brain structure that is capable of change in many ways yet set in other ways. Healthy brain development, and hence healthy development of the self, happens in the context of warm relationships with significant others, sufficient resources to meet basic needs, and enriching experiences to motivate learning. Teaching and learning are seen as interactive processes in this view. Adler's premise, early on, that mental health is a function of the developing mind's ability to make sense of experiences and relationships can be associated with the construct of the integrated self.

Readers are probably quite clear about the theoretical position regarding the self taken in this book. In my view, the integrated-self viewpoint best supports reciprocal human relations in modern democratic society. I'll now highlight eight individuals associated with this viewpoint. They are important to include because of their clear articulation of concepts integral to the democratic life skills and because they articulated principles generally applicable to, or distinctly focused on, early childhood education. The perspectives are those of

- Five "self" psychologists of the 1960s
- Lilian Katz
- David Elkind
- Howard Gardner

## The Sixties "Self" Psychologists

During the 1960s the writings of psychologists including Abraham Maslow (1962), Carl Rogers (1961), Arthur Combs (1962), Erik Erikson (1963), and William Purkey ([1970] 2006), among others, brought attention to the developing self as the primary dynamic in human learning and behavior. These "self" psychologists shared Adler's premise that to the extent children feel safe in their circumstances and valued as members of the group and as a worthy individual (the first democratic life skill), they see themselves in a positive light and can express strong emotions in non-hurting ways (the second democratic life skill).

DLS 1: Finding acceptance as a member of the group and as a worthy individual

DLS 2: Expressing strong emotions in non-hurting ways

DLS 3: Solving problems creatively—independently and in cooperation with others

DLS 4: Accepting unique human qualities in others

DLS 5: Thinking intelligently and ethically

These children become open to future learning experiences (DLS 3, 4, and 5).

For example, a 4-year-old looks up at the moon as she is riding in a car and tells the family, "The moon is coming home with us." Her parent asks, "I wonder why?" The 4-year-old replies with a smile, "'Cause Moon likes it at our house." At night in the car four years later, the same child comments, "The moon looks like it follows us when we drive. It just looks that way 'cause the car is moving. I like looking at the moon . . . in the daytime, too."

Affirmed in her developmentally rooted perceptions at age 4, the child remains willing and able to further experience this celestial body as she grows. Her positive self-image relative to experiencing the moon was confirmed; she feels empowered to further investigate. Preventing discouragement by acknowledging children's ideas describes much of what the self psychologists were about, although they put the matter in their own various terms.

The theory that healthy personal development leads to societal progress underlies the works of the self psychologists. This is not to say that life is not without problems and challenges; however, according to this theory, with adult guidance, even young children can make progress in learning to civilly manage them. We look briefly at these psychologists' contributions in relation to the five democratic life skills.

**Abraham Maslow** (1962), who studied under Adler, wrote of two coexistent motivational sources—the needs for safety and growth—as fundamental in human life. He contributed the landmark construct of a hierarchy of needs: that individuals, especially the young, must meet their safety needs—for physical security and psychological nurturing—before they can focus on growth needs—for experiencing, learning, and finding meaning. His concept is fundamental to the dynamic underlying the democratic life skills.

DLS 1 and 2 have to do with finding acceptance and expressing strong emotions in non-hurting ways. Only as children find personal acceptance and gain skill in expressing strong emotions can they progress to DLS 3, 4, and 5, which relate to a willingness and ability to undertake new experiences. The dynamic is illustrated in this adaptation of Maslow's ideas:

### Democratic Life Skills as Related to Maslow's Theory of Human Motivation

| Motivational Source for Human Behavior | The Five Democratic Life Skills |
|---|---|
| Safety motivation: the needs of the individual for basic security such as through food, shelter, consistent nurturing, and unconditional acceptance | • DLS 1: Finding acceptance as a member of the group and as a worthy individual<br>• DLS 2: Expressing strong emotions in non-hurting ways |
| Growth motivation: the needs of the individual for exploration, engagement, creation, cooperative endeavor, effectiveness, attainment, and actualization | • DLS 3: Solving problems creatively—independently and in cooperation with others<br>• DLS 4: Accepting unique human qualities in others<br>• DLS 5: Thinking intelligently and ethically |

**Carl Rogers** (1961) popularized the concept of unconditional positive regard for others, in particular between the significant adults and the children in their care. When applied in education settings, Rogers's idea means that teachers accept children even when they experience conflicts and that an unwavering relationship of acceptance is central to the guidance teachers use to help children see the world as trustworthy and to help children learn and grow. Rogers opposed the practice of teachers giving reinforcement to some, but not others, based on the children's behavior.

The guidance teachers use to forge and sustain unconditional acceptance even in conflict situations is illustrated by the following anecdote from a preschool classroom:

> Sherry, not quite 5 years old, and two other children of similar age were playing with Lincoln Logs and a plastic train set on the floor of the building area. Sherry told Paula and Delsey she was making a station with the Lincoln Logs next to the tracks. Sherry was almost done when Paula said, "We don't want that station."
>
> Showing some exasperation, Sherry picked up the Lincoln Logs. She then said, "I will use the little ones and make a bridge for the tracks to go on."
>
> "No," said Delsey. "We don't want that."
>
> Really frustrated, Sherry hit a cardboard box with two long logs and yelled, "I am very angry!" The teacher, who had been observing, helped Sherry cool down. She then explained that the three girls were playing together and they needed to figure out how all three could be happy. She asked the three how Sherry could use the Lincoln Logs to "add to the railroad, maybe here" and pointed to a spot away from Paula and Delsey at the end of tracks.
>
> Paula paused, looked, and said, "Maybe a train garage."
>
> "Yeah," said Delsey.
>
> Looking relieved, Sherry said, "Yeah, I could make a really big one." While Sherry was building the "garage," the teacher commented on how they had a problem but solved it together. She added that this was something they might remember they could do next time. The three girls played together for the rest of the time block, including using the train garage. The teacher quietly talked with Sherry later to affirm the child's sense of worth in her own eyes.

Among the sixties psychologists, Rogers held a high profile for defending education for healthy personal development. Kirschenbaum (1989) provided an account of a famous debate held between Rogers and the behaviorist B.F. Skinner, documenting Rogers's place as an advocate for his psychology of acceptance.

**Arthur Combs** (1962) furthered the idea that reality for the individual is what he or she perceives, including in the classroom. Combs's perceptual-field theory has helped many educators move past having moralistic reactions to children's behavior. For example, in the preceding anecdote the teacher did not scold Sherry for hitting the box and yelling—acting "inappropriately" in the classroom. Instead, the teacher perceived that Sherry was frustrated at being left out and helped the children to resolve their conflict. When adults suspend value judgments and instead seek to understand the child's perceptions of events, they are in a better position to respond in ways that resolve, rather than aggravate, problems. Galinsky (2010) calls this skill *perspective taking*, a direct, contemporary application of perceptual-field theory. Even when teachers do not observe a situation firsthand, by responding as a mediator rather than enforcer, they can learn what happened and guide children through a conflict-resolution process that teaches rather than punishes. Chapter 9 discusses specific guidance practices for doing so.

When conflicts occur, teachers who use guidance to investigate and mediate rather than punish make a great difference in the child's personal development (Gartrell, forthcoming). Readers can probably recall experiences of a teacher wrongly (or mostly wrongly) blaming them or a classmate for a perceived failing or transgression. Vivid and lasting emotional memories of such events testify to the impact that teacher responses have on self-concept and self-image. An important contribution of Combs has been the importance of teachers responding to students' perceptions of events rather than just their own.

**Erik Erikson** (1963) is well known for his construct of eight fundamental conflicts that human beings experience during different stages across the lifespan, infancy through old age. The first four conflicts, occurring during childhood, indicate the importance of parenting and teaching that is responsive to the child's physical and psychological needs. With "good-enough" parenting—a term that describes the notion that parenting doesn't have to be perfect to be effective (Bettelheim 1987; Hoghughi & Speight 1998; Winnicott 1953)—and the support of early childhood teachers, children make progress toward the healthy resolution of these four developmental challenges:

◆ Trust versus mistrust during infancy

◆ Autonomy versus shame and doubt during toddlerhood

◆ Initiative versus guilt in the preschool years

◆ Industry versus inferiority during middle childhood

I once asked a college student why she wrote in a tiny handwriting style. Elissa chose to share in class that in third grade she had been publicly embarrassed by a teacher who criticized her sloppy handwriting. From that day on, Elissa dedicated herself to writing so small that teachers could not tell if her writing was sloppy or not. (It wasn't. She had to concentrate so much on writing small that she perfected the technique.) This student expressed relief at being able to share this emotional memory. For a joke, she submitted her next paper in 8-point type size. (Fortunately for me, she had a backup in 11-point Helvetica.)

Erikson's construct harmonizes with Maslow's concept of safety needs and growth needs and with Bowlby and Ainsworth's attachment theory, discussed in the next chapter. David Elkind (profiled later in this chapter) builds upon Erikson's theory by arguing that children should not be forced to grow up too soon, including in the classroom, by being pushed toward mistrust, shame and doubt, guilt, and feelings of inferiority. (Think of Elissa's handwriting, described in the sidebar.) Erikson's construct explains the effects of factors that make healthy development challenging for children, and suggests that the healthy characteristics of the self—such as openness to new experiences—develop as children successfully resolve each life challenge.

The democratic life skills reflect Erikson's construct in their emphasis on personal development requiring the support and guidance of caring others. His construct broadens the scope of traditional schooling by reinforcing the need for teachers to address not just academic concerns but also children's social and emotional needs. Erikson reminds us that children grow in all developmental domains, and therefore education needs to address the whole child.

**William Purkey** ([1970] 2006) in particular related the new psychology to education and schooling practice. Known for memorable quotes, Purkey often clearly explained educational issues from a progressive perspective. Two statements from his still widely used book *Self Concept and School Achievement* ([1970] 2006) follow:

The indications seem to be that success or failure in school significantly influences the ways in which students view themselves. Students who experience repeated success in school are likely to develop positive feelings about their abilities, while those who encounter failure tend to develop negative views of themselves. (26)

Purkey went on to discuss the culture of school that reinforces failure and frustration:

Traditionally, the child is expected to adjust to the school rather than the school adjusting to the child. To ensure this process, the school is prepared to dispense rewards and punishments, successes and failures on a massive scale. The child is expected to learn to live in a new environment and to compete for the rewards of obedience and scholarship. . . . Unfortunately a large number of schools employ a punitive approach to education. Punishment, failure, and depreciation are characteristic. . . . The principle that negative self-concepts should be prevented is ignored by many schools. (40)

In response to what he saw as a stultifying effect on the self in traditional schooling, Purkey developed an *invitational approach* to education. Invitational education addresses all domains of development and focuses on fully developing the potential of each individual. Embedded in intentionally inviting education is the use of discipline that guides rather than punishes (Purkey [1978] 2006)—guidance that is required if teachers are to assist children in gaining the democratic life skills.

Over the years, Purkey wrote of the need for not just teachers but also counselors, school administrators, and leaders in general to be *intentionally inviting*. Like Dewey, Purkey recognized the need for education to model and teach the skills of democratic life. He saw and wrote of the connection between how schools treat individual children and how the adults they become respond to the issues of social living in modern society. Purkey wrote of an education that kindles and nurtures the skills I call democratic life skills in all students.

# Katz: Realism in Early Childhood Education

Lilian Katz is an emerita professor at the University of Illinois in Urbana, past president of NAEYC, cofounder of the [Erik] Erikson Institute, and lecturer and consultant on educational issues. Of the psychologists and educators profiled in this chapter, Katz has focused her authorship most directly on early childhood education. One of her many areas of study—the kind of teaching that builds children's self-esteem rather than encourages narcissism—adds a reality check for democratic life skills.

## Self-Esteem, Not Narcissism

Katz joins Dewey ([1899] 2010) and Purkey ([1970] 2006) in arguing that self-esteem in children is critical to learning, and that psychological support for building self-esteem is different from engendering narcissism. She defines self-esteem as "feelings derived from evaluations of the self." In contrast, narcissism "is a preoccupation with oneself and how one is perceived by others" (Katz 1995, 13), and it can result when we provide an education environment that is too child centered.

By emphasizing "all about me" and "I am special" messages with children, educators indulge children's vanity and fail to assist them to look to the world beyond themselves (Katz 1995, 16–17). We risk having children become self-centered and self-indulgent. Better messages to convey are "what I am interested in" and "all about us"—messages that build consciousness about what children can become and who they are sharing life with.

Katz speaks of the "cyclic nature" of self-esteem and effort. A feeling of confidence, related to self-esteem, promotes effort. The resulting accomplishment reinforces the child's self-esteem. For the cycle to continue, the individual must feel that she herself is the primary cause of the results. Classrooms that provide both intellectually intriguing challenges and support in meeting those challenges are esteem-building places. The benefit of positive self-esteem for the child is the confidence it engenders to tackle new experiences and to progress in the democratic life skills.

## Teacher Interactions That Build Self-Esteem

Katz makes the case that self-esteem cannot be directly taught. She states, "Constant messages about how wonderful a person is may raise doubts about the credibility of the message and

### Self-Esteem and Culture

In her analysis of self-esteem across cultures, Katz (1995) comments that self-esteem and its reinforcement have different contexts, depending on the culture:

The distinctions between the Western independent and the non-Western interdependent construal of the self indicate that the sources of self-esteem are also distinctive. For Westerners, independent self-esteem is achieved by actualizing one's own attributes, having one's accomplishments validated by others, and being able to compare oneself favorably to others. In Asian and other non-Western cultures, self-esteem is related to self-restraint, modesty, and connectedness with others. (30)

the messenger" (1995, 36). Her contention is that comments offered to children that are nonspecific and evaluative, such as "Good job" and "That is a pretty outfit," influence children to depend on how they are viewed by others and undermine, rather than build, self-esteem. In contrast, when adults convey specific appreciation for the details, efforts, and progress they see, they tell children they care about them enough to pay nonjudgmental attention (Katz, 1995), as in "You are working hard on that picture" and "Your outfit is red and blue and yellow. It's very colorful." The conversation that generally follows such statements, as much as the acknowledgment given, bolsters children's feelings about themselves. Katz (1995) states:

> Self-esteem is most likely to be fostered when children are esteemed. Esteem is conveyed to them when significant adults and peers treat them respectfully, consult their view and preferences (even if they do not accede to them), and provide opportunities for real decisions and choices about events and things that matter to them. Young children's opinions, views, suggestions, and preferences about relevant activities and events should be respectfully solicited and considered seriously. (34)

Katz's thoughts about interactions that build self-esteem are essential for the positive adult-child relationship that empowers learning and growth. Her observation that individual self-esteem must develop within, and with regard for, the child's social communities moves forward the ideas of Froebel, Montessori, and Dewey. Guidance for progress toward the democratic life skills begins with teacher support for true self-esteem in the individual child. Katz makes this argument uniquely, and in a manner cogent for the times.

## Elkind: An Understanding of the Child in Society

In his lifelong effort to make child development theory and research accessible to parents and practitioners, David Elkind has provided a clear illustration of how social forces in contemporary society undermine healthy development in children. Much of the following is based on his classic work, *The Hurried Child,* first published in 1981 and again as a revised 25th anniversary edition in 2006. In the book Elkind makes the case that children are hurried by social pressures into growing up too soon, and that this rushing of development makes for undue stress. He points out that social pressures begin in early childhood with an inappropriate emphasis on school readiness, which is taken to excess in many affluent families in order to get children admitted to prestigious private schools (Elkind [1981] 2006). Pressures continue throughout childhood with huge backpacks of homework and the spate of organized sports and activities that harried parents transport their programmed youngsters to and from.

As well, given the high number of families with dual and single working parents, many children and youth face inadequate out-of-school supervision and forced premature self-care—often resulting in a retreat to television and digital games (Elkind [1981] 2006). Media and peers pressure even very young preteens into sexualized pop-culture emulation and commercially engineered desires for material possessions.

Nearly one-third of America's children are raised by single parents or surrogate family members, such as grandparents, and even two-parent families are facing unprecedented financial difficulties (Children's Defense Fund, 2011). Many children, Elkind says, are growing up without the family structure of two parents and an in-the-home parent, as was more common in the past. These changing social conditions mean that children are subject to the influence of peer pressures and sophisticated multimedia in ways qualitatively different from in the past. Elkind makes the case that these pressures cause children to develop habits of behavior beyond their years that may be detrimental to long-term social and emotional development.

Elkind believes that given this state of affairs, the need for family-school partnerships is ever more important. Beginning in preschool, teachers and families pooling their resources can result in an unforced, more naturally occurring childhood.

Still, just at a time when schools might and must provide a supportive climate and services to help students and families cope with the stressors of modern life, in Elkind's view some educational practices are actually contributing to the problem (Elkind [1981] 2006). He notes that the widespread reaction of schools to lags in student achievement has been to heighten academic expectations, but without providing adequate supports for achieving these high expectations. He argues that much of the "reform" in education over the last 15 years has not been reform at all, but simply an institutionalized preoccupation with test scores. He writes,

> Accountability and test scores are what schools are about today, and children know it. They have to produce or else. This pressure . . . is bound to be bad for those who can't keep up. Their failure is more public and therefore more humiliating than ever before. Worse, students who fail to achieve feel that they are letting down their peers, their teachers, the principal, the superintendent, and the community. . . . The effect of these new reforms is the opposite of what was intended. The high school drop-out rate, which had been level for many years, is on the rise again. In part this is the result of having raised the standards for graduation without giving children the wherewithal to meet those standards. (Elkind [1981] 2006, 55)

Elkind laments a system that continues to emphasize test scores and grades over the learning actually gained. He warns that the result is young people who will go into the work world more concerned with pay and benefits than with the work itself. In this regard, he says, even employers have a role to play that will benefit society. The best companies treat their employees as worthy individuals who can have a say in the workplace and take reasonable pride in their work. Elkind ([1981] 2006) states,

> Such an approach, in industry or schooling, is not permissive—it is democratic in the best sense of the term. Individuals need direction and limits, but they also need to be able to make choices that are appropriate for them to make and to take appropriate responsibilities. And teachers need to be empowered to have a say in the governance of the schools in which they teach. Democracy is the balance between total control and total freedom, and what we need in education, as in industry, is true democracy. Only when the values upon which this country was founded begin to permeate our educational and industrial plants will we begin to realize our full human and production potentials. (70)

Elkind argues that intensified pressures on educators cause them to be defensively self-centered and less responsive to students' needs than they otherwise would be. Just as in overburdened families, if we can take some of the pressures off teachers and administrators, we will take some of the pressure off children as well (Elkind [1981] 2006). Elkind's words, first written 30 years ago, apply as well, perhaps even more so, today. His understanding that the raising and education of children are interdependent and demand family-teacher partnerships underscores a best practice of early childhood education. When children know that significant adults in their lives are working together on their behalf, stressors decrease, and they are able to move forward with healthy development.

# Gardner's Psychology: Multiple Intelligences for Responsible Citizenship

Developmental psychologist Howard Gardner's scholarly activity includes research, education, writing, and social commentary around the development, disruption, resiliency, and expression of higher cognitive processes (Gardner 2006). According to their online profiles, Howard Gardner and his wife, Ellen Winner, credit much of his intellectual development not just to his aptitude for diverse studies, but also to lasting relationships and meaningful acquaintances with the likes of psychologists Erik Erikson, Jean Piaget, and Jerome Bruner; the philosopher Nelson Goodman; and the neuropsychologist Norman Geschwind (Gardner 2010; Winner 2006).

## Multiple Intelligences

Although he has written some 25 books on broad issues exploring cognition and the interface of the self and society, Gardner is best known for developing the construct of **multiple intelligences** (Gardner 2006). To Gardner, the century-old notion of a fixed, genetic entity called *intelligence* is outdated (Gardner 1993a, 1999). Longitudinal studies of children's development in the 1950s and 1960s, followed by the beginnings of neuroscience in the 1980s, argued for separate, multiple intelligences that have a genetic basis but that can be facilitated.

### Eight Multiple Intelligences

1. Musical intelligence—the ability to enjoy, create, and perform music

2. Bodily-kinesthetic intelligence—the ability to use large and small muscle activity to express ideas, solve problems, and produce results

3. Logical-mathematical intelligence—the ability to use reason, logic, and mathematics to solve problems

4. Linguistic intelligence—the ability to use written and oral language

5. Spatial intelligence—the ability to perceive, orient oneself in relation to, graphically represent, and think creatively in relation to visual and spatial phenomena

6. Interpersonal intelligence—the ability to perceive and interpret the behaviors, motives, feelings, and intentions of others

7. Intrapersonal intelligence—the ability to understand one's own skills and their limits, motivations, self-perceptions, emotions, temperaments, and desires

8. Naturalist intelligence (the eighth intelligence, added later)—the ability to perceive and understand the meaning of features and phenomena of the natural world (Gardner 1999)

Source: Gardner 1993a

A list of Gardner's eight multiple intelligences is shown here. Gardner has considered adding a ninth and even a tenth intelligence, in the existential and spiritual domains (Gardner 1999, 2006). Although the eight, nine, or ten intelligences are all harmonious with the democratic life skills, Gardner (2006) has stated that the eight intelligences listed here have for him the most definitive neurological basis.

Gardner's theory supports opposition to such practices as ability tracking and special education placements based on intelligence tests. His theory, as well, gives credence to the argument that early environment impacts both learning abilities and inabilities in children and youth. For Gardner, intelligence is more than the inherited ability to use linguistic and analytic skills in test situations. Countless educators find gratification in the author's criticisms of the limited utility of most standardized tests.

Gardner's concise definition of intelligence (1999) provides a purpose and direction for what education in a diverse society should be:

> A biopsychological potential to process information that can be activated in a cultural way to solve problems or create products that are of value to a culture. (33–34)

Noteworthy in Gardner's definition is the interplay of culture and biology in intelligences that are developed and expressed. For Gardner, environment fundamentally impacts the development of human abilities. Further, he broadened the arena for the expression of intelligence to extend beyond the academic, legal, and scientific settings where the capacity to reason with words and/or numbers is paramount (Gardner 1993a, 1999, 2006).

If, as Gardner's definition of intelligence states, the problems solved and the creations made must be of value to a culture as a whole, then there are multiple intelligences and many expressions of intelligence in ways that benefit a culture.

## Implications for Education

Gardner's construct emphasizes the development of abilities in relation to culture. Different social groups value some intelligences over others—for instance, linguistic over logical-mathematical, or interpersonal over intrapersonal (Gardner 1999; Schickedanz & Schickedanz 1998). Each child is born with unique potential relative to the intelligences, and education becomes the empowering of those potentials in the context of, though not limited by, cultural predispositions.

In Gardner's view the purpose of education should be progressive, to assist learners in the development and expression of their total unique abilities for the benefit of others and oneself within the dynamic element of culture (Gardner 1995). Education for the whole child includes curriculum and methods that focus on multiple intelligences, leading to teaching that is developmentally appropriate in multiple domains. The goal of such education is individuals who can function intelligently in multiple spheres of human endeavor, particularly displaying intrapersonal and interpersonal intelligence—social-emotional competence—in a highly interactive society.

## The Matter of Assessment

An overriding issue in education today is accountability. Many critics believe the discussion of accountability has been politicized, driving classroom practice toward undue emphasis on preparation for standardized tests (Elkind 2006; Rose 2004; Wolk 2008). Gardner considers aggregated standardized test scores to be skewed indicators of learning, biased and incomplete. He argues the need to measure academic performance by cumulative patterns of **authentic assessment** of children's progress in multiple intelligences (Gardner 1995). (Authentic assessment uses tasks that are as close as possible to real-life practical and intellectual challenges. It is based on observations and samples of children's classroom work and so can accommodate multiple intelligences.) Gardner (1993b) states the matter this way:

> We believe that it is essential to depart from standardized testing. We also believe that standard pencil-and-paper short-answer tests sample only a small proportion of intellectual abilities and often reward a certain kind of decontextualized facility. The means of assessment we favor should ultimately search for genuine problem-solving or product-fashioning skills in individuals across a range of materials. An assessment of a particular intelligence (or set of intelligences) should highlight problems that can be solved in the materials of that intelligence. (31)

Those who, like Gardner, advocate for observation-based assessment risk the criticisms about observer reliability and testing validity that have been around for years. Formalized assessment systems such as the HighScope Preschool Child Observation

---

### Ten Educational Principles Compatible with Multiple Intelligences Theory

This list, adapted from the works of Charlesworth (2010), Gardner (1993a, 1995, 2006), and Gartrell (2011), offers 10 educational principles compatible with multiple intelligences theory. The principles also reflect the whole-child approach to early childhood education and are compatible with practices needed for children to progress in the democratic life skills.

1. The gifted artist, athlete, carpenter, or teacher is no less intelligent than the scientist, physician, or lawyer—just differently intelligent.

2. Schooling must expand to educate children in each of the intelligences.

3. As families and educators partner in children's education, progress is facilitated across the intelligences.

4. Each kind of intelligence is relatively independent, engages particular parts of the brain, and shows itself in different behaviors.

5. Children have different potentials for development in the eight intelligences, determined by each child's genetic makeup and brain formation due to experiences.

6. Children progress in developing all intelligences through the use of those intelligences in which they are more comfortable and capable.

7. As children construct meaning for themselves from engagement in activities, they make progress in the intelligences.

8. Children make progress in developing their intelligences when they are intrigued (challenged positively) by learning opportunities but not threatened by them.

9. The teaching style that facilitates children's progress in the intelligences is encouraging and interactive, not didactic and dictatorial.

10. Progress in relation to the intelligences is best measured by authentic assessment of samples of the child's everyday work.

---

Record and the Work Sampling System for Preschool to Grade 5 have attempted to address these criticisms. Reliability training and certification, as is done for the Classroom Assessment Scoring System (CLASS) of teacher performance, provides one model for where authentic assessment efforts might go in the future.

## Multiple Intelligences and the Democratic Life Skills

The connection between the democratic life skills and multiple intelligences lies in the foundation that the intrapersonal and interpersonal intelligences (in the domains of emotional and social development) provide for the democratic life skills. At the same time, the capacities to solve problems creatively, both independently and cooperatively; accept unique human qualities in others; and think intelligently and ethically (DLS 3, 4, and 5) are key learning dynamics in the development and expression of all eight intelligences. There is considerable overlap in indicators of healthy development under both constructs.

For example, at the beginning of the kindergarten year, Amanda, just 5 years old, has difficulty bringing herself to sit with others in large groups, let alone singing with the other children. After a week or so, during choice time the teacher notices Amanda singing to herself the songs the group has sung. After two weeks, with the teacher's encouragement, Amanda begins to sit with the group and sometimes sing quietly. With continued encouragement, after two months, she is singing as loudly as any child in the class. Amanda, therefore, has made progress in the development of the following intelligences:

- ◆ Intrapersonal intelligence, through the expression of increased individual strength
- ◆ Interpersonal intelligence, through a demonstrated willingness and ability to participate in the singing with the group
- ◆ Musical intelligence, through increased enjoyment of and making of music

In terms of the democratic life skills, Amanda has made progress with

- ◆ DLS 1 by (with the teacher's encouragement) finding acceptance as a member of the group and a worthy individual

**DLS 1: Finding acceptance as a member of the group and as a worthy individual**

- ◆ DLS 2 by overcoming her reluctance to participate and experiencing positive emotional expression through the music

**DLS 2: Expressing strong emotions in non-hurting ways**

- ◆ DLS 3 by creatively solving her problem with participation and cooperation with others in song

**DLS 3: Solving problems creatively—independently and in cooperation with others**

**DLS 4: Accepting unique human qualities in others**

**DLS 5: Thinking intelligently and ethically**

In my judgment, intrapersonal and interpersonal intelligences are prime mover intelligences, motivating development in, more than co-existing with, the other intelligences. But what is important is to identify elements in early childhood education that help children like Amanda make progress in the multiple intelligences and democratic life skills. Part Two of this book discusses the educational environment conducive to both development of multiple intelligences and progress toward the democratic life skills.

## Toward Responsible Citizenship

Although his name will long be associated with the theory of multiple intelligences, Gardner's theoretical work has since moved to a focus on broader issues of the self in society (Gardner 2010). Building from his own personal history with music and the arts, as well as a keen awareness of social processes, Gardner's perspective has been to apply research to broad questions of the creative and ethical expressions of thought.

Out of the work that led to the development of the multiple intelligences, Gardner has initiated large collaborative projects continuing to this day. His first was Project Zero, an ongoing research collaborative on the interaction of artistic expression and cognitive processing. Again with associates, the GoodWork Project was started— dedicated to "the study of work that is at once excellent in its technical aspects, ethically responsible, and personally engaging" (Gardner, Csikszentmihalyi, & Damon 2001).

Gardner has written of the states of mind in exemplary individuals able to transform their educations into three essential human endeavors: engagement in life, excellence in effort, and ethics as personal guide (Gardner 2010). With this focus he harkens back to an early influence on his thought and work, Jean Piaget, whose goal for education was autonomy, the ability to think intelligently and ethically (Piaget [1932] 1997). Similarly, Gardner moves forward the ideas of other progressive thinkers over the years who have understood the importance of educating the young for civil, democratic living and of teaching for the integrated self.

For me, Gardner serves as a transitional figure between psychological constructs for healthy personal development of the twentieth century and constructs for healthy psycho-neurological development (involving the new neuroscience) in the twenty-first. Fascinating to me is the congruence in the conclusions of the psychologists and educators of this chapter that schooling can no longer be restricted to narrowly defined academic gains. Education for the twenty-first century must respond to the developing whole child, to the expression of multiple intelligences, and to the social-emotional skills all citizens need in order to sustain civilization into the century to come (Cloud 2010). In the next chapter we continue the discussion by looking at the emerging neuroscience and its connection to education for the democratic life skills.

# Neuroscience and Nurturing Relationships

This chapter explores the connection of neuroscience (the study of the structure and functioning of the brain) to teaching for the democratic life skills. Neuroscientists hypothesize that nurturing relationships build trust and lower stress levels in children (Cozolino 2006; Siegel 2001). My view is that such relationships in the classroom can empower children to gain the safety-oriented democratic life skills (1 and 2) and make progress in the growth-oriented skills (3, 4, and 5). We start with the key ideas of two innovative psychologists whose classic work on mother-child relationships is being supported by brain research. During the second half of the twentieth century, their work updated how we think about the interface of family and school in the healthy development of the young child.

DLS 1: Finding acceptance as a member of the group and as a worthy individual

DLS 2: Expressing strong emotions in non-hurting ways

DLS 3: Solving problems creatively—independently and in cooperation with others

DLS 4: Accepting unique human qualities in others

DLS 5: Thinking intelligently and ethically

## The Attachment Theory of Bowlby and Ainsworth

Established in the traditional approach to psychotherapy—providing therapy to an individual in an office or clinic—John Bowlby looked in new ways at the closeness of the mother-child relationship as the foundation for the child's mental health. He developed the concept of **attachment,** which is a "lasting psychological connectedness between human beings" (Bowlby [1969] 1982, 194). He concluded from his research that when the mother-child attachment is based on consistent maternal warmth, responsiveness, and support, the child gains a lasting sureness in the affairs of life ([1969] 1982). Over time, Bowlby's work caused many in his field to look anew at the focus and location of psychotherapy.

Mary Ainsworth was a specialist in cross-cultural psychological research whose early studies on mother-child relationships were conducted in east Africa. Ainsworth furthered attachment theory by arguing that the attachment *style* of the mother predicts the coping abilities of the growing child (Ainsworth et al.1978). Ainsworth documented the differing impact on children of attachment styles that were *secure, ambivalent-insecure,* and *avoidant-insecure.* A fourth style, *disorganized-insecure,* later was documented by Main and Solomon (1986).

The work of Bowlby and Ainsworth perhaps is due some criticism for underplaying the role of fathers, surrogate parents, and secondary attachments with persons outside of the family, such as teachers. Also, the theory was developed largely before much was known about atypical gene neurostructures responsible for conditions such as autism spectrum disorders. It thus does not take into account the fact that adults can do little to change a child's atypical neurostructure and must work very hard to accommodate it. Children with atypical neurostructures respond differently to a parent's attempts to build positive bonds, which makes it challenging to build secure attachments.

Bowlby and Ainsworth nonetheless advanced a now widely accepted paradigm for active professional support of caregivers to ensure a child's healthy development. Studies, books, and dedicated journals continue to show the impact of relational therapy on the quality of attachments and children's consequent behaviors and development (Friedman & Boyle 2008). That is, assisting caregivers to improve the quality of attachments leads to greater mental health in the developing child.

**attachment:** a lasting psychological connectedness between human beings, particularly between a child and parent or other meaningful adult

## Attachment Styles

The following is an adaptation of Ainsworth's three attachment styles (Ainsworth et al., 1978), together with a fourth style developed later by Main and Solomon (1986).

**Securely attached** children readily accept contact initiated by a parent and greet the parent's return with positive behavior. Parents of securely attached children tend to play more with their children. Additionally, these parents react more quickly to their children's needs and are generally more responsive to their children than are the parents of insecurely attached children. Securely attached children are described as less disruptive, less aggressive, and more mature than children with ambivalent or avoidant attachment styles and have been shown to be more empathic during later stages of childhood.

Children who are **ambivalently attached** tend to be extremely suspicious of strangers. In some cases, the child might passively reject the parent by refusing comfort, or may openly display direct aggression toward the parent. Ambivalent-insecure attachment in children often is associated with parents who do not respond promptly to their children's needs and are less responsive to their children in general. As these children grow older, their teachers often describe them as clingy and over-dependent. Without clear direction and support, venturing forth into new learning experiences tends to be a major challenge for these children.

Children with an **avoidant attachment** style tend to avoid parents and caregivers. These children might not reject attention from a parent, but neither do they seek the parent's comfort or contact. Children with an avoidant attachment show no preference between a parent and a complete stranger. As they become adults, those who experienced avoidant attachment tend to have difficulty with intimacy, empathy, and close relationships. Other common characteristics include a failure to support partners during stressful times and an inability to share feelings, thoughts, and emotions with partners.

Children with a **disorganized-insecure attachment** style show a lack of clear attachment behavior. Their actions and responses to caregivers are often a mix of behaviors, including avoidance or resistance. These children are described as displaying dazed behavior, sometimes seeming either confused or apprehensive in the presence of a caregiver. Parents who elicit a combination of both fear and reassurance in a child contribute to a disorganized attachment style. As adults, children who experienced disorganized-insecure attachment patterns tend to feel ambivalence in relationships and have difficulty making decisions.

With advances in neuroscience, researchers are documenting the validity of the dynamics undergirding attachment theory—that the quality of the parent-child relationship is predictive of the child's developing mental health (Fisher et al. 2006; Shonkoff & Garner 2012). In the balance of the chapter I'll discuss the neuroscience of caregiver[1]-child relationships. The discussion identifies by name a few of the key brain systems in the social process of "the making of a mind" (Galinsky 2010). A helpful primer for readers on the vocabulary of brain development and functioning is the fourth edition of *How the Brain Learns* by David A. Sousa (2011).

The rationale for the discussion is straightforward. *It is toxic stress that overwhelms healthy brain functioning in young children—not mis-attributed "character flaws"—and causes the fight-or-flight behaviors teachers find so challenging* (Shonkoff & Garner 2012). The mitigating dynamic that reduces stress, builds trust, and empowers healthy brain development and prosocial behavior is the positive adult-child relationship (Cozolino 2006).

## Healthy Brain Development

An authority on relationships and the developing mind, Daniel Siegel (2001) begins his classic work, *The Developing Mind: How Relationships and the Brain Interact to Shape Who We Are,* with a basic neuroscience concept: The brain is an open system that physically changes throughout life in response to experiences, especially those that occur in the context of close relationships. Experiences shape not only the information that enters a child's brain but also the way in which the brain processes that information. Siegel emphasizes that the most important experiences for building healthy brains occur through the bonding relationships of early life.

During the early years, the making of a mind results from an amazing dual function of the genes each person is born with (Siegel 2001): a template function, and a transcription function.

**template function**: the working of genes to build the basic structure of the brain

Through a **template function**, genes build the foundation of the brain, which includes billions of neurons with up to 100,000 synaptic connections for each. Many neurons develop elaborate interconnecting branches, called dendrites. Some of these neural clusters grow and define the different regions of the brain, operating all human functions from keeping us breathing to empowering us to engage in socially responsive actions (Siegel 2001; Sousa 2011).

But genes also serve a **transcription function** through the brain's transforming of perceived experiences into the synaptic connections across the neural structures of the brain. Siegel and Cozolino (2006) agree that brains are *social organisms*. Infants are born with more neural architecture than they will ever use. As a result of social experiences,

---

[1]Significant numbers of children are being raised by family members other than parents—such as grandparents—or in foster homes or orphanages. I use *parent/parenting* and *caregiver/caregiving* as synonymous terms.

some synaptic connections in the brain develop, and other connections, circumvented and unused, are pruned back; neurons originally present in the neuroarchitecture die off. In this way, relationships fundamentally affect how our brains function and develop (Shonkoff & Phillips 2000). The transcription of experience into synaptic matter is best understood by recognizing that 70 percent of the brain's neural structure forms *after* birth (Cozolino 2006), largely in the connecting cell structures (synapses and dendrites) among neurons (Sousa 2011).

For most infants, during the first months of life, good-enough caregiving facilitates healthy development of the limbic system—including the regions of the brain known as the amygdala, the hypothalamus, and the hippocampus (Cozolino 2006; Siegel 2001). The limbic system mediates the emotional aspects of experiences and interactions. If the brain perceives threat in the immediate environment, the amygdala and other elements of the limbic system trigger a stress hormone reaction and fight-or-flight reaction tendencies in the individual (Sousa 2012).

> There are about 100 billion neurons in the adult human brain—about 16 times as many neurons as people on this planet and about the same as the number of stars in the Milky Way galaxy. Each neuron can have up to 10,000 dendrite branches. This means that it possible to have up to one quadrillion (1,000,000,000,000,000) synaptic connections in one brain (Sousa 2011, 22).

For a young child with a consistently secure attachment, brain development is not dominated by fear and stress. The amygdala does not become hypersensitive to perceptions of threat. The hypothalamus is able to maintain homeostasis, a dynamic state of mind and body balance (Sousa 2011). The hippocampus is able to generate not just normal synaptic connections but also, research now indicates, new neurons that facilitate its chief operations: processing long-term and working memories and integrating new information with what has been already learned (Shonkoff & Phillips 2000; Sousa 2011). During the preschool years, the hippocampus operates in conjunction with the frontal lobe, temporal lobe, and prefrontal cortex development, gradually making language and conscious thought possible.

**transcription function:** the working of genes to continue brain development by converting the individual's perceived experiences into brain matter

Good-enough caregiving empowers the child to begin developing **executive function** as the child moves into the preschool years. Executive function refers to the coordinated abilities to stay on task in attending and thinking; plan and organize thoughts as in problem solving; and use short- and long-term memory to facilitate thought processing (Copple & Bredekamp 2009; Galinsky 2010). The prefrontal cortex region is principally responsible for executive function, which remains a work in progress until adulthood. As a result of the interplay of experiences within the child's stress tolerance, synaptic connections across the frontal lobes, prefrontal cortex, and hippocampus (among other systems) develop normally, and emerging executive function works as it should. Development progresses in harmonious ways across the various domains—physical, emotional, cognitive, linguistic, and social (Shonkoff & Phillips 2000). (The importance of developmentally appropriate practice is paramount here, facilitating the learning and development of the whole child. This is further discussed in Part Two.)

**executive function:** the coordinated abilities to stay on task in attending and thinking, plan and organize thoughts as in problem solving, and utilize short- and long-term memory to facilitate thought processing

## Windows of Opportunity

A noteworthy occurrence in healthy brain development during the earliest years involves **windows of opportunity**—"important periods in which the young brain responds to certain types of input from its environment to create or consolidate neural networks"—the transcription gene function at work (Sousa 2011, 25). The foundations of emotional control (via healthy attachments) must be consolidated by about age 3 for healthy social-emotional capacities to continue developing throughout a lifetime (Sousa 2011). Likewise, the windows of opportunity for the basics of cognitive, linguistic, math/logic, and foundational motor skills all occur during the first few years.

**windows of opportunity:** important periods in which the young brain responds to certain types of input from its environment to create or consolidate neural networks

For most children, during the earliest years windows of opportunity are open wide for transactions between the brain and the environment. This is why healthy adult-child attachments are so crucial during this time, when caring adults can most effectively nurture the young child's boundless potential for learning.

## The Effects of Stress in Early Life

**toxic stress:** high levels of stress not ameliorated through a secure attachment; causes neurochemical reactions that overwhelm the hypothalamus, the center for maintaining the normal state of functioning, and hyperstimulate the child's fight-or-flight reactions

As part of the limbic system, the amygdala controls the child's interpretation of possible threat (Sousa 2011). (Threat, in line with attachment theory, often comes down to feelings of abandonment.) Perceived threat causes the amygdala, in concert with the hypothalamus, to induce the adrenal glands to secrete stress hormones. This can trigger reactions in a child ranging from crying and tantrums, to overtly acting out, to psychologically or physically withdrawing from situations (all fight-or-flight reactions) (Gunnar, Herrera, & Hostinar 2009).

**Toxic stress**—high levels of stress not ameliorated through a secure attachment—causes neurochemical reactions that actually overwhelm the hypothalamus, the center for maintaining the normal state of functioning (Shonkoff & Garner 2012). The priority of brain functioning then switches to maintaining basic needs rather than pursuing the more cognitively demanding tasks associated with learning and social interactions.

LeDoux (1996) has documented that over time toxic stress causes physical deterioration to the receptors of the hippocampus, undermining the individual's ability to process memory and thought. Shonkoff and Garner (2012) argue that without the buffeting effects of secure attachments, adversities experienced by the young child cause a long-term decrease in the child's abilities to trust the world, develop feelings of self-adequacy, manage emotions, and engage effectively in learning and social transactions. Young children subject to toxic stress develop long-term tendencies toward anxiety and depression (Gunnar, Herrera, & Hostinar 2009).

### Unmet Caregiver Survival Needs

In a classic early childhood book titled *Caring: Supporting Children's Growth,* Rita Warren (1977) observed that inside every inadequate parent is a child who has not been allowed to grow up. Some parents, as children, were subjected to insecure parenting attachments themselves and never experienced the resiliency (the ability of the brain to heal itself) that can come from later buffering relationships (Lowenthal 1999). Their own brain development was adversely affected.

Less-than-secure attachments may be due to

- The caregiver's own unmet safety needs
- Special needs of the child due to atypical template and transcription patterns in the developing brain
- Adversity/trauma experienced by family members that undermines the attachment
- A combination of these factors

Without ongoing support from partners or other family members, these parents predictably are challenged in forming healthy attachments with their own children (Ainsworth et al.1978). A benefit of attachment theory is the documented importance of direct support that such programs as Head Start can provide for adults still struggling with survival needs. Lowenthal (1999) and Gunnar and colleagues (2009) stress that with directed therapeutic actions by significant adults, children can develop secure attachments, and due to the plasticity of their developing brains (the ready ability to build synaptic connections and networks), they can heal and become resilient.

### Special Needs, Diagnosed and Undiagnosed

Since I began doing training and conference sessions 35 years ago, I have noticed a trend in participants' comments about the number of children they serve who have diagnosed or strongly suspected special needs. In general they estimate that compared to the late

1990s, the percentage of children in their classes who have special needs has increased from around 10 percent to about 30 percent. While many of these teachers work in Head Start programs, which serve families who tend to be confronted with high levels of stress, I hear these same comments from many teachers in other early childhood settings. I continue to be surprised by the consistency in the percentages given.

These teachers include in the special needs category children who have brains with neural structures that seem to process experiences differently. Most obvious are children who are on the fetal alcohol or autism spectrum or who have attention-deficit/hyperactivity disorder. Children who have genetically related mental health problems—those with depression, bipolar disorder, or schizophrenia, for example—also would be included among those who process experiences differently, as would children with disabilities such as Down syndrome or cerebral palsy.

Less obvious are children with "extreme" temperaments—for example, children who are severely shy or impulsive, whose brains may be hypersensitive to challenge, criticism, or overload. One illustration is an infant who, because of his particular neural architecture, has difficulty responding to and showing affection. The caregiver may interpret distancing by the infant as a reflection on her parenting, become depressed, and show less affection toward the infant. The infant then feels and reacts to the additional stress, probably with continued withdrawal. Ainsworth would say that such a child has an avoidant-insecure attachment style. A long-term cycle of stress—moving from fight-or-flight reaction, to parental rejection, to heightened stress, and then to reinforced fight-or-flight reaction—becomes a worrisome possibility (Gunnar, Herrera, & Hostinar 2009).

Raising children with diagnosed or undiagnosed special needs is challenging for all parents, and particularly so for single parents, surrogate parents, and those dealing with financial and environmental stressors. Teachers and other supportive professionals can partner with families to sustain secure parent-child attachments (Davis & Yang 2005; Galinsky 2010). I address the vital nature of reciprocal teacher-family member relations in Chapter 6.

## Trauma in the Life of the Young Child

Neuroscience has increased our understanding that physical and psychological trauma to the brain can result in post-traumatic stress disorder (PTSD). Although PTSD has long been associated with the violence of war and physical assault, we now know that because of the sensitivity of the child's brain during early development, post-traumatic stress reactions can be caused by less severe trauma (psychological as well as physical) than previously believed (Gunnar, Herrera, & Hostinar 2009; Lubit 2010). These authors argue that post-traumatic stress in young children can disrupt healthy patterns of attachment already forming and aggravate the complications of insecure attachments.

An example is a preschooler whose brother was wounded in the first war with Iraq, sometimes referred to by their family as the Gulf Coast War, during the 1990s. While the brother was still away, the child began to have panic attacks whenever the family drove to a nearby town. Mom and his preschool teacher were able to help only after they talked with the child. They came to realize that the family often drove "the golf course

way," a shortcut identified by this landmark. The child heard the words "golf course" as "gulf coast." They figured out that he thought the family would be driving through a war zone that had taken his brother away from him. For adults to recognize that panic attacks and other fight-or-flight reactions are not problem behaviors but may be post-traumatic stress reactions, they must take the time to know the child well.

Other, more insidious adversities frequently cause post-traumatic stress in children (Lubit 2010). Going hungry or being homeless, and experiencing disruption to family structure or dynamics are all events that contribute to potentially toxic childhood stress.

The effects of trauma can affect children at any age, disrupting healthy patterns of adult-child attachment that may have already formed. The younger the child, the fewer resources the developing brain can muster to protect itself from harm and initiate resiliency (Lowenthal 1999; Lubit 2010). Children who have difficulty with finding acceptance and expressing strong emotions in non-hurting ways (DLS 1 and 2) often seem to have the high stress levels caused by acute or chronic trauma. The situation is made worse if adults are unable to provide the (clearly focused) nurturing care that the child needs— and/or if they punish the child for expressing fear, anxiety, or other strong feelings by acting out (Gunnar, Herrera, & Hostinar 2009).

## Stress-Caused Behaviors

With young children it is helpful to think of stress reactions in terms of degrees. A child dealing with unmanaged stress may show, at varying levels of intensity, behaviors such as an inability to stay focused, frequent emotional outbursts, and the rejection of relationship overtures (Gunnar, Herrera, & Hostinar 2009; Lowenthal 1999). These fight-or-flight behaviors make secure attachments difficult to sustain. More specifically, toxic stress characteristically shows itself in children's

- ◆ Being hyper-sensitized to the threat aspect of situations, making fight-or-flight reactions more likely and positive interactions more difficult

- ◆ Imprinting hurtful experiences as emotional memories, thus endangering the child's later ability to regulate and manage emotions and impulses

- ◆ Generating a self-fulfilling expectation of rejection based on an emerging negative self-image, a possible long-term effect on personality (Gunnar, Herrera, & Hostinar 2009; Lowenthal 1999; Lubit 2010)

These behavior patterns are challenging for most adults. Tantrums, dramatic moping, reactive aggressive outbursts, and instrumental aggression such as bullying can test any adult's emotional and social intelligence. Still, meting out punishment in an attempt to stop the behavior keeps the child's stress levels high and makes it even more difficult for the child to develop healthy executive functioning (Gartrell 2011a). Without a buffering relationship and guidance, the child is in danger of falling into a cycle of conflict, adult and peer rejection, and renewed stress (Gunnar, Herrera, & Hostinar 2009; Shonkoff & Garner 2012).

So, I agree with many who see a child's acting-out behavior as a symptom of a hurting brain, the child's cry for help (e.g., Cozolino 2006; Montessori [see Chapter 2]; Siegel 2001). The studies of Ladd and associates (Ladd & Dinella 2009; Ladd & Ettekal 2009) have documented a pattern of aggression and rejection in early childhood as predictive of continued rejection, behavior problems, and academic underachievement in later school life. As noted by Ladd and other authors referenced in this chapter, including Galinsky (2010), the importance of caregivers and teachers in the life of the young child is clear. Brains develop differently depending on the attachments that adults and young children are able to form, including in the face of adverse life situations.

## The Internal Dynamic, Neuroscience, and Education

Education for democracy, as explored by Froebel, Montessori, Dewey, Purkey, Katz, Elkind, and Gardner, includes a common abiding respect for the internal dynamic of development within each child. None of these individuals argues that the developmental dynamic is self-defining—that education should be without structure except for the whims of the child. Collectively, they claim that effective education results when teachers attune themselves to the template and transcription processes of development within each child. These educators see teaching and learning as interactive, or in Vygotsky's ([1935] 1978) terms, a mutual scaffolding of each other's learning. They regard education as a fundamentally social process—children learning in unique ways, but through cooperative transactions with other minds (Galinsky 2010).

The message of this chapter is that neuroscience positively identifies, in ways that social scientists could only intuit before, the internal dynamic of developing brains (if not the miracle behind the dynamic). The scanning equipment used by neuroscientists helps us understand not just how brains develop but also the kinds of experiences that either contribute to or undermine healthy brain formation. By understanding the dangers of dysfunctional relationships for the dynamic brain, society has an opportunity to reframe how we look at the functions of significant adults in the lives of children. The relationships that effective caregivers and teachers build with children help the young meet their needs for safety and acceptance, and then progress in ways that can, ultimately, transform our society.

We hear in education circles that children must be challenged to do their best. The neuroscience of nurturing relationships suggests that perhaps a better expression is that children should be intrigued in the process of learning. In an encouraging classroom, in which children are not just expected to learn but are also supported in learning through positive relationships with others, children can better manage stress and are more motivated to learn (Baker & Manfredi/Petitt 2004; Gunnar & Quevedo 2007; Ostrowsky & Jung 2003).

Along these lines, an important term in progressive education is ***mastery motivation*** (Reineke, Sonsteng, & Gartrell 2008). Mastery motivation refers to the intrinsic drive for learning within the child when the miraculous psychological dynamic of brain development is aligned with concrete opportunities for engagement in meaningful activity (as when the program is developmentally appropriate for the learner). When teachers appreciate and guide the internal dynamic of intrinsic motivation within each child, learning becomes active, interactive, and significant (Gartrell 2011b; Maslow 1988).

**mastery motivation:** the intrinsic drive for learning within the child

An honest appraisal in the twenty-first century is that schools do not just educate; they also socialize the young for modern society. Many early childhood educators accept this point of view. When the interface of healthy brain development, developmentally appropriate education, and the furthering of democracy is made clear, we have a definite direction in which the socialization of schooling during this century should go. Families and teachers should work together. Curricula should be less prescribed and more emergent. Assessments should be less standardized and more authentic. Guidance that teaches, rather than discipline that punishes, should be practiced. And classrooms should become encouraging communities. We explore these topics in Part Two of the book.

# The Early Childhood Lead

# PART TWO

# Best Practices in Early Childhood Education: Not Just for Young Children

art One established historical and intellectual roots for progressive education—education that prepares the whole child for effective, civil participation in a diverse, modern democratic society. In addition, Part One profiled education innovators and psychological and neuropsychological insights that set the foundation for teaching the democratic life skills.

Part Two provides the superstructure for that teaching. It develops the idea that best practices in early childhood education, when applied at all levels of education, define a schooling approach that effectively supports the development of the democratic life skills. We'll take an in-depth look at the umbrella concept of developmentally appropriate practice, focusing on three elements: family-teacher partnerships, classroom programming that is responsive to individual learners' levels and interests, and the use of guidance to teach for social-emotional development.

In Part Two of the book I posit the following:

1. Schools and education programs are successful, especially with children from families with low incomes, when they provide comprehensive education services. Such services begin with ongoing reciprocal relationships between educators and family members.

2. Best practices in early childhood programs, specifically in high-quality preschool programs, have long-term, beneficial socialization effects for children.

3. Comprehensive, nurturing, and developmentally appropriate education provides the socialization *all* children, at *all* levels of education, need in order to be productive citizens and healthy individuals in modern democratic society.

This chapter will focus on quality, comprehensive early childhood education, which has much to offer education at all levels.

## Not an Achievement Gap, an *Education* Gap

During the 1960s social observers Edgar Friedenberg (1962) and Paul Goodman (1966) provided cogent commentary on American education. They argued that even more than educating youth, schools served a socializing function, acculturating the young for compliant membership in society for whatever roles they may fill. Other educational reformers during this time, including Herbert Kohl (1967) and Jonathan Kozol (1967), spoke out against what they perceived to be a continuation of regressive schooling for students of color. The term *regressive schooling* refers to public school policies and practices that lagged behind other aspects of the civil rights movement of the time—socialization practices in classrooms that on a de facto basis perpetuated second-class citizenship for children from minority groups. The combined argument of these critics was that, more than educating for intellect, schools were socializing American students to assume compliant roles as adults along the social strata of society. In the case of students from minority groups, this socialization was toward a lower social status.

Kozol (1991) and others (Barton & Coley 2009; Boyd-Zaharias & Pate-Bain 2008) have continued the criticism of underequipped, understaffed, and underfunded schools in inner cities and less affluent suburbs. A lack of effective education in significant social groups means widespread future unemployment, an untenable situation for the students it impacts and for society.

Years of experience working with gifted students in underresourced communities and schools—some of whom became successful and some of whom did not—have convinced me that American society has an *education gap* rather than an *achievement gap*.

**achievement gap:**
the disparity in academic performance among different groups of students, as determined by standardized tests

The **achievement gap** in education refers to the disparity in academic performance among different groups of students, as determined by standardized tests. The problem with this term is that it narrows the criteria for success in education to easily computed but overly simplistic standardized test scores (Barton & Coley 2009). This narrow focus leads to a mistaken conventional wisdom that the problem resides only in underachieving students and underachieving teachers (Barton & Coley 2009; Kozol 1991; Rose 2004). The term deflects attention away from the underlying causes of unmet educational outcomes and erroneously implies a level playing field among students, schools, and communities, regardless of the differences in the resource base across those settings (Boyd-Zaharias & Pate-Bain 2008).

**education gap:**
the disparity in the quality of education experienced by different groups of learners due to an inadequacy of targeted, coordinated resources to overcome the pervasive impact of poverty

In contrast, the term **education gap** refers to the disparity in the quality of education experienced by different groups of learners. This term identifies a cause—the inability of society to provide the focused resources needed to overcome the pervasive impact of poverty on learners from low-income households (Jensen 2009; Kozol 1991). Imperfect school funding practices, with resources for schools largely tied to the affluence of their communities, are a primary cause of educational and social inequities.

The model of effective, comprehensive early childhood programs can help meet the needs of children *and* their families, by offering families physical and psychological support, guidance, and education in community-based schools. As described in the sections that follow, families and schools working together can accomplish what neither socializing entity can accomplish alone.

# Comprehensive Education Services

## Head Start

Comprehensive early childhood education became a coordinated, nationally available service through Project Head Start in 1965, as one of the War on Poverty bills signed into law by then-President Lyndon Johnson. Focused on preschool children and families with low income, **comprehensive education services** through Head Start typically include physical, mental, and dental health screenings for the child with follow-up assistance; nutrition support for the child and nutrition education for the family; parenting education and counseling; family literacy assistance; and career support services for families. Through the programs' sponsoring

agencies, many Head Start families also receive a variety of financial support services, referrals (with support) for social services from other agencies, counseling, fuel assistance, and weatherization improvements for homes (L. Pigatti, pers. comm.).

Head Start's support of families is perhaps most visible in its many types of parent involvement activities (National Head Start Association 2012). Family members are welcome to visit and volunteer in classrooms. Home visits, either as a primary program delivery option or as a supplement to classroom programming, have for years been an operational priority. Family members are encouraged to join in program events and activities, engage in supplementary family services, serve on committees and councils, and even to become staff members.

Head Start programs have been responsive to changes in family needs over the years, such as higher numbers of families needing full-time child care and support services for children with special needs. In many cases Head Start programs contract and work with area child care providers and school district special education personnel to come into classrooms.

## Public Schools

Influenced by innovations and accomplishments within Head Start, other schools, programs, and projects have picked up on the importance of comprehensive education services as a means of closing the education gap (Daggett 2005). This section profiles two of those efforts to illustrate how public schools can serve as community centers and provide programs that further society's democratic ideals.

### School of the 21st Century

One national effort in comprehensive education is School of the 21st Century (21C), begun by Edward Zigler with Matia Finn-Stevenson at Yale University (1999). While Zigler is noted for his leadership role in the founding of Head Start, 21C is a separate, interstate venture initiated not by a government agency but by a nonprofit group affiliated with Yale.

21C is a national network of locally funded public schools that meet specific standards for the integration of preschool care and education, supplemental family support services, and primary-grade public education. 21C takes the concept of **community**

**comprehensive education services:** family and child support services incorporated into schools, such as child care, parent education, and health and nutrition support

**community schools:** schools that serve as community centers with close ties to families

**schools**—schools serving as community centers with close ties to families—to a polished demonstration level.

Six criteria must be met by 21C schools and illustrate the comprehensive approach taken by the project (Finn-Stevenson & Zigler, 1999):

+ Guidance and support for parents

+ Early care and education

+ Before-school, after-school, and vacation programs for school-age children

+ Health education and services

+ Networks and training for child care providers

+ Information and referral services for families

### Harlem Children's Zone Promise Academy Charter Schools

A second illustration of a public school initiative in providing comprehensive education services is the Harlem Children's Zone's three Promise Academy Charter Schools—two elementary schools and one middle school. (Charter schools are publicly funded schools that usually have a unique philosophical perspective and are often sponsored by outside agencies.) In addition to operating the charter schools, the Harlem Children's Zone Project supports children attending the public schools within the zone with classroom assistants and after-school programs.

The Harlem Children's Zone Project grew out of social service efforts in this large neighborhood of New York City during the 1970s (Harlem Children's Zone 2009). By 2009, the Children's Zone Agency was serving more than 8,000 children and 6,000 adults in a nearly 100-block section of Harlem.

The website for the Promise Academy Charter Schools opens with this snapshot:

> The mission is to give children in Harlem a high-quality, well-rounded education. To do so, the schools have assembled talented, loving staffs that create safe, enriching environments where children know they are cared about and that there are high expectations of them.

> The children at the three Promise Academy schools have an extended school day and year, giving them the time they need to master basic skills as well as explore the arts and sciences. To make sure they are ready for the rigors of the school day, the students receive healthy, freshly made meals and participate in daily physical activity. (Harlem Children's Zone 2009)

Students at the Promise Academy schools have demonstrated academic success. In 2008, the percentage of third graders who scored at or above grade level on the statewide math test was at or near 100. Middle school students have likewise made great strides, with 87 percent of eighth graders scoring at grade level in math, up from 40 percent when students entered the school in the sixth grade.

This success has been attributed to the project's ability over time to counter the pervasive impact of poverty with comprehensive cradle-to-college services, both in school and out of it, for the children and their families (Tough 2008). The schools themselves are not necessarily the prime movers of comprehensive education services; rather, they are part of a cohesive community effort dedicated to concrete social progress for all—particularly the children.

Perhaps the defining feature of these and other schools that provide comprehensive education services is reciprocal partnerships with parents above and beyond the schooling of the child. Schools and programs that are community centers, building from the comprehensive education and service model first provided by Head Start, make a lasting difference in children's lives and help to close the education gap.

# Long-Term Benefits of Comprehensive Early Childhood Education

Carefully designed early childhood models have been operating since the 1960s. These programs have been developed by researchers using particular theoretical frameworks, and many have been the subjects of long-term research. The most-studied models are the Perry Preschool Project in Michigan, the Chicago Child-Parent Centers, and the Carolina Abecedarian Project (for descriptions of these programs, see Promising Practices Network 2011a, b, c). But meta-analysis reports (critical summaries of longitudinal, experimental, and other studies) indicate that other quality programs have similar lasting benefits for children. The following section provides annotated summaries of four large-scale meta-analyses of published early childhood studies in the United States.

## Princeton University/Brookings Institute Meta-Analysis

A 1995 meta-analysis examination was part of a collaboration of the Woodrow Wilson School of Public and International Affairs at Princeton University and the Brookings Institution. Barnett (1995) investigated 36 studies that looked at a number of model programs, including the three identified above, and also several large-scale public programs of reputed quality.

Barnett's analysis showed that the early childhood care and education programs significantly reduced rates of grade retention and special education placements, while increasing levels of high school completion and postsecondary program attendance. The longer term studies showed higher employment levels and lower incarceration and welfare rates than in the control groups—indicating significant paybacks to society. The Princeton/Brookings report (Barnett 1995) concludes,

> These effects are large enough and persistent enough to make a meaningful difference in the lives of children from low-income families: for many children, preschool programs can mean the difference between failing and passing, regular or special education, staying out of trouble or becoming involved in crime and delinquency, dropping out or graduating from high school. (43)

## RAND Corporation Meta-Analysis

Ten years after the Princeton/Brookings report, the RAND Corporation released a meta-analysis report of 20 research studies on comprehensive early childhood education programs (RAND 2005). The report concludes,

> Even though findings suggest that early benefits in terms of cognition or school achievement may eventually fade, the evidence indicates that there can be longer-lasting and substantial gains in outcomes such as special education placement and grade retention, high school graduation rates, labor market outcomes, social welfare program use, and [lower rates of] crime. (2)

The RAND report found that the financial benefits to society from investment in quality early childhood education was consistently positive, as high as $17.07 for each dollar spent on the program (determined for the longest running studies analyzed). Benefits included reduced welfare use among participants, greater income earned, and more taxes paid.

Parents were also found to have benefitted in programs that specifically included parental supports. Relevantly degreed teachers, positive home-school connections, developmentally appropriate practice, and small group sizes were characteristics of the most successful programs analyzed in the studies.

## National Early Childhood Technical Assistance Center Meta-Analysis

In a 2005 compilation of abstracts on studies of the efficacy of early intervention programs, the following is noted by the National Early Childhood Technical Assistance Center (NECTAC) Clearinghouse (Diefendorf & Goode 2005):

> An extensive body of research indicates that high quality early intervention for at-risk infants, toddlers and young children and their families is a sound economic investment. Studies have found a number of long-term cost savings in terms of decreased grade repetition, reduced special education spending, enhanced productivity, lower welfare costs, increased tax revenues, and lower juvenile justice costs. (1)

## Public Policy Forum Meta-Analysis

Public Policy Forum (2008), which "serves as a neutral, independent forum for open dialogue on public policy," published a report of 26 separate studies, experimental and cross-sectional, as well as longitudinal. Two-thirds of these studies were done after the year 2000. Findings were similar to the previous reports discussed. Across the types of studies analyzed, the 18 that addressed educational issues such as grade-retention rates, special education placements, and graduation levels all found statistically significant long-term positive gains for preschool attendees.

Further, the 11 studies that addressed external benefits to society found positive gains at a statistically significant level, up to a 13:1 dollar rate of return. As indicated, the positive return to society in quality preschool attendance is from increased work productivity as well as decreased social services and law enforcement costs. The comparisons in the 11 studies were with control groups who did not attend comparable early childhood programs.

## Inferences

Whatever the causes of a leveling effect seen with early academic gains among children, I think the lasting "mega benefits" shown by these studies deserve our full attention. As they grew, children who attended high-quality preschool programs—when compared with peers who did not attend comparable programs—experienced long-term benefits. Trends in the studies indicate that these individuals

- Were retained at grade level less often
- Were more likely to complete high school
- Were more likely to attend post-secondary programs
- Received welfare services less often
- Were incarcerated less often
- Experienced better personal and family health outcomes
- Became productive enough to more than justify the costs to society of their preschool programs

My hypothesis about these effects is that the best practices used in these programs allowed for a positive socialization process during this time of maximum brain plasticity in the life of the child.

In the remaining chapters of Part Two we take an in-depth look at the umbrella concept of developmentally appropriate practice, but we'll begin the discussion of it here.

## Developmentally Appropriate Practice/Best Practice

As explained in Chapter 4, learning experiences that inspire children to investigate further ignite mastery motivation—an inherent drive in children to be active in the process of making meaning from experience and to master tasks (Reineke, Sonsteng, & Gartrell 2008). On the basis of what they have learned, children become intrigued with the prospect of related further learning. The children's interest in the activity is real, their engagement is total; their perseverance often is surprising and impressive. Through mastery motivation children act in intentional ways relative to intellectual exploration of a task or material at hand (for example, a 5-year-old asks to keep working during play time to complete a goodbye book for a student teacher; a 7-year-old sneak-reads his library book during arithmetic work time).

Learning experiences that encourage mastery motivation in children can be defined as *developmentally appropriate*. Developmentally appropriate practice "refers to decisions that vary with and adapt to the age, experience, interests, and abilities of individual children within a given age range" (Copple & Bredekamp 2006). For me, the definition is even simpler: Developmentally appropriate practice means providing learning experiences that ignite mastery motivation for each child in the group.

Effective teachers pick up on children's unique interests and expressions of their developing minds (Hyson 2012). They assist children in developing and honing their emerging intellectual talents along the directions of their particular abiding interests—and all within the purview of the curriculum (Copple 2012).

Quality comprehensive early childhood education—birth to age 8—can take many forms. The point is that developmentally appropriate practice has much to offer education beyond early childhood. Developmentally appropriate practice, in the context of comprehensive education services, provides the most promising approach to closing the education gap. And developmentally appropriate practice makes possible, through its emphasis on the whole child and healthy brain development, children's progress toward the five democratic life skills.

Chapters 6–9 explore the three elements of developmentally appropriate practice mentioned at the beginning of this chapter—parent-teacher partnerships; appropriate, responsive classroom programming; and the use of guidance—that can be applied at all levels to teach intelligent and ethical decision making, something children will use throughout their lives.

# Family-Teacher Partnerships: An Early Childhood Approach

**E**arly childhood educators long have understood the importance of homes and schools working together (NAEYC 2009). Froebel emphasized the need for home visits and mothers' meetings. In the Casa dei Bambini, Montessori held that regular mother-directress conferences were essential to children's progress. Moving beyond the expectation that mothers would be the only family members involved in children's education, James Hymes ([1953] 1973) is among those who began to frame "effective home-school relations" in more inclusive terms. Coming from a tradition of early childhood education as a service to families, Hymes was, with Edward Zigler and others, a key person in the founding of Head Start.

As we saw in Chapter 5, reciprocal teacher-family relationships are an integral part of Head Start. The approach to building reciprocal relationships as laid out in this chapter is clearly influenced by Project Head Start, but my hope is that readers will find the approach relevant to American schooling in a more general sense.

## Home and School Together

Parents generally recognize the importance of children's formative years and of positive adult-child relationships during those years. Early childhood professionals build partnerships with families and establish attachments with children to sustain the continuity of relationships for children. This is why NAEYC's position statement on developmentally appropriate practice so thoroughly documents the importance of family-teacher partnerships, particularly when families and early childhood professionals come from different cultural backgrounds (NAEYC 2009). The encouraging early childhood class-room expands upon home life for the child without trying to replace it (Gonzalez-Mena 2006).

In 2009 Halgunseth and colleagues published the NAEYC document *Family Engagement, Diverse Families, and Early Childhood Education Programs: An Integrated Review of the Literature.* The report details how parent involvement in education has been histori-cally viewed from a deficit model—that is, involvement with the school was to correct implicit weaknesses in the family that might detract from the child's education. The contemporary model, delineated in the report, is strengths based: Through a reciprocal relationship, the family and educator combine their separate knowledge and skills to forge a positive education for the child together. The importance of family engagement for children's healthy development and successful learning makes family-teacher part-nerships essential with older learners as well, beyond the early childhood years. At any level, the relationship needs to be reciprocal. It is part of a teacher's job to initiate such partnerships and collaborate with families to maintain and develop them.

## Building Trust Through Communication

The teacher's goal with family members is to establish and maintain a relationship based on mutual trust. As teachers learn more about the children's families and as fam-ily members learn more about the teacher and the program, they begin to work together on behalf of the children. Establishing communication to build this level of cooperation early in the year is essential. A teacher does not want the first significant contact with a parent to center on negative circumstances, such as scratches or bite marks caused or received by the parent's child. With a trust level built between parents and the teacher, when children encounter problems, the focus becomes how to work together to resolve the matter.

Here are five basic practices for cooperative communication that help teachers build partnerships with children's families.

### Written Notes (Even in This Electronic Age)

Many adults associate notes sent home with critical messages from the teacher. In en-couraging classrooms, however, the reason for notes is to announce events and to build relationships with families. In addition to describing upcoming events, notes should be either happygrams (notes complimentary of a child's efforts) or progress statements as follow-up to a conference. Because children wonder about the content of personal notes from the teacher, it is important to read them to the child before sending them home. If the tone of the note is encouraging, children generally will take pride in seeing that it is delivered.

### Digital Communication

More and more teachers and families with young children use Facebook, Twitter, You-Tube, email, interactive websites, texting, and other means of virtual connection. It is important to remember, however, that some families are not connected at all.

Through greeting meetings at the beginning of the school year, informal survey let-ters, and early conferences, teachers can discover which parents are and are not users of the different types of digital technology. The teacher needs to make sure those who do not use technology will not be disadvantaged in teacher-parent communication. One way is to ask parents if they would prefer hard-copy notes sent home or emails and whether they would prefer hard-copy newsletters or a regularly updated website. (If necessary, teachers can print out and send home paper versions, including photographs of children in action in the program.)

Teachers might find that some families would appreciate classes or assistance with technology use. Providing such assistance is another way to build relationships with families.

## Telephone Calls

Telephone calls to families are more direct than either notes or emails. Many teachers call or text parents regularly. Especially with parents who are nonreaders, phone calls allow for important connections. However, there is a note of privilege associated with being given a parent's cell phone number, and respect for this access is important.

Telephone calls allow for actual conversation but not for physical proximity and face-to-face contact. So, under normal circumstances I don't recommend that a teacher conduct a serious conference on the telephone; instead, use the call to set up a time to meet with the caregiving family member.

Telephone conversations are helpful for establishing and maintaining relationships with families, delivering happygram messages, following up on conference topics, and inviting parents to participate in special events. If the teacher wants to communicate more directly than with a note, a friendly phone call means a lot to a parent.

Some teachers use a phone answering machine as an electronic billboard. Each night they record assignments, upcoming events, and do-together ideas for families, which they can access at their leisure. Other teachers post phone call-in times when they are available to speak to families about their needs and concerns.

## Home Visits

Head Start and other comprehensive early childhood programs have long included home visits as a strategy to get to know and work with families and as opportunities for families to get to know program staff. Head Start home visitors work with both family member and child, and act partly as social workers and partly as early childhood teachers.

Home visits help teachers learn about family dynamics and children's response styles in ways they cannot within the confines of the classroom. The visits are also opportunities for teachers to learn about the families' cultural contexts and home languages so they can make decisions about what is developmentally appropriate for the children in their class.

> In a tongue-in-cheek list of the most difficult jobs in the world that I sometimes share in trainings, teachers have the third most difficult job, and being a parent comes in first. There is a three-way tie for second place: being a home visitor, a family child care provider, and a substitute middle school teacher.

When families are faced with difficult circumstances, home visits can be challenging. If educators see signs of possible child maltreatment, mandatory reporting requirements certainly apply. Short of that, however, the early childhood professional can use the information gained during visits to work with both family members and the child. Depending on the program and the circumstances, if the family would like assistance, the home visitor can also make referrals to other helping agencies. Programs need to establish and communicate clear policies spelling out what is and is not part of the home visitor's role. Supportive, ongoing relations between home visitors and supervisory administrators are essential.

## Family-Teacher Conferences

Except for home visits, conferences provide the most direct link between teacher and parent. Much has been written in recent years about family-teacher conferences (e.g., Gestwicki 2013; Gonzalez-Mena 2008). Gonzalez-Mena emphasizes that early childhood professionals need to see themselves as learners as well as teachers, especially when cultural differences, including a home language other than English, are involved. Gestwicki suggests that successful family-teacher conferences consist of three phases: *preparation, conduct,* and *evaluation.*

When *preparing,* the teacher needs to make sure families know the reasons for the conference. A program guidebook can include a statement about conferences that is repeated in follow-up communication. As appropriate, this information should be in the home languages of the program's children and families. Giving time options is helpful for families, including both night and daytime slots if possible. An informal, private setting, in which parents and the teacher can sit side by side at a table, is preferable to conversing across a desk. Teachers should plan adequate time for the discussion so parents do not feel hurried.

The teacher should have a folder or portfolio for each child with samples of the child's work over time, including photographs of the child's activities and projects. Dated observational notes are helpful. Some teachers may include video clips of the child at work, shared via a laptop or computer screen or tablet (preferably not on tiny-screened personal devices). This strategy is particularly useful when holding conferences with families of children who are dual language learners. A form to record notes from the conference, in preparation for a later written summary, rounds out this stage (Gestwicki 2013).

For the *conduct* of the conference, the teacher sets the tone with positive statements about the child, such as: "I really enjoy having Maybelle in class. She works hard and has such a sense of humor." The teacher asks the parents to share what they would like to see the conference accomplish. The teacher goes over the materials she has prepared, and invites the parents to discuss them. When the teacher talks about the child, she uses the technique known as the **compliment sandwich**—giving *at least* two positive statements about effort and progress that frame one suggestion for further growth.

The teacher also encourages family members to share information about their child's home life and experiences. She acknowledges the parents' comments and uses *reflective listening,* which means repeating back the thoughts and feelings the other person is expressing (Pappano 2007). Reflective listening helps ensure that the parents' messages have been received as intended. As the conference wraps up, the teacher summarizes decisions made and any follow-up plans, checking to make sure family members agree. The teacher ends the conference on a positive note (Gestwicki 2013).

Following the conference, the teacher *evaluates* the session by reviewing notes and completing a brief summary, perhaps on a prepared form. She files the original form and, when a follow-up plan has been agreed to, sends a copy to the parents—in their home language, if needed. The teacher reflects in personal terms about the success of the conference, initiates agreed-to follow-up actions, and notes plans for conferences to come.

An important trend in conferencing for children at all age levels is to include the learner along with the parents. Teachers' first reactions to this idea can be guarded; they (and the parents) may have to approach both the material and the communication process differently with the learner present. After teachers get used to this format, they commonly say that under most circumstances, they wouldn't have conferences any other way. Often a young child will sit in on part of the conference, then be free to play in the classroom if the discussion gets too involved.

**The Conference Setting**

Providing a comfortable setting for parent conferences is important. At one parent's suggestion, a teacher held conferences in a small Parents' Corner already established in the classroom. The corner included bulletin board dividers, two easy chairs, and a coatrack. The parents loved this.

In a primary school, a mother shared with a teacher that her husband literally had a gag reflex when he entered the doors of a school due to his own distressing experiences as a student. The teacher and couple then held the first conference in a neighborhood fast food restaurant. Dad later decided he could make the next conference in the classroom—the teacher had communicated clearly and consistently that their son was doing very well.

**compliment sandwich:** an encouragement technique that provides at least two positive statements about a child's effort and progress and one suggestion for growth.

**reflective listening:** repeating back the thoughts and feelings the other person is expressing

Gestwicki (2013) imparts this important point in her discussion of parent-teacher conferences:

It should be remembered that nonattendance at a conference does not necessarily indicate disinterest in the child or the school. Instead, it may be a reflection of different cultural or socioeconomic values, of extreme pressures or stress [on the] family or work demands. A teacher's response to nonattendance is to review the possible explanations . . . see if different scheduling or educational action will help, persist in invitations and efforts, and understand that other methods of reaching a parent will have to be used in the meantime. (288)

## Responding to Diversity in Families

In its many forms, cultural diversity is becoming ever more visible in American communities. Two explored here are linguistic diversity and religious diversity.

### Linguistic Diversity

According to a 2010 US Census Bureau report, a growing number of families in the United States speak a language other than English in the home—19.7 percent in 2007 (Shin & Kominski 2010). In 2009 Marian and colleagues examined 43 studies of differences between single-language and multi-language speakers. The following are just a few of the authors' findings:

◆ Early bilinguals use more neural regions for language processing.

◆ Bilingual children have been found to exhibit superior performance in divergent thinking and other related metacognitive skills.

◆ Bilingual adults are better than monolingual adults at learning new words.

The conclusion of these authors as well as of Genishi & Dyson (2009) is that American schooling, beginning in the early years, should help learners to become multilingual. Teachers who view dual language usage as a lasting neuropsychological gift for all children proactively accept this cultural strength in participating families (Genishi & Dyson 2009).

With families whose home language is not English, teachers work to build strong relationships and to make them feel welcome in the classroom. Nemeth (2010) suggests these practices for effectively including children whose home language is other than English:

◆ Have parents spend some time in the classroom with the child before leaving the child, if possible.

◆ Use pictures and languages on signs and displays that reflect children's home cultures and languages.

◆ Have teachers learn a few words in the children's home languages. Ask families for assistance with these words, or find translations online.

◆ Reflect each child's language and culture throughout the classroom—in children's books, on labels, on dolls, and in toys. Add foods and cooking tools that are familiar to the children to the kitchen area.

Nemeth (2012) also offers several suggestions for conducting conferences with parents who do not speak English or whose English is uncertain, particularly when challenging topics arise. These comments supplement the earlier comments on parent-teacher conferences:

◆ Seek to establish a positive relationship with families before a challenging situation arises. Share photos and videos of children's activities with parents.

◆ Have an interpreter attend a conference. If it is not possible to include a certified interpreter, ask a trusted staff member or member of the family to help. Seek out individuals from community organizations who are knowledgeable about a family's culture and language.

◆ Promote mutual understanding using aids such as a message board with photos and words in both English and the family's home language. Teachers and parents can point to what they wish to communicate.

◆ Keep information brief and clear to avoid overwhelming parents and to increase the chances that they will understand the most critical points you want to convey.

◆ Resolve differences together. To understand a family's concerns and priorities, it is critical that teachers get to know family members and what is important to them.

Through each of the communication practices used, the teacher remains unconditionally positive in efforts to form reciprocal relationships with all families and to encourage their engagement in furthering their child's learning in the home as well as at school.

## Religious Diversity

Linguistic diversity can be challenging for teachers, as can differences in religious beliefs between teachers and families. Whatever the specifics involved, cultural responsiveness in matters of religion requires openness and understanding on the part of the teacher.

The profile that follows is compiled from papers written by two teachers who were graduate students in my classes some years ago. Their experiences were remarkably similar and engendered the following case study (which the teachers approved and first appeared in Gartrell 2000). Mary Beth recalls her experience with a family that other teachers had found difficult to work with.

In my first year, another teacher told me to "watch out" for a certain family whose younger child was to be in my kindergarten class. As Jehovah's Witnesses, and as part of their faith, the family had taught their children not to salute the flag or celebrate birthdays and holidays.

This teacher told me that in the previous year the parents had become irate when they were not told of a Halloween party in the classroom of the older child, even though their child had not participated. The teacher then tried to let the family know of upcoming events, but she felt they remained distant and uncooperative.

There were instances when the older child, now a third grader, had been made fun of by classmates. Arlys, the mother, had reported these incidents, but the teacher apparently told the family there was not much she could do.

I took this teacher's comments as a personal challenge, and decided to work hard to learn about this family and to work together with them. It was my practice to send home notes of introduction to each family before school began and then continue with happygrams on a rotating basis for each member of my class. I made sure the child, Wilma, went home with at least one happygram every week. This was not a hard task. I enjoyed the child's pluckiness. (I read each note to her before giving it to her to bring home.) I called the home a few times as well, but always got an answering machine. I left messages that I hoped the parents would find friendly.

Other teachers told me not to expect this family to attend the fall parent conference, but Arlys did come. I was very pleased to see her, and she seemed rather surprised at my reaction. I decided to let Arlys bring up issues related to their religion. My job was to let her know that I valued working with families and how well her daughter was doing in my class. Well, she did bring it up. I told her I was interested to hear about her faith (because I was).

Arlys told me about the flag salute, and I said not to worry—we wouldn't be doing the Pledge until close to the end of the year because I didn't think the children could understand it. She smiled at this. About birthdays, I told her what I told all the parents: I preferred that the children had parties at home, but we let the children wear a "birthday crown" for the day if that was okay with the parents. Arlys said no crown for Wilma, but otherwise she liked what I did.

About holiday activities, I asked her what she would like me to do, and we had quite a conversation about that. I was very surprised when she said Wilma could stay in the classroom if I could figure out a way to have her fit in without participating. That year I kind of downplayed the holidays, explaining to parents who asked that not all of the children in the class celebrated all holidays. I did more with the ideas behind the holidays—for instance, having the class consider why should we be thankful—rather than hold Thanksgiving pageants and have the children make crafts. This is a practice I still use today.

What I am still the proudest about with this family has to do with the flag salute. Before we started doing the flag salute in April, I asked three parents to come in to discuss with the class what saluting the flag meant to them. One was Arlys, and she did a fine job of explaining why Wilma would stand up (out of respect for the class), but wouldn't be doing the rest. (All three parents knew that they were part of a panel and that the three might be expressing different opinions about the flag salute.) I do not remember any of the children making fun of Wilma that whole year—they liked her, just as I did.

There are many religious differences we could discuss, but as I said, the matter comes down to openness toward the belief systems of others—whatever those sources of faith happen to be.

## Levels of Family Engagement

In the development of their family engagement model, Halgunseth and her colleagues build upon Epstein's (2001) influential criteria for assessing parent engagement in school programs. This section also begins with Epstein's criteria, modifying them as four levels—a system of indicators that might be helpful in building partnerships with families that enable the full effectiveness of the guidance approach (Gartrell 2011, 2012). Encouraging parents to move through the levels of engagement depends on trusting, reciprocal relationships. Such relationships help teachers understand and respond to children's behavior with appropriate guidance strategies intended to build the democratic life skills. Also through partnerships, the teacher supports family members in reinforcing the life skills with children at home.

The four levels are

- ◆ One—Acceptance of program information
- ◆ Two—Active educational engagement with one's child
- ◆ Three—Program participation
- ◆ Four—Personal/professional development

To illustrate the stages, I refer to Mary Beth's experience with Arlys and Wilma discussed in the previous case study.

## Level One—Acceptance of Program Information

Showing unconditional acceptance, the teacher warmly introduces family members as well as children to the program. Families differ in the level of participation they are ready to engage in (Coleman 1997). Most families, if they feel accepted, are willing to participate at Level One, at least accepting information about the program and what their child is doing and learning. Level One extends to attending meetings, conferences, and class events as parents can find the time.

In order to encourage families to solidify their engagement at Level One, teachers recognize the importance of both direct, friendly communication with family members *and* the impact on the family of a child who is happy at school. Families who sense that their child has positive feelings toward the teacher are inclined to interact positively with the teacher.

In the case study above, Mary Beth did not let herself be influenced by the other teacher's attitudes toward the family. She enjoyed having Wilma in class and conveyed this acceptance quietly and consistently to the child. She sent home happygrams and left positive phone messages about Wilma for the family. When the mother attended a first conference, Mary Beth showed friendliness to Arlys and a genuine interest in Wilma and the family, including the family's religious values. That Arlys attended the conference—in response to the teacher's friendly inclusiveness—indicated that she felt comfortable enough about communicating with the teacher and about Wilma's acceptance in the class to move to engagement at Level One.

## Level Two—Active Educational Engagement with One's Child

Engagement at Level Two means that parents move from accepting information about their child in the program to positively acting on the information received. Typically families at Level Two actively follow up on activities and projects begun or assigned in the classroom. Perhaps even more important, families use more fully the resources in the home and community as teaching and learning opportunities with their child. Teachers help families muster available resources and reach out for additional resources to further support their children's learning (NAEYC 2009).

In helping families move from Level One to Level Two, the teacher's goal is motivation toward and reinforcement of parenting practices that further children's education and learning in and around the home. Encouraging an extension of classroom practices, such as reading to the child each day, is an important component of this communication. The teacher works with the family to help family members see their everyday activities as essentially educational for children. For example, an adult might take the child on the bus or subway that the adult takes to work or to do shopping, or the adult and child might take walks or garden together. The teacher helps parents understand the importance of adults talking with children during these activities.

At Level Two, mutual trust is growing, and parents begin to work together with teachers on behalf of their children. By attaining Level Two, parents together with teachers can do so much for children, more than either party could alone (Pappano 2007). Children know when the principal adults in their lives, in this case teachers and parents, get along and cooperate. For the child, continuity then exists between home and school, and a basis for progressing in the democratic life skills is established in the child's life.

As evident from Arlys's participating during the conference, the teacher's notes and phone messages had a positive effect. The transition for Arlys from Level One of parent engagement to Level Two was shown during the conference. She and Mary Beth openly discussed the Pledge, holidays, and birthdays, topics that might have caused alienation. Mary Beth indicated that the two reached understandings about these topics that sustained their growing partnership on Wilma's behalf at school.

Wilma was adjusting well at school, experiencing no academic or behavioral problems. When children do encounter problems, the focus of the teacher and family member becomes how to work together to resolve the matter, whether it is extra help with reading or writing, coordinated support for self-esteem, or parental agreement for special education assessment and possible services. Cooperative engagement on behalf of the child indicates family members have progressed to Level Two. All early childhood programs, at a minimum, should have a goal of parent engagement at this second level.

## Level Three—Program Participation

Families are engaged at Level Three when they participate in program activities in a way that goes beyond their own child. When family members reach Level Three, they take an active role that benefits the program—the goal of establishing truly reciprocal interactions has been reached.

Commonly—though not necessarily—this kind of engagement involves volunteering in the classroom. When family members first come into the classroom, teachers encourage them to take part in informal ways, like helping out and visiting with children and other adults.

When families cannot easily come into the classroom, the teacher actively seeks parental support in other ways, perhaps by asking for donations of needed materials or services or participation on committees or at special events (Kersey & Masterson 2009). Parents ready to engage at a program level may be willing to sit on parent advisory and policy committees, and even to help represent the program to the public. Sometimes out-of-class parent participation can lead to a classroom visit. Working parents can sometimes build an occasional visit into their schedules—eating with a child during a lunch break is one example; taking time off work to go on an end-of-year field trip is another.

In the case study Mary Beth mentioned that she delayed having her kindergarten children learn the Pledge until spring. (Mary Beth did this at the suggestion of a veteran kindergarten teacher who one September heard a child proudly reciting, "I pledge

Norwegians to the flag.") Mary Beth was delighted that Arlys accepted her invitation to share the family's beliefs around the flag salute. When Arlys and the other two parents spoke with the class, all three showed parental engagement at Level Three.

Whether on a formal basis or for an occasional visit, family members who come into the classroom benefit their children greatly. A teacher once shared a story with me about an unemployed father who accompanied his daughter to preschool one day. He looked unsure as he entered the classroom, but the teacher welcomed him, introduced him to the children, and helped him begin reading stories. As he was reading, he overheard three children, including his daughter, talking about what their parents did. One child said his dad was a teacher. Another said her mom was a dentist. The man's daughter said with a smile, "My dad is here!"

It does not take special knowledge or a degree to talk with a child, read a story, help in an interest center, do a family share, or assist with a trip. Parents who come into the classroom can contribute to the program in any of these ways. The teacher whose goal is to build a two-way bridge between home and school knows that the children, the program, the teacher, and the child's whole family gain when family members come into the classroom (Crawford & Zygourias-Coe 2006).

## Level Four—Personal-Professional Development

For some early childhood programs, Level Two parent engagement is a reasonable goal for most if not all families in the classroom community. Level Two marks the baseline for reciprocity in the parent-teacher relationship, the two functioning as a team to benefit the child. For other programs, teachers have as a goal Level Three engagement for many if not most family members. Head Start programs and many comprehensive early childhood programs set Level Four as a goal at least for some parents. At Level Four, as a result of successful experience at the first three levels, family members engage in significant personal or professional development encouraged or inspired by the program.

Examples are pursuing significant civic participation (such as traveling regularly to serve on a regional council), furthering one's education, or progressing in a career. Additional schooling could mean getting a high school diploma, job training, or a bachelor's degree. The family member might become a teacher assistant or a teacher, enter another field—or take on substantial new activities as an at-home parent. With support from a teacher, these parents choose to improve life circumstances for themselves and, by their example, for their entire families.

Level Four of parent engagement happens as a result of a family member feeling accepted by a teacher, taking more of an interest in her child's learning, and volunteering in the program. The parent gains so much in self-image and concept from the first three levels of engagement that she embarks on new paths for personal and professional development as a result.

In our earlier example, Arlys seemed to be engaged at Level Three and not yet at Level Four. She would be emerging into Level Four if, for example, she became an ongoing assistant to Mary Beth or, in another direction, wrote a children's book about a child from a Jehovah's Witness family and her experiences at school. These aspects of personal/professional growth might reasonably be attributed to the parent's time in working with this teacher.

In my university classes over the years, some of the most dedicated and responsive students have been parents of young children who chose teaching careers after finding their niche by volunteering in classrooms. In these classrooms, teachers welcomed them warmly, helped them locate activities to do, thanked them for volunteering, and invited them back. Finding the experience exhilarating, the parents returned to the classroom

and became regular volunteers. They then made the decision and the commitment to become teachers.

## Summation and Segue

This chapter has looked at ways that teachers can make the family ties that are so important to children a natural and accepted part of the encouraging classroom. As children mature, there will be time enough for them to separate more fully from the family. While they are young, these connections should be celebrated in the classroom so that each child feels a healthy sense of belonging at both home and school. By doing so the child gains a foundation in DLS 1 (finding acceptance as a member of the group and as a worthy individual) and has a solid start on the other four skills.

The importance of teacher-parent partnerships does not diminish as children enter middle childhood. The community-school model discussed in Chapter 5 keeps home-school partnerships paramount—for example, with parents sitting on committees that advise educators on the mix of matters that are a part of modern school operations. In my view, only as schools for older learners pick up on the partnership paradigm can full progress toward education for a civil society be made.

We turn next to a chapter on developmentally responsive teaching in the classroom. What happens in this milieu to foster the cognitive and physical gains vital to the democratic life skills is the subject of Chapter 7. Chapters 8, 9, and 10 then carry through with developmentally appropriate teaching for social and emotional development. Together, the chapters round out the conceptual basis for each of the five democratic life skills, explored in a concise and concrete fashion in Part Three.

# Developmentally Appropriate Practice: In the Classroom

evelopmentally appropriate practice, which was touched on in Chapter 5, consists of teaching that is attuned to the developmental level of a group of children as a whole, to the individual learning patterns and interests of each child, and to the societal and cultural contexts of the child's home and community (Copple & Bredekamp 2009). The previous chapter explored family-teacher partnerships, also an essential aspect of developmentally appropriate practice. In this chapter we'll look at what developmentally appropriate practice is and isn't, as well as an application of it in a Head Start preschool classroom and a public school second grade classroom.

## Developmentally Appropriate Practice: What It Is and Isn't

Key to developmentally appropriate practice is the idea that young children's development is dependent upon learning experiences that are tied to their own life experiences. The child's learning mode is essentially active, the direct experiencing of what life has to offer, mediated by teachers (NAEYC 2009). It is critical that for extended time blocks each day, the child has a choice of type and level of activity. The teacher supports and extends the child's learning by linking her interests and engagement with interactions that lead to further learning experiences (Hyson 2008).

Certainly education must be rigorous, and learners should be persistently nudged to learn and grow. But the motivation for significant learning, the kind attained through developmentally appropriate practice, comes from within the child. Teachers need to *intrigue* children to learn—challenge them, but in a supportive way, without the stress that often accompanies "challenging" tasks that are imposed in school. If the child's personal interest is awakened in an activity, full engagement and real learning are probable (Hyson 2008).

The following quote (NAEYC 2009) comments on high-pressure classrooms that jeopardize children's full, healthy development by emphasizing academic performance at the expense of development in other domains:

> There is concern that schools are curtailing valuable experiences such as problem solving, rich play, collaboration with peers, opportunities for emotional and social development, outdoor/physical activity, and the arts. In the high-pressure classroom, children are less likely to develop a love of learning and a sense of their own competence and ability to make choices, and they miss much of the joy and expansive learning of childhood. (4–5)

Such an environment places inappropriate behavioral expectations on children, often making even the desired academic performance more difficult. Education must accommodate all domains of development and build on the child's intrinsic (mastery) motivation.

## Mastery Motivation

Rather than focusing specifically on children's attainment of narrowly defined academic knowledge and skills, the goal of education must be what Dewey argued for 100 years ago: enabling students to *learn how to learn* (Jacobs 2010; Smilkstein 2011; Thomas & Seely Brown 2011). We should want our graduates at any level to have a growing willingness and ability to

- Engage in activity
- Conceptualize problems to be solved
- Formulate plans of action, alone and with others
- Put the plans into effect with needed modifications, individually and cooperatively
- Solve the problems successfully (Smilkstein 2011; Thomas & Seely Brown 2011)

To help children learn how to learn, adults must kindle and nurture intrinsic motivation in the young (Smilkstein 2011; Thomas & Seely Brown 2011). Intrinsic motivation, or mastery motivation (see Chapter 5; also Reineke, Sonsteng, & Gartrell 2008), signifies the brain's willingness to engage with a world perceived to be more intriguing than threatening. It includes being open to new information. It gives learners the ability to persist at the task. It is the essential dynamic in building executive function.

The knowledge that mastery motivation generates is experiential and highly individual (Combs & Gonzales 2008). Still, knowledge *is* shared and modified through human interactions, experience, and development (Thomas & Seely Brown 2011). That is where caregiving and teaching come in. Teachers who respect the fact that knowledge is personal but changes with experience, thought, and brain development over time actively support mastery motivation (Combs & Gonzales 2008; Smilkstein 2011).

Every day, early childhood educators see the benefits of nurturing mastery motivation, but the push to spur academic achievement (i.e., high test scores) increasingly discourages teachers from nurturing this fragile organic energy as a learning source (Elkind [1981] 2006). Teachers may feel forced to replace teaching that supports intrinsic motivation with a reliance on external rewards (Rose 2004).

Knowledge—information transactions within the child's brain—is important, but it should not be the sole purpose or outcome of the learning experience. Knowledge is a tool for ongoing engagement with life (Thomas & Seely Brown 2011). For schooling to help children grow in the democratic life skills and contribute to civil society, teachers must make the *affect* of the learning positive. Only then can stress hormones in the brain be kept manageable, and executive functioning develop and thrive.

# The Fish Case Study

Let's bring the discussion of developmentally appropriate practice into the classroom via a case study at the preschool level. I'll apply core considerations in the use of developmentally appropriate practice (NAEYC 2009) to analyze the activities, and then use elements of the HighScope Preschool Child Observation Report (COR; HighScope Educational Research Foundation 2003) to analyze learning that occurred. Educational accountability through intentional assessment is part of developmentally appropriate practice.

As previously mentioned, learning begins when children can tie interesting school activities to their own life experiences. Picture a Head Start classroom in northern Minnesota near the beginning of fishing season. With 11,842 lakes in the state, lake life is a staple throughout the state (Minnesota Department of Natural Resources 2008). Not surprisingly, Minnesota has the second highest per capita fishing rate in the country, second only to Alaska (Department of Natural Resources 2003). A large percentage of the state population is on the lakes during the weekend of "fishing opener."

## Planning

The week before fishing season opens, the Head Start teachers in this rural town organized materials for many fish-related projects in the classroom. Going a step beyond conventional theme construction, staff members planned experiences to accommodate the needs, abilities, and interests of individual children in their class—sixteen 3- to 5-year-olds, six of whom had special needs.

The teachers used the HighScope Preschool Child Observation Record, and while planning the fish-related learning experiences, they consulted the HighScope key developmental indicators (KDIs). These milestone statements, based on the school readiness dimensions of the National Education Goals Panel (Kagan, Moore, & Bredekamp 1995), guide teachers as they plan experiences and support learning. The teachers looked for indicators that might be addressed through the project activities. They discussed assessing specific children and, keeping the children firmly in mind, planned the related experiences.

## Diving In

The teachers use the HighScope plan-do-review sequence to bring intentionality to the children's learning process. This sequence is a part of the daily routine in which children plan their activities, carry them out during work time, and review what they did. After breakfast each day, the class clumped around three teachers in a large group and reviewed the activities that were available. With an adult's help, the children each marked the activity they selected on a low white board and left for that area. Choices included the following:

- A "fish camp" with an inflated fishing boat, hookless lures on small poles, life jackets, a couple of fish-net scoopers, plastic worms, some full-size plastic fish of local varieties, a "campfire" with cooking utensils, and a small pop-up tent, all in the active play area

- Three species of live minnows and nets for catching them, in the science center water table

♦ A magnetic fishing pole game with real, child-size fishing poles. To provide functional literacy experiences, teachers labeled the fish on different days with fish names, the names of children in the class, and words from *One Fish, Two Fish, Red Fish, Blue Fish* by Dr. Seuss. With the latter, the children and teacher put the words together in sequence once all the fish were caught.

♦ Homemade puzzles portraying people from different cultures fishing

♦ A variety of materials in the art center for creating underwater pictures/scenes (to encourage creativity, no outlines or replication projects were included)

♦ Labeled but blank "fish journals" for emergent literacy reflections and scientific observations, in the writing center

♦ Books on fish, including *Rainbow Fish* by Marcus Pfister; *Swimmy* by Leo Lionni; *Mister Seahorse* by Eric Carle; and *One Fish, Two Fish, Red Fish, Blue Fish* by Dr. Seuss, in the library (*The Dead Bird* by Margaret Wise Brown was also included—more on this later.)

♦ A creative fish-related game on the computer that two children could play together

In the science center the featured project involved three kinds of live minnows in the water table—fatheads, golden shiners, and chubs. On an adjacent table that held three dishpans of water, the teachers had placed a photo of one kind of minnow next to each dishpan. During work time each morning four different children donned "anglers'" (paint) smocks and became "fish biologists." Some used minnow nets to practice catch and release. Some used the nets to transfer the minnows to the dishpans—for the younger children any dishpan, for the older ones mostly the labeled dishpans. Henri, a veteran 5-year-old, assisted the younger ones (when they wanted the help) to place their minnow in the labeled dishpan.

Sharlene, a younger preschooler, stood for an entire work time watching the minnows and the fishing activities. Terry, a teacher, held a minnow for her to touch, but she couldn't quite do it. Terry told her it was just fine to watch.

Two other children caught minnows in their hands. They engaged in biological field analysis, noting details of the two fish with the assistance of a teacher. Jasmin told the teacher, "The line on the [side of the] shiner goes down and the chub is fat. But they both catch bass [when they are on hooks]." She continued, "We gotta put them in the dishpans so they don't die."

Terry talked with every child several times during the activity, asking questions and acknowledging the thinking of each. She jotted down on sticky notes what each child said and did, for later COR scoring (see Assessing Learning Through the Theme).

The writing and art centers were open for the children to express their in-class and out-of-class experiences on paper and in the fish journals. In the daily brief and interactive large group, the children sang fish songs using motions and words adapted to familiar tunes, such as "Five Little Fishies Swimming in a Brook."

During the week as minnows died, the teachers and children placed them in plastic bags in the freezer. (On Monday and Tuesday during small-group time, the groups had read and discussed Margaret Wise Brown's classic, now out-of-print *The Dead Bird*, relating the story to the fish.) The following Monday, they buried the dead minnows in the newly planted class garden. The group discussed the concept of fish as fertilizer—which two children further explored on their own by digging some up days later. They discovered the fish were, in the teacher's words, "partially decomposed."

## Reflections

All week during the 1¼-hour work time, the experiences were a hit with the children. The staff reported that not one child's interest span sputtered during the minnow experience. Within the limit of showing respect for the fish, teachers allowed for a variety of modes of engagement—no one set of actions was the correct one. Observing the individual ways the children engaged in activities, the teachers recognized that learning is an individualized experience.

An example was the difference in the ways Sharlene and Henri had approached the water table. Though Sharlene had been hesitant, staff members guessed that in another year she would be happily participating. Henri, a class veteran, showed patience and helpfulness with the younger children as they put their minnows into the dishpans. Terry recalled that the previous year, when he was new to the program, Henri had seldom initiated a conversation and often played by himself.

One 4-year-old stayed at the "fish camp" all week. Jason organized experiences ranging from fishing trips to shore lunches to rainy-time activities in the tent—not surprising, as Jason's older brother was a fishing guide.

Louella, who chose not to do the minnow activity, did most of the other activities during the week. One day at the writing center she worked very hard on a *story picture*, a creative picture that tells a story—the kind of pictures children see every day in books. Her picture showed three fish in water, each with a big smile. On the lines beneath, the child used developmental spelling (Copple & Bredekamp 2009) to write her story: "M n m fm dt ct fs." ("Me and my family don't catch fishes," she read to the teacher.) During review time, Louella added that the family does go boating and swimming.

---

### Sample Interaction Between Terry and Martin on Martin's Water Table Experience

**Terry:** Martin, I wonder how the minnow swims?

**Martin:** 'Cause it has fins on top and bottom and a sideways one on the back. It moves them, and he swims.

**Terry:** It pushes the water with its fins? All of them or just some?

**Martin:** The one on the tail, Terry, 'cause I saw it wagging.

**Terry:** You saw the fish push the water back and forth with its tail fin?

**Martin:** Yep, and it can go fast, but I am going to catch him.

Later at review time, held during snack, Terry asked, "Martin, what did you have a good time doing today?" Martin grinned and said, "The water table. Two fish died 'cause their bellies was up and they just lay there, but the others swam fast, and you had to make your net go like this [sweeps his arm through the air quickly] to catch 'em."

Martin spoke more during this activity than he usually did. During review time, he used the longest sentence Terry had ever heard him use, which included three conjunctions. She was impressed with his vocabulary, sentence structure, and analysis of events. He observed closely and analyzed how he thought fish swam, how he knew they were dead, and how he had to swoop the net to catch them.

---

## Core Considerations Applied

To help teachers implement developmentally appropriate practice, NAEYC'S 2009 position statement includes these three core considerations.

> The core of developmentally appropriate practice lies in this intentionality, in the knowledge that practitioners consider when they are making decisions, and in their always aiming for goals that are both challenging and achievable for children. In all aspects of their work with children, early childhood practitioners must consider three areas of knowledge. (9)

Following are the three areas, with a brief application of each to the fish theme.

> 1. What is known about child development and learning—referring to knowledge of age-related characteristics that permits general predictions about what experiences are likely to best promote children's learning and development. (9)

A variety of experiences were provided. Children could choose those that reflected their interests and styles of learning. Recognition was given to the fact that young children learn best through body-integrated experiences—when physical, social and emotional,

cognitive, and language/literacy dimensions of learning are all involved. All center activities required movement, gross motor, and/or fine motor use. The center activities and the large-group activity also required integrated activity across developmental domains.

All activities were either open ended or (like the puzzles and fishing pole game) at different levels of difficulty, so allowing for various stages of development and styles of learning. Through the plan-do-review sequence, the children used intentionality in their learning.

2. What is known about each child as an individual—referring to what practitioners learn about each child that has implications for how best to adapt and be responsive to that individual variation. (NAEYC 2009, 9)

The teachers knew the children and their families and planned experiences that built on this knowledge. For instance, they knew that fishing was not something Louella's family did. The staff provided a range of experiences that allowed her to successfully engage in choices she was comfortable with.

At the art and writing tables, children worked at various stages of art development and writing development. In addition to Louella, who created the three-fish picture and used invented spelling, one younger preschooler completely covered his picture in brown and blue paint. When the teacher acknowledged his hard work, he replied proudly, "Yep, this is a lake, but the water is dirty so you can't see the fishes."

By allowing the children to choose activities and engage in them in their own unique ways, teachers set the stage for "a natural integration of maturation and experience" (NAEYC 2009, 2). One child, with a high need for physical activity, spent most of the week in the fishing boats leading "fishing trips," as his family was doing with him. The teachers understood that he would probably feel constrained by some of the other activities that did not allow for as much physical engagement.

3. What is known about the social and cultural contexts in which children live—referring to the values, expectations, and behavioral and linguistic conventions that shape children's lives at home and in their communities that practitioners must strive to understand in order to ensure that learning experiences in the program or school are meaningful, relevant, and respectful for each child and family. (NAEYC 2009, 10)

The Head Start staff knew the importance of lake life in the lives of the children in the program and used this knowledge to reinforce what were for some children actual experiences, and to inspire the imaginations of other children. The staff also tied the fishing theme into another real-life activity in northern Minnesota, gardening. By using the minnows as fertilizer for the class garden, the staff showed respect for a Native American gardening tradition.

Because the teachers had applied the three core considerations during their planning—taking into account the children's general ages, their individual preferences and characteristics, and the social and cultural context of the group—this fish theme was developmentally appropriate not just for most of the children in the group but for *all* the children, including a child whose family chose not to fish.

## Assessing Learning Through the Theme

Authentic assessments analyze observed samples of the child's everyday activity for progress in relation to set standards. Authentic assessment is a central tool for evaluation of child progress, not to be limited to prekindergarten education (NAEYC 2009).

The Preschool COR (HighScope Educational Research Foundation 2003), an authentic assessment system, has six categories representing broad domains of child development:

I. Initiative                    IV. Movement and Music

II. Social Relations             V. Language and Literacy

III. Creative Representation      VI. Mathematics and Science

Each category contains between three and eight items that describe developmentally important behaviors. Each Item has five levels ranging from simple (1) to more complex (5). For each of the six categories, I have selected one item and briefly analyzed and scored a child's responses in relation to it (see the table).

| COR Scoring Sample from Fish Theme | | | |
|---|---|---|---|
| **Category** | **Item** | **Notes on Child's Response** | **Level** |
| I. Initiative | D. Taking care of personal needs | Henri helped younger preschoolers place minnows in the labeled dishpans. | 5. Child helps another child in a self-care activity or program routine. |
| II. Social Relations | F. Relating to other children | Jason organized and led other children on "fishing trips." Most accepted his invitations for cooperative play. | 4. Child invites another child to play. |
| III. Creative Representation | J. Drawing and painting pictures | Louella drew three fish, each with two eyes and a smile. Louella's picture also showed a sense of perspective—a horizontal lake line with water below and a sky with clouds above. | 5. Child draws or paints a picture with details on one or more of the basic parts. |
| IV. Movement and Music | M. Moving with objects | Jasmin and others caught minnows in the minnow nets or in their hands and often carried them to the labeled dishpans. | 3. Child coordinates both hands to manipulate one or more objects. |
| V. Language and Literacy | S. Uses complex patterns of speech | Louella: "Me and my family don't catch fishes." | 4. Child uses a compound subject or object in a sentence. |
| VI. Mathematics and Science | Y. Sorting objects | Jasmin: "The line on the shiner goes down and the chub is fat. But they both catch bass." | 4. In sorting, child groups objects that are the same in some way and identifies the similarity. |
| | FF. Identifying natural and living things | Robert and Jonathan dug up the minnows and said they were slimy. They agreed with the teacher that they were "decomposing." | 4. Child identifies a change (in a material or the environment) and a possible cause. |

# Rigorous and Developmentally Appropriate: The Birds Project

The idea that developmentally appropriate practice is less than rigorous is, unfortunately, common. Especially at the K–12 grade levels, developmentally appropriate practice is thought to be somehow custodial—that it means gearing instruction to learners at the lowest levels in the class. Developmentally appropriate practice, however, can be attuned to the child's intrinsic mastery motivation and still be rigorous and standards based. The following composite case study, combining elements of themes I've observed in a few different primary grade classrooms, illustrates how developmentally appropriate practice can be not just intriguing but also robust in its implementation at the primary level.

In Ms. Ryan's second grade class of 21 students, mornings are reserved for specific skill development in reading, writing, and math. Afternoons are split between specialist time (library, music, art, physical education, technology) and instruction in social studies, science, and the arts. Working with the specialists when possible, Ms. Ryan does much of the afternoon instruction using theme-based, integrated curriculum.

The sixth grade class in this school built a bird sanctuary on the playground, a collection of different kinds of feeders, birdhouses, and (as temperatures warmed) a birdbath. During early April, Ms. Ryan's second graders notice the large number of birds visiting the sanctuary. Ms. Ryan decides that "Birds of a Feather" would make an interesting theme for them. Spanish is the home language of one of the students, so Ms. Ryan researches the English and Spanish words to describe the birds. Ms. Ryan also enlists the help of one family member who is an expert birder.

Ms. Ryan divides her planning for this theme into four parts:

1. Academic standards to be addressed

2. Theme grand plan

3. Coordination with specialists

4. Center activities

5. Assessment

## 1. Academic standards to be addressed

Consulting her state Department of Education's academic standards to be addressed in second grade, Ms. Ryan decides to assess for benchmarks (points of achievement) in the areas of Writing, Life Science, and Mathematics/Data Analysis, as shown in the table.

| Academic Standards to Be Addressed | | | |
|---|---|---|---|
| **Curriculum Area** | **Strand** | **Sub-strand** | **Benchmark** |
| 1. Language arts | Writing | Types of writing | Use informal writing skills such as note taking, listing, mapping to record information or observations. |
| 2. Science (Animals) | Life Science | Diversity of organisms | Recognize and describe life cycles of plants and animals. |
| 3. Mathematics | Data Analysis, Data and Statistics | | Collect and represent data in statistics and real-world probability. |

## 2. Theme grand plan

a. Ms. Ryan divides the class into five teams. At a convenient time for both classes, the five groups go with two sixth grade "expedition guides" to observe the sanctuary. The guides point out different birds, give information about the sanctuary, and take photos with a digital camera. Team members take notes in their own bird journals.

b. The five teams research the birds they observed using library books and the digital photos. The sixth grade expedition guides work with them. The children write further notes in their bird journals.

c. Ms. Ryan and the class develop a web on the chalkboard for center activities related to the theme. Each day the teams rotate through the centers and complete these activities.

d. At the end of the theme, the teams present their bird journals and findings to the class. Each child shares something learned from the theme. The class writes thank-you letters to the sixth graders.

## 3. Coordination with specialists

Ms. Ryan speaks with the music teacher about learning bird songs; the art teacher about a possible mural featuring birds; the physical education teacher about doing bird-related creative movement and games; and the technology teacher about bird-identification programs and websites.

## 4. Center activities

Ms. Ryan monitors how the children are using the centers and offers assistance when needed. She also records observations about the children's activities using the still camera and video functions on her smartphone.

a. Writing Center *(teacher-instructed/exploratory use of center)*: Students transpose their observation and research notes from their bird journals into a team Bird Sanctuary Book. They include photos and illustrations.

b. Reading Center *(self-directing/open-ended use of center)*: Students read books about birds and write reviews of the books. They share their reviews and revise them as a final draft to go into their portfolios.

c. Math/Manipulatives Center *(self-directing/self-correcting use of center)*: There are two activities in this center: 1) Team members complete puzzles made from laminated photos of birds, then group them into migrating birds and resident birds. 2) Each team fills in one block of the class bar graph for each bird they saw in the sanctuary.

d. Art Center *(self-directing/open-ended use of center)*: Using realistic and colored feathers, glue, colored paper, and markers, children make pictures of two or three birds—either fanciful or realistic—that might be of the same species. To support the children's creativity, no models are provided.

## 5. Assessment

For this theme Ms. Ryan is focusing her in-depth assessments on six students for whom she has incomplete data for the three benchmarks she has chosen. For each of the six selected students, and depending on the item, Ms. Ryan completes one of two authentic assessment forms: 1) a two-part anecdotal observation—a specific description of what the child says and does and her own assessment of the child's work; or 2) a checklist/rating with interpretative comments. She will use the interpretative comments on both forms to share her assessment with the child's family. The completed forms are included in each child's portfolio to document progress toward the state academic standards.

Ms. Ryan states that using the thematic approach "takes real work, especially the first time you do a theme." But she believes the children's learning touches on so many different dimensions of development that the extra planning, teaching, and assessing make the effort worthwhile. She concludes, "Nothing the students do during the year is more challenging than the themes. And usually, no learning experience is more developmentally appropriate for my second graders."

This kind of learning, which Dewey ([1916] 1997) believed was the only true learning and Rogers (1962) called *significant learning,* registers in the brain as a pleasant emotional experience. The developing mind builds positive emotional memories associated with the learning activity (Siegel 2001). Mastery motivation is sustained. Such learning motivates children to want to learn more and brings meaning, social and emotional as much as cognitive, to their lives.

## Conclusion

Progressive educators have long recognized that every act of learning has an affective as well as a cognitive component. For learning to impact healthy executive functioning, and not generate fight-or-flight reactions, the experience has to be intriguing rather than stressful. The learning experience has to be positive for the child.

Elkind ([1981] 2006) and Galinsky (2010) tell us that the context of healthy learning is essentially social and cooperative, like brain development itself. Individual strength comes from secure relationships with adults and friendly peers. Through both the fish theme and the bird theme, the teachers created a world with the children that allowed for the expression of interest, engagement, persistence, healthy human interaction, the solving of problems, and the creation of products and ideas. At the same time the children were progressing toward nationally accepted standards in developmentally appropriate ways.

By providing a learning environment that respects children's own experiences and cultures, developmentally appropriate practice increases the likelihood that family-teacher relationships will be positive. By creating a learning environment that is encouraging to all, developmentally appropriate practice makes possible the practice of guidance. Developmentally appropriate practice, therefore, provides a foundation for an education relevant to the twenty-first century, one that can sustain democratic principles in social life.

The next two chapters give a picture of the component of developmentally appropriate practice referred to as *guidance.* Chapter 8 covers guidance practices with the group; Chapter 9 addresses guidance with individual children. Chapter 10 addresses guidance to include every child.

# 8

# The Encouraging Classroom: Using Guidance with the Group

I n education for a civil society, early childhood professionals model and teach a key democratic principle: the worth of each individual. The term *encouraging classroom* describes the physical and social-emotional environment of a community of learners that empowers all children to develop and learn. This is a place where pressures for measurable academic performance are kept in balance with the broader educational goals of teaching learners to become productive citizens and healthy individuals, goals of progressive social thinkers for the last 400 years.

In practical terms, an **encouraging classroom** is a place where children want to be even when they are sick, as opposed to a place they do not want to be when they are well (Gartrell 2011). An encouraging classroom is where developmentally appropriate practice happens. NAEYC (2009) describes the environment of such a classroom this way:

> In developmentally appropriate practice . . . the role of the community is to provide a physical, emotional, and cognitive environment conducive to that development and learning. The foundation for the community is consistent, positive, caring relationships between the adults and children, among children, among teachers, and between teachers and families. It is the responsibility of all members of the learning community to consider and contribute to one another's well-being and learning. (16)

The management approach used in encouraging classrooms is *guidance*, which teaches for the healthy social-emotional development of individual children and enables democratic principles to take hold within the community of learners as a group. As the leader of the group, the teacher is firm when there is a prospect of harm or disruption but remains always friendly. By safeguarding positive relationships with individual chil-

**encouraging class-room:** the physical and social-emotional environment of a community of learners that empowers all children to develop and learn

dren, and mutual trust and a cooperative spirit within the group—which we'll discuss in this chapter—the early childhood professional teaches for Piaget's noble sense of the goal of education ([1932] 1960): for individuals to be able to think intelligently and ethically. This is the highest democratic life skill.

In this chapter we explore four guidance practices that define, build, and sustain the encouraging classroom. I refer to this set of four as *public* guidance practices, primarily intended for use with the group as a whole in ways that do not single out individuals. A sense of community happens only when individual children know that their place in the group will not be endangered by public criticism (Gartrell 2011).

These four guidance practices have been discussed in the Guidance Matters column in *Young Children* (Gartrell 2006, 2007, 2012) and in my books (Gartrell 2004, 2011). The four practices are as follows:

- ◆ Leadership communication: encouragement, not praise

- ◆ Moving to the positive: guidelines, not rules

- ◆ Class meetings to build the encouraging classroom

- ◆ Class meetings to sustain the encouraging classroom

## Leadership Communication: Encouragement, Not Praise

In a Guidance Matters column, "'You Really Worked Hard on Your Picture!': Guiding with Encouragement," (Gartrell 2007), I discuss public and private encouragement. Public encouragement, given to the entire group, is the focus of this chapter; private encouragement, quietly shared with an individual child, is addressed further in Chapter 10.

**praise:** general, evaluative statements given to recognize an accomplishment

### Praise vs. Encouragement

Educators often confuse **praise** and **encouragement**. The distinction was first popularized in the writings of Dreikurs (1968) and Ginott (1972). Since then Hitz and Driscoll (1988), Kelly and Daniels (1997), and I (Gartell 2004, 2011) have written about the crucial difference between the two concepts.

- ◆ *Praise*—evaluative; indiscriminately public; usually given for an accomplishment; often given in the form of a quick generalization: "Good job."

**encouragement:** specific, supportive statements that acknowledge effort and progress

- ◆ *Encouragement*—supportive; when given publicly addresses the whole group (does not single out individuals); often given to recognize effort, not just a completed task; is specific: "All of you are working hard to get this room cleaned up."

Here are two examples of praise:

- ◆ *Praise* in a prekindergarten classroom at large-group time—Teacher in front of group: "Peter is sitting straight and tall. His lips are zipped, and his hand is up. I will call on him. Peter?"

- ◆ *Praise* in a second grade class during a math assignment—Teacher in front of group: "Marcella, you worked quietly and did a great job. You get to line up first when we go outside today."

When teachers single out a child for praise in front of the group, they are usually trying to influence the behaviors of the rest of the group. They believe they are setting up positive competition—other children will want the recognition that Peter or Marcella received and will try harder. But Kohn (1999), Dreikurs (1968), Ginott (1972), and others argue that these actions inadvertently institutionalize winners and losers in the class. This sets up negative group dynamics that can actually work against the teacher's management design (Reineke, Sonsteng, & Gartrell 2008).

Tasks such as sitting up straight and persisting on math problems are just easier for some children than others. Because the teacher is looking for examples to use in order to influence the group, she often overlooks children who are trying hard. By being passed over, children who already may perceive themselves as marginalized feel even further so. Rather than try harder, they become discouraged and may give up (Gartrell 2011; Kohn 1993).

Resentments can build in under-acknowledged children, especially if they perceive an unequal differential in teacher recognition. Stress hormones increase, which makes it even more difficult for them to learn the behaviors that will help them succeed in school and in life. The dynamics of evaluative praise make classrooms unencouraging places (Reineke, Sonsteng, & Gartrell 2008).

In order to prevent public encouragement from sliding into praise, the teacher directs positive acknowledgement to the entire group. Individuals are not singled out for praise, just as they are not singled out for criticism. She talks with individuals privately. For example, say a class is cleaning up the room and one child in particular is working very hard. Two other children, though, grinning, have disappeared around a corner in the room. The teacher enthusiastically makes the case that the *group* is working hard and the room is really getting cleaned up fast.

Privately, and maybe even later, she talks with the two children about what the problem was. She thinks about next time giving the two specific cleanup options that they can handle and using enthusiastic private encouragement to get them going. Also privately, she thanks the child who worked especially hard, which lets the child know that the acknowledgment is meant just for her. Here are some further examples of encouragement.

- *Public encouragement* in a prekindergarten class at large-group time—Teacher: "Girls and boys, you are sitting straight and tall and everyone can see the book. We are ready for this story!"

- *Private encouragement* in a second grade class during a math assignment—Kneeling down next to a child, the teacher whispers, "Janelle, you are working really hard on those problems and you have correct answers for almost all of them. You just need to double-check these two. You are almost done."

Public encouragement builds group spirit, and it builds pride in all children just for being part of the group. Children who opt out of group doings are given private, selective attention so as to neither embarrass nor reinforce them. In this way, the teacher preserves the relationship with individual children and sustains the pride all the children feel in their group.

# Moving to the Positive: Guidelines, Not Rules

At the end of a wing in an elementary school, a prekindergarten class walks past primary-grade classrooms four times a day. The preschoolers have trouble remembering not to talk. With doors open due to the school's old air-conditioning system, the preschoolers' chatter distracts the primary-grade children and their teachers. The principal discusses the problem with Renilda and Cathi, the prekindergarten teachers. They agree to figure out a way to have the preschoolers walk in line more quietly.

Renilda recalls a group punishment from her own school days—when some children talked in line, the entire class had to "practice" walking up and down the hall five times in complete silence. Renilda shares with Cathi how the experience still upsets her —she wasn't one of the ones talking—and how negative the class felt toward the "talkers" and upset they were with the teacher.

Not wanting to introduce the negative dynamics of group punishment in their classroom, the two teachers hold a class meeting. They matter-of-factly explain the problem to the children and ask what would help them remember to walk quietly. The teachers acknowledge each idea the children offer. One child says, "We could be mommy and daddy elephants. We have to tiptoe so we don't wake the babies." Everyone likes this idea, and they decide to try it.

As the children line up the next day, the teachers ask them if they remember how they are going to walk quietly. The children remember. When the class tiptoes by the principal's office, he notices them and declares, "I like how you boys and girls are walking quietly down the hall."

"Shh," one child says. "You'll wake the babies." (Gartrell 2012)

Think about the differences in the learning climate of these two settings—Renilda's childhood class, and Renilda and Cathi's present-day class:

- One classroom has the rule "No talking in line." The other has the guideline "We are quiet in line so we don't wake the babies." (With older students, it might be " . . . so we don't bother children in other classrooms.")

- One classroom has the rule (probably unstated) "All members can be punished for the mistakes of some." The other has the guideline "Mistakes are okay. We just need to learn from them."

In a *Young Children* article, Wien (2004) makes the case that rules tend not to be helpful in early childhood communities. Rules are usually stated as negatives. In fact, the way most rules are worded, it seems as if adults expect children to break them (Wien 2004). For example, with the rule "No hitting," teachers often feel pressure to be hypervigilant for this behavior, but then can only ignore the behavior or punish the child when it actually happens—limited options indeed. Even when rules are not entirely negative, such as "Be nice to your friends," they may have an unspoken "or else" implication in teachers' minds.

When the adult enforces rules with children, the children know they have done something wrong. However, the typical punishment associated with rule enforcement does not teach the children what to do *instead* (Readdick & Chapman 2000): "You know the rule—no hitting! Go to the time-out chair." Busy with enforcement, adults can easily forget the importance of teaching children positive strategies, such as using words or walking away, as alternatives to expressing frustration by hurting a classmate.

Rules can lead to teachers labeling children, lumping them in groups, and enforcing rules accordingly: Teachers might be lenient with the "good children" who obey the rules most of the time but be strict with the "naughty children" who often break rules.

Studies show that children who frequently are subject to punitive rule enforcement feel rejected, develop negative self-images, and may have long-term problems with aggressiveness in school and life (Ettekal & Ladd 2009; Ladd 2008). Rules can make teachers stricter than they want to be, and that is an unhappy situation for everyone in a classroom community.

In contrast to rules, guidelines are stated as positives. They identify social expectations that teachers assist children (and other adults in the classroom) to learn and to use. With the guideline "We are friendly with our mates," the adult can calm down an upset child, then teach the child how to use friendlier words to express her feelings. (This teaching is built on a positive adult-child relationship that the adult is always working to improve [Watson 2003].) In this sense, guidelines are not just "permissive rules"—a common misperception (Gartrell 2010). When there is danger of harm, teachers must be firm—but again, firm and friendly, not firm and harsh.

When adults model positive expectations, they teach children the skills they need for civil living (Copple & Bredekamp 2009). From the guideline "We are friendly with our mates," a child learns to say, "Please share the markers." With the teacher's help, the comment may lead to dialogue and problem resolution. This set of interactions is far more effective than demanding, refusing, grabbing, pushing away, and the teacher's enforcing a "No fighting" rule.

With preschoolers, writing and posting guidelines provides a functional literacy activity as well as a quick visual reminder. Having just a few guidelines works well; in fact, Renilda and Cathi's classroom had only one: "We are friendly with our mates." (These teachers preferred the term *mates*, as in *classmates*, to *friends*. They respected the children's right to define their own friendships.)

In the primary grades, three or four guidelines work well; too many makes things complicated (Gartrell 2010). The following are examples:

- We are friendly with others.
- We solve problems together.
- Mistakes are okay. We just need to learn from them.

## Class Meetings to Build the Encouraging Classroom

Circle gatherings long have been used by Native Americans and other cultural groups for matters of public deliberation in a spirit of equality. The circle suggests the equality and worth of each individual and lends itself to the building of a community spirit.

Circle times in the classroom go back to Froebel's first kindergartens in Germany. These times usually include daily activity routines such as finger plays, songs, stories, movement activities, weather and calendar, and an introduction to the day's activities.

Class meetings (sometimes called *community meetings*) transcend daily routines to deal with life in the classroom. On occasion circle times flow into class meetings, but the two have a different focus. The class meeting is expressly designed for the active involvement of each child. Its purpose is to encourage thought and sharing by children and teachers about their experiences, needs, concerns, and triumphs (Vance & Weaver 2002).

William Glasser is credited with popularizing the use of class meetings (1969), which he called "magic circles." Countless teachers, and writers such as McClurg (1988), owe a debt to Glasser. McClurg (1998) notes,

> The purpose of the community meeting is to create an intentional community devoted to a common project: learning to live with and take in the realities and perspectives of others. Here young children encounter and learn to acknowledge multiple realities, discover that they have choices, and realize that they are responsible for their decisions. (30)

In "The Beauty of Class Meetings" (Gartrell 2006), I discuss why I believe class meetings are the single most important institutionalized function in the encouraging classroom: They provide opportunities for the teacher and children together to set guidelines for the class; discuss and make decisions about events, issues, and procedures; appreciate individual members of the group; and build an inclusive, noncompetitive group spirit. Teachers often hold class meetings at the beginning of the year to invite the group to develop a few overall guidelines (Vance & Weaver 2002).

Class meetings empower children to be contributing citizens of a learning community, to work together to attain a sense of belonging, and to develop individual responsibility (DeVries & Zan 2003; Vance & Weaver 2002). The following anecdote relates events that took place during my first year of teaching in a Head Start program in which the families celebrated Christmas.

---

It was December. The holiday open house for families was coming up, and we needed to decorate the room, especially one large, high bulletin board (not placed well for young children). It was time for a class meeting. The assistant teacher and I asked the group of eighteen 3-, 4-, and 5-year-olds: What could go on the bulletin board that would look nice for the open house?

After a few moments of thought, Karen (age 4) said, "We could make "The Night before Christmas."

I said that sounded fine, but how would we do that? Joey (age 4) said, "I make the Santa on the roof. I need cotton." Two girls (ages 4 and 5) said they would make the tree, "with lights even." Rita (age 4) added, "I will make the guy coming down the stairs."

"OK," I commented, "How about if I make the house with a room and a roof." Various other older preschoolers volunteered to make the sled and some reindeer. Buddy (age 4) drew and cut out stairs.

Five 3-year-olds didn't say anything. But at the end of the class meeting they all went to the art center, cut out small pieces of paper, and drew crisscrosses on them. I went over, curious to see what they were doing. Darwin said, "We're makin' presents, Teacher." The kids brought me their pieces as they finished them. I asked them where each piece should go and tacked the pieces wherever they indicated, which created a wonderful scene.

On the big day the families, who were used to commercial, professional-looking bulletin boards, arrived. They looked at this one, and there were smiles all around. They knew the children had made just about all of it. The kids all pointed out the pieces they had made. The parents were very pleased.

> Yet this is not the end of the story. On the first day back to school in January after our break, I was beginning to take the bulletin board down when the children came in from the buses. "What are you doing, Teacher?" asked Karen. I told her and the others that I was taking the bulletin board down because Christmas was over. "No," said Joey. "We made it. We take it down." And with me spotting for the tallest children as they stood on chairs, the children did.

This anecdote illustrates how class meetings are a key practice in creating an inclusive community. As more and more children contributed ideas about what to do on the bulletin board, it truly became a group effort, and the children took responsibility not only for creating it but also for taking it down.

In an account of Glasser's writing on building "a sense of togetherness" within the class, Charles (2005) states,

> To foster a sense of togetherness, the teacher should continually talk with the class about what they will accomplish as a group, how they will deal with the problems they encounter as a group, how they will work together to get the best achievement possible for every individual in the group. In order to bring this about, responsibilities are given and shared, students are encouraged to speak of their concerns while the class attempts to find remedies, and the teacher takes special steps, when necessary, to incorporate every student into the ongoing work of the class. (142)

McClurg (1998) points out that meetings help teach the skills of group living that adults generally want all children to learn:

> Some children may be too self-conscious; others may need to become more self-aware. Some may need to take control, while others are learning how to give. It is good news that, with a little leadership from an understanding adult, young children can learn these and many other things from each other. (30)

Class meetings, then, become a primary method for teaching democratic life skills. Each time a meeting occurs, children are reminded that the classroom is a community that includes each one of them as well as each adult (Vance & Weaver 2002). Class meetings help to define the encouraging classroom.

## Guidelines for Holding Class Meetings

Regardless of the immediate purpose for a class meeting, guidelines such as these should consistently apply:

- Anyone can talk.
- Take turns and listen carefully.
- Be honest.
- Be kind.

Wolfgang (1999) points out that in Glasser's conception of classroom meetings, there are no wrong answers; every child can successfully participate without fear of correction. The teacher works toward this goal by offering direct teaching about the meeting process and also by using ongoing verbal and nonverbal support. An example of verbal support during class meetings follows, in which the teacher uses reflective statements that affirm what a child has said or meant in order to reduce her own personal judgments during meetings:

**Third-grader:** It made me mad that someone took my pencil. Chaz thought it was his, but he gave it back.

**Teacher:** You were upset that your pencil was gone. How did you feel when he gave it back to you?

The teacher also may use nondirective statements:

**Child:** I could write in a story about Buddy getting lost, but I don't know how to say it.

**Teacher:** Well, you think about how to draw or write about your dog and do it any way you want. Do other children have suggestions?

As much as verbal support, the teacher relies on the staple nonverbal responses of nods and smiles, allowing the children as much as possible to guide the discussion's flow (Wolfgang 1999).

Writers have different ideas about how often to hold class meetings and how long they should be. McClurg (1998) suggests a weekly meeting of at least a half hour for a first grade class. In contrast, at a kindergarten/first grade level, Harris and Fuqua (2000) recommend three meetings a day. Harris and Fuqua state: "Twenty minutes, three times a day spent in building a sense of community, we predict, will have an impact on all aspects of the day and make all other times more productive with less time spent in overt management" (46).

Because class meetings are central to the encouraging classroom, I recommend two 5- to 10-minute meetings each day in a full-day program at both the prekindergarten and primary-grade levels—after arrival (and breakfast when possible) and just before going home. The teacher can also call a special meeting if something eventful happens that needs immediate discussion.

Vance and Weaver (2002) offer helpful advice for teachers ready to try class meetings:

If you're just beginning to use class meetings and are weighing the benefits, make a commitment to hold them for at least three months before judging the results. It may take that long for children to incorporate their new social skills, begin to use them regularly, and learn to trust one another. The change in the classroom's social climate will be noticeable. (24–25)

## Class Meetings to Sustain the Encouraging Classroom

An essential use of class meetings is to solve problems that involve the whole group. Renilda and Cathi, for example, held a class meeting to address the noise problem when the class walked in the hall. On the other hand, if one child calls another "butthead," that in itself is not usually enough to hold a class meeting—the teacher deals with it privately. If that term or a similar one catches on with other children, however, then a class meeting can help address the issue with all.

Class meetings are the guidance alternative to *group punishment.* Group punishment may occur when *some* children in the group are engaging in mistaken behavior, the teacher does not know who was involved, and the entire class endures the consequences. An example of this was Renilda's childhood experience. Unfortunately, group punishments set teacher and students against each other (Gartrell 2011). By instead using class meetings to address an issue together, teachers prevent and, if necessary, repair this fundamental disruption to the dynamics of the group. Rather than the emotional message "The teacher finds us unworthy," the message children receive from class meetings is "We can solve this together."

Three examples of class meetings—in second grade, prekindergarten, and toddler classrooms—show the problem-solving function of class meetings at work:

**Second grade class meeting:** In an urban second grade classroom, some members of Julie's class were leaving the restroom a mess. Julie wasn't sure who was responsible, but instead of punishing everyone, she held a class meeting, nonjudgmentally mediating the process. She passed around a talking stick so that individual children could discuss the problem, identify possible solutions, and agree on a course of action. It worked—the custodian no longer noted any issues (Gartrell 2006).

**Prekindergarten class meeting:** In a Head Start classroom, children were having problems when playing on a new climber that had been set up to promote physical activity. During a class meeting, the teacher used the following social problem-solving steps with the children.

1. She identified the problem and set the scene for the meeting.
2. The teacher had the children share specific issues, such as pushing while on top of the climber.
3. She brainstormed solutions with the group.
4. The teacher decided on three guidelines for use of the climber.
5. She posted the written guidelines by the climber, which the teachers and children monitored together.

The guidelines, which the children came up with and the teacher helped to word and write down, were as follows:

1. Give kids room when climbing up the ladder.
2. Use only careful touches on the top.
3. We go down the slide except on Fridays.

The teachers loved the third guideline—a wonderful, child-devised solution to the perennial problem of children trying to climb up the slide when others are coming down. This solution also provided a functional use of the class calendar and allowed for upper-body exercise. (Children often come up with solutions adults would never think of. If these solutions have a chance, make them work—for the benefit of the group.)

**Toddler class meeting:** In the toddler room of an urban child care center, two children had developed a habit of biting other children. Children were going home with bite marks, and parents were upset. The teachers held a class meeting with the toddlers, explained the problem, and taught the children to hold up a hand and say "Stop" loudly if they thought biting was about to happen. The class practiced the response, and the next day a 2½-year-old used the strategy. The toddler who was about to bite had his impulse broken and hesitated; the teachers intervened quickly. The teachers made much of the first toddler's proactive response, and other children began to try it.

Over time, one of the toddlers who had been biting began to cry when yelled at to stop. The other child who had been biting would grin and run away when told to stop. The staff felt that these behaviors were a vast improvement over the biting, and biting behaviors were greatly reduced. By using the class meeting to both stop the aggressive behavior and give potential victims a proactive response, these teachers were perhaps preventing the beginnings of the bully-victim syndrome. The syndrome can be reinforced when teachers respond to aggressive behavior only by comforting the victim and punishing the child responsible (Gartrell 2011).

The message is that class meetings to solve problems and sustain the encouraging classroom can work even with very young children. Class meetings not only help children identify problems and work toward solutions but also help them build language arts and social studies skills—and progress toward the democratic life skills.

Class meetings to address serious conflict situations often can and do make things better. However, I must mention one caution in relation to using class meetings to resolve public problems. Teachers must always balance the need of the group to feel secure with the right of an individual child for the dignity of privacy. Meetings to address one child's actions that are posing a threat to others take careful thought and preparation. They may include informing other adults, such as parents and administrators, beforehand.

Perhaps the child causing harm need not be at the meeting, or perhaps the child is present and sits next to the teacher or on the teacher's lap. If the child is present, the teacher reinforces a basic premise of class meetings: that the meetings are respectful to all, and are held only for the purpose of making a difficult situation better. Not holding a class meeting when a single child's actions are posing a threat may hurt a teacher's effort to sustain a classroom that is encouraging for all. Still, it can be a difficult decision. I talk more about this issue in Chapter 7 of Gartrell (2011).

As class meetings become established in the encouraging classroom, children value them. The teacher will know that community meetings are having an impact when children take more responsibility for running them, and the teacher is sometimes able to sit back and watch (McClurg 1998).

> Over time, children will begin to care for one another, solve their own problems, feel more empowered and more in control of their learning, and come to view all in the community as their "teachers." It will be time well spent when the teacher sees what happens during [class meetings] coming around again and again. (Harris & Fuqua 2000, 47)

The long-term benefits of class meetings to children are society's, too: class meetings build individuals' confidence at using language to solve human problems, develop the ability to balance the needs and viewpoints of others with one's own, and offer the experience of speaking in public. With years of experience in the democratic functioning of groups, a new generation would be well prepared to face and respond positively to society's—and the world's—problems, and to implement the democratic life skills.

# The Guidance Approach: Guidance with Individual Children

I n Chapter 8 we explored using guidance techniques with a group of children, techniques that lead to the creation of an encouraging classroom and assist children in attaining the democratic life skills. In this chapter, we turn to guidance with individual children. Specifically, this chapter is about helping individual young children to develop the social-emotional capacities of the democratic life skills.

The following anecdote conveys the theme of the chapter perfectly:

> When teacher Beth first came to her preschool center, young Jeremiah was having angry outbursts and was often placed in time-out, which consisted of, as Beth referred to it, "the dreaded green chair." Beth built a relationship with Jeremiah and learned that his parents, who struggled financially, had recently separated. The turmoil in their lives showed in his behavior. Beth became aware that he was a very bright child who was affectionate toward animals and most living things, and really just needed some stability in his life. Beth built a relationship with each parent separately outside of class. In class she used peer mediation, a particular form of conflict mediation. She taught all of the children, especially Jeremiah, the technique. Beth related the following incident, which occurred after Jeremiah had had considerable experience with peer mediation.

> One day I overheard a fracas in the block corner: I stood up to see what was going on, ready to intervene. The youngest child in the room, who was just 2 and only talking a little bit, and one of the 4-year-olds were in a dispute over a truck. I took a step forward, ready to go to their aid, and then I saw Jeremiah approach them.

"What's going on?" he asked (my standard opening line when addressing children having a conflict). He proceeded to facilitate a discussion between the two children that lasted for five minutes. He made sure both kids got a chance to speak; he interpreted for Jordan, the younger child.

"Jordan, what do you think of that idea?" Jeremiah asked. Jordan shook his head and clutched the truck tighter. "I don't think Jordan's ready to give up the truck yet," he told the 4-year-old.

It was amazing. Jeremiah helped the kids negotiate an agreement, and then he walked away with a cocky tilt to his head I'd never seen before. His competence was without question; his pride was evident. (Gartrell 2006b, 105)

**liberation teaching:**
helping children who are vulnerable for stigma (exclusion from the group) overcome their vulnerabilities and find a place of acceptance, perhaps even leadership, with their peers

When a teacher guides a child to meet the safety needs shown in DLS 1 and 2 and to progress in meeting the growth needs outlined in DLS 3, 4, and 5—as Beth did with Jeremiah—I call this ***liberation teaching***. By liberation teaching, I mean helping children who are vulnerable for stigma—exclusion from the group—overcome their vulnerabilities and find a place of acceptance, and perhaps even leadership, with their peers. Liberation teaching is guidance at its best. It occurs when teachers see children who have a lot of conflicts and, rather than turn their backs on them and write them off, open their arms to them again and again.

Ladd and associates have documented that children who are unable to form peer relationships during the preschool years are likely to have continuing behavioral and educational problems (Ladd & Dinella 2009; Ladd & Ettekal 2009). Therefore, with any child, educators should work toward preventing a cycle of stress—a cycle that begins with aggression, leading to an adrenalin rush, and eventually rejection and, in turn, renewed stress—which can lead to a poor self-image and a possible negative self-fulfilling prophecy (Gunnar, Herrera, & Hostinar 2009).

DLS 1: Finding acceptance as a member of the group and as a worthy individual

DLS 2: Expressing strong emotions in non-hurting ways

DLS 3: Solving problems creatively—independently and in cooperation with others

DLS 4: Accepting unique human qualities in others

DLS 5: Thinking intelligently and ethically

As we discuss what teachers can do to help children avoid these outcomes and work toward developing DLS 1 and 2, keep in mind that first and foremost, a developmentally appropriate program will prevent many problem behaviors. When adults have appropriate expectations for children, children are less likely to feel frustrated and act out. Of course this will not prevent all of children's conflicts, so let's start this chapter by exploring the dynamics that cause children to have serious conflicts in the classroom, and how children benefit when teachers use guidance instead of discipline.

## Beyond Discipline

A *conflict* is an expressed disagreement between individuals. Because young children have limited experience interacting with others and are still developing their abilities to self-regulate and express themselves, their conflicts often involve behaviors that adults find unacceptable: namely, verbal and physical acts that can potentially cause harm. In a classroom that depends on rules to keep children in line, individuals who cause unacceptable conflicts are disciplined. The problem with discipline, however, is that the consequences too often slide into punishment (Gartrell 2011b; Reynolds 2006).

Merriam-Webster's definition of *punishment* is "suffering, pain, or loss that serves as retribution." Young children cannot think rationally in the face of punishment (Readdick & Chapman 2000). A child put in time-out does not think, "I will be a better child for having this experience!" With the hurt and embarrassment of public, forced removal from the group (temporary suspension) comes an onslaught of stress hormones, a negative self-message, and often stimulation of the fight-or-flight reaction (Gartrell 2011a, c, d). It is neither appropriate nor effective to inflict pain and suffering on children for causing conflicts that they haven't yet learned how to manage.

Instead, adults should help children develop the ability to identify, handle, and express their emotions. The capacity of the teacher to build a positive relationship—a healthy teacher-child attachment—provides the classroom security children need to progress in this (Ostrowsky & Jung 2003). Much comes down to how the teacher regards a child's behaviors.

In contrast to discipline, teachers who use guidance see their approach as consisting of these two fundamentals:

◆ Teaching children to learn from their mistakes rather than punishing them for the mistakes they make

◆ Helping children learn to solve their problems rather than punishing them for having problems they cannot yet solve on their own (Gartrell 2011b)

In a guidance approach, there are consequences if a child causes a conflict. But the consequences are for the teacher as well as the child. The consequence for the early childhood professional is to teach the child less hurtful ways to manage the conflict. The consequence for the child is to gain from the experience and learn less hurtful ways. In this fundamental use of guidance, teachers base their interventions on relationships with children that have been forming since the beginning of their time together.

Sometimes the progress a child makes through the use of guidance is only a small improvement. For example, one day a child who previously hit her classmates when she was angry or frustrated instead uses angry words to communicate her feelings. Yet this is still the beginning of an improvement! The early childhood professional is committed to teaching what the child can learn on *this* day, at *this* time. Scaffolding a child's social-emotional learning requires a positive teacher-child relationship, which lowers the child's stress and builds his trust in the teacher. With the relationship growing, the child can gradually begin to learn to use less hurting words during a conflict, such as "I am angry" instead of "You dumb butthead."

## Misbehavior, Conflict, and Mistaken Behavior

Like *discipline,* the term *misbehavior* carries connotations of judgment, not only about a child's behavior but also about the child (Gartrell 2011b). *Conflict* is a less emotionally charged term for an interpersonal problem. When a conflict occurs, even adults have to work at expressing strong feelings in non-hurting ways, and adults have years of experience and mature brains to assist them. Children are just learning how to manage strong emotions; they are really better thought of as months old, not years old. A 4-year-old only has between 48 and 60 months of life experience. A 5-year-old is very much a work in progress, and executive function in younger children has just barely begun to develop (Galinsky 2010). Young children are only beginning to learn skills that they will still be working on decades later.

**mistaken behavior:** an intentional or unintentional action that causes a conflict or contributes to complications in getting the conflict resolved; error in judgment

Having conflicts is part of being human. When many little bodies spend long hours of the day with a few big bodies in a relatively enclosed space, conflicts are going to happen. With only months of brain development and experience, 4-year-olds are not going to be able to say to each other, "I see you have a high need for an extra portion of playdough. It is all right that you take mine; maybe just return a bit when you are done." No, most are going to do whatever it takes to get their playdough back.

This is why, during the 1980s, I began using the term ***mistaken behavior*** instead of *misbehavior* (Gartrell 1987, 2004, 2010). A mistaken behavior is an intentional or unintentional action that causes a conflict or contributes to complications in getting the

conflict resolved—like screaming and trying to grab back your playdough or pushing the other child off his chair. Though it may seem unusual to consider acts done on purpose as mistaken behavior, I view them as errors in judgment.

One argument for thinking of actions that cause or contribute to conflicts as mistaken behavior is this: In contrast to misbehavior, which teachers typically expect more of in certain children, *everybody* makes mistakes in their behavior. In the process of learning the democratic life skills, certainly children, who are just beginning that process, are going to make mistakes. Teachers who accept "misbehavior" as mistaken behavior are in a good position to help children learn from their mistakes. This assistance will help children gain DLS 1 and 2, so that they can make progress with DLS 3, 4, and 5.

## Three Levels of Mistaken Behavior

Thanks in large part to the work of my doctoral advisor, Dr. Steve Harlow, I have developed the concept of three levels of mistaken behavior, which help to explain the kinds of conflicts children experience (Gartrell 2004, 2010). The levels clarify distinct sources of motivation for children's conflicts and suggest guidance-related practices to use in response.

With any level of mistaken behavior, teachers should be firm when they need to be. Guidance is not hesitant or tentative in the face of possible harm, ever. But as mentioned, guidance means that teachers are firm and friendly, not firm and harsh. A friendly sense of humor is an asset; it helps us remember how young the children really are. An assistant teacher I worked with once asked a 3-year-old to use his magic words. With great seriousness he exclaimed, "Abracadabra!" (The assistant excused herself to the hallway and came back in the room after having a good laugh.)

For consistency across the three levels of mistaken behavior, I'll use examples of children's swearing/pejorative use of language to illustrate the differences in the behaviors and the type of guidance useful for each type.

### Level One: Experimentation Mistaken Behavior

Situations sometimes go differently than children expect, and they fall into *uncontrolled experimentation mistaken behavior.* An example is a child who is busily building with blocks when another child grabs several from her. The first child screams, "Stop it, Stupidhead!" and grabs them back.

Another type of experimentation mistaken behavior—referred to as *controlled*—is seen when children try things to see what will happen, and their "experiment" results in a conflict. In the previous example, the child who intentionally grabbed the blocks may have been exhibiting controlled experimentation mistaken behavior.

Four-year-old Karen once came up to me with a big grin on her face and said, "Shit, Teacher." This was definitely an example of controlled experimentation mistaken behavior. She said something purposely to see what her teacher would do. I knelt down on her level and said, "Karen, I like how you are always learning new words in our Head Start program, but that one bothers people. You should keep using new words, just not that one." Karen rolled her eyes, but I didn't hear her use that word again. If I had made a big deal of her experiment—lectured her, disciplined her—she would have noted the emotional significance of the situation and likely used the word again at a choice time.

If experimentation mistaken behavior is public and others notice it, it is helpful to place yourself on the child's eye level, calm the child if necessary, and use a low-key compliment sandwich (two positive statements surrounding the one correction requested, as I used with Karen). This will address the mistaken behavior but avoid reinforcing its significance, which might lead to its becoming a mistaken behavior at Level Two or even Level Three. If the experimentation mistaken behavior is private and no one other than you is aware of it, sometimes the behavior is best ignored.

## Level Two: Socially Influenced Mistaken Behavior

*Socially influenced mistaken behaviors* may be exhibited by an individual child or by a group. The source of a Level Two behavior for an individual is often significant persons outside the classroom. An example is a child who learns a swear word from someone in the family or neighborhood and repeats it exactly as that person would say it.

In addition, a socially influenced mistaken behavior may show as a ripple effect in a group, such as when a word like *butthead* catches on. When Level Two mistaken behaviors are observed in a group of children, class meetings conducted in a manner respectful of all children can help. The following anecdote illustrates the contagious type of socially influenced mistaken behavior, the kind that children can learn from each other, and how using the guidance approach through a class meeting can help correct a group's socially influenced mistaken behaviors.

---

Charley had crutches but got them replaced with a new leg brace. It squeaked, and by the end of the first day a few kids started laughing and repeating "Squeaky-Leg Charley."

The teacher noticed, talked with Charley, and the next day at the class meeting Charley showed everyone his new leg brace. The class had a chance to look at the brace closely and become familiar with it. The teacher then explained that Charley didn't need the crutches anymore and had made real progress by getting the leg brace. The children's use of the pejorative term ended there. The following day the teacher was absent. When the substitute teacher walked in, three children came up to her and said, "Charley got a new leg brace. It squeaks, but he gets around on it really good."

---

Class meetings raise children's awareness, as this one did, as well as teach guidelines about behavior.

## Level Three: Strong Unmet Needs Mistaken Behavior

At Level Three a child intentionally uses hurtful language with obvious strong emotion and may attempt physical acts of harm as well. The reason for these behaviors is that, in an intense state of perceived unmet safety needs, the child feels threatened. The child is using **reactive aggression** to protect himself against the perceived threat (Gartrell 2011a).

A second kind of aggression at Level Three, **instrumental aggression,** is using force to get what one wants. A similar initial cause operates in instrumental aggression as in reactive aggression: the child feels threatened by life experiences. In instrumental aggression, however, the aggressive behavior becomes a strategy for the child to cope with stress by asserting his will (Dodge 1991). Aggression becomes a learned behavior (Gartrell 2011b; Kaiser & Sklar-Rasminsky 2012). Instrumental aggression is particularly bothersome to teachers because children are intentionally inflicting harm on others.

**reactive aggression:** behaviors used in self-defense when a child perceives a situation as threatening

**instrumental aggression:** the use of force to get what one wants

Bullying is a classic example of instrumental aggression. Besides the serious effects—immediate and potentially long-term—of bullying on the victim of the aggression, bullying affects the person using the instrumental aggression. According to the *Surgeon General's Report on Violence* (1999) and the American Medical Association's *National Study on Bullying* (Nansel et al. 2001), children who bully tend to be bullied themselves as they age and may experience mental health and aggression problems into adulthood.

Teachers who are able to see a child's emotionally intense words and actions as cries for help—even if the behaviors are quite challenging—are acting as a guidance professionals (Ostrowsky & Jung 2003). These teachers understand the importance of assisting children whose unmet needs are bigger than they are. Through a caring relationship, the child is able to lower stress levels, build trust, and work on DLS 1 and 2 (finding acceptance as a member of the group and as a worthy individual; expressing strong emotions in non-hurting ways).

## Guidance Interventions

In the remainder of the chapter I'll discuss guidance techniques for assisting children to work through their conflicts. Four key guidance intervention strategies are

1. Calm everyone down.

2. Use guidance talks with individuals.

3. Practice conflict mediation with disputing children in small groups.

4. Use comprehensive guidance.

### 1. Calm Everyone Down

When a conflict occurs, teachers naturally want to get the situation back under control. But with a guidance approach, the teacher responds to the conflict *more* like a first responder and mediator, and *less* like a police officer and instantaneous judge. So, after checking for injury, the first step is to calm everyone down, starting with yourself if necessary.

Remember that high stress levels in children and adults make it more difficult to resolve a problem. Your goal is to help everyone cool down so they can talk about what happened. Three common techniques are these:

- ◆ Have everyone take deep breaths. Model deep breathing if this will help.

- ◆ Have the children choose their own calming technique—deep breaths, counting slowly, sitting in another area. Support the children's choices.

- ◆ Remove the children from the conflict situation; provide the space and time children need for a cooling-down time.

Please note that a cooling-down time is different than a time-out. Time-out, or temporary expulsion, is punishment, a consequence of something a child has done. A cooling-down time is for the purpose of helping the child regain composure so you can talk about what happened. In deciding whether or not to have a child move away from the conflict, it helps to remind yourself of this difference. Some children will require minutes, not seconds, to regain composure.

Staying with the child during the cooling-down period is sometimes, but not always, effective. Use your knowledge of the child to determine whether to stay with her. Explain that after everyone is calm you will talk about the situation and think of ways to make it better. (If your effort is well intended and considerate—even if not perfect—it *will* make things better.)

## 2. Use Guidance Talks with Individuals

Teachers use guidance talks when individual children show mistaken behavior at any level and need to learn an alternative behavior. A guidance talk is *not* a lecture. Instead, teachers use what I call the five-finger formula for solving social problems, although in guidance talks the steps are more informally used than in mediations, and sometimes steps can be combined (Gartrell 2011b). See the figure.

During a guidance talk, the teacher speaks individually with the child. An example of a guidance talk was shared previously, involving Karen. Guidance talks are important because, as mentioned previously in this chapter, there is a consequence for a child who causes a conflict: Learn a better way to handle the situation. And the child learns that better way from the teacher. Through guidance, the teacher scaffolds the child to progress from where she is on her own to where she can act on that particular day. The following is another example of a guidance talk, reported by Francisca with Roland, who had just turned 5.

> **Five-Finger Formula for Social Problem Solving**
>
> 1. Thumb: Calm everyone down—yourself, too.
> 2. Pointer: Help the parties to accept how each person sees the conflict. (This may not be what happened as you saw it.)
> 3. Tall guy: Brainstorm possible resolutions. (Provide suggestions for children with limited language ability or who are dual language learners. Respect nonverbal signs of agreement or disagreement.)
> 4. Ringer: Agree to one solution and try it. (This is not your imposed solution but one that all agree to.)
> 5. Pinky: Monitor the solution and provide follow-up feedback to individuals. (Talk especially with children who need to manage emotions more effectively during conflicts. Use compliment sandwiches in these follow-up guidance talks.)

Roland was having a tough day, and nothing was going right. He spilled his juice during breakfast. Other children took all the slots for his favorite activity, water play, during center time. Two children got on the other teacher's lap first for reading a story. When he was building with the unit blocks, another child accidentally knocked over part of his castle. At this point, Roland lost it. He kicked at the child as she walked by, threw a block at the wall, and sat down and cried.

I went over and sat by him and put my arm around his shoulders. After a minute, he snuggled against my side, and we sat there. I said, "Things don't seem to be going your way today." He shook his head and sniffled a bit, and stopped crying. I asked, "I wonder what you can do when things bother you to help you feel better?"

Roland said, "Tell you." I said that I thought that was a good idea. I said he could either call for me or come over to get me. I told him he could count on me to try to help. We talked about how a child could get hurt if kids threw blocks. He listened, looked down, and gave a nod. I reminded him that Katrina maybe felt bad about what happened. I asked Roland how he could help her feel better.

"Tell her sorry," he said. I asked Roland if he would like me to go with him or if he could do it by himself. He said he could do it, and while I watched, he did. Roland was able to work some more on his castle, and then he put away the blocks himself.

Using guidance is not always easy. The only thing harder than learning the democratic life skills is teaching them to others. Guidance talks that reaffirm a relationship with the teacher, as Francisca accomplished here, are very important for helping children work on DLS 1 and 2.

## 3. Use Conflict Mediation with Disputing Children in Small Groups

Conflict mediation is appropriate when two or three children have lost control in a situation, a fracas has started, and the teacher decides to intervene. The teacher becomes a firm but friendly mediator, leading the children through each of the steps in the five-finger formula while expecting, encouraging, supporting, and acknowledging each child's participation.

The five-finger formula in conflict mediation is explained more fully in Chapter 9 of Gartrell (2010), and an illustration and discussion of the technique is found in Gartrell (2006a). Another example appears in Chapter 14 of this book with Ben, Will, and Nouri. The discussion of conflict mediation here covers basic elements of this guidance intervention.

A key feature of conflict mediation is that it allows children who are at a power imbalance during a conflict to move to a balanced power status. Conflict mediation reduces the bully-victim syndrome (reinforced when a teacher comforts the "victim" and punishes the "bully") which is an important benefit of the approach for both parties in the conflict (Gartrell 2011b).

In fact, this outcome alone makes conflict mediation worth the effort to learn and use. In addition, each time the teacher mediates a conflict—or uses any of the other guidance interventions—children gain in language and social studies skills, and the entire class sees democratic life skills being modeled as well as taught.

In modeling and teaching conflict mediation, teachers work to move children from *high-level mediation* to *low-level mediation* to *child negotiation*.

Most students in my classes have had relative success with the five-step approach, even in their first couple of tries. In the following example of **high-level mediation,** the student teacher, Jenner, uses each of the five steps in a clear and instructive fashion.

---

One morning two kindergarten boys were arguing over some LEGO wheels. Their faces were getting really intense, and their voices were getting louder.

Dylan: Hey, those are my wheels. You took my wheels. [whining loudly]

Austin: [yelling] No, I had them first.

[Dylan grabs at the wheels. Austin pulls them away.]

Jenner: Boys, I can see you are upset. Please come sit with me for a minute. I will hold the wheels just for now. [The boys say okay and come over.]

Jenner: Thank you. First, let's all take a couple of deep breaths and then we will see what's going on. Ready, 1 ... 2 ... 3 ... Okay, now let's talk about what happened. Dylan, you can start and then I will ask Austin next.

Dylan: He took my wheels that I was using yesterday and was gonna use today.

Jenner: Done? Okay. Austin, now you tell me what happened.

Austin: He wasn't here yet so I thought I could use the wheels.

Jenner: It sounds to me like we are having trouble figuring out who should get the wheels, huh?

Boys: Yeah.

Jenner: Okay, let's see if we can't come up with a way that you will both get a chance with the wheels. Do either of you have an idea?

Dylan: He should give them back to me.

Jenner: Austin, do you think that is a fair idea?

Austin: No, then when do I get to play with them?

Jenner: Can you think of another idea, so you both will have a chance to use the wheels?

Dylan: He can keep using them today and then tomorrow I will get to use them.

Jenner: Austin, what do you think of that idea?

Austin: Okay.

Jenner: Great, but next time something like this happens we need to use our words and not get mad right away. Then if it is still a problem, come and get me or another adult in the class. How does that sound to you?

Boys: Good.

Jenner: Okay, go play!

[The boys go over and play together with the LEGOs. Austin uses the wheels. Dylan finds an older, broken-down set but makes them work. There are no more problems.]

Typically in a successful **low-level mediation,** after calming down and having the teacher get them started, the children basically take over the process at step three or four and solve the problem themselves. The following example was written by Camille, a prekindergarten student teacher. At the time of this conflict Camille and the two children were already accustomed to working out conflicts through mediation.

Dakota and Chante were in the classroom store. Dakota was using the cash register, and Chante was talking on the telephone. Dakota picked up another telephone and started talking to her. Chante turned to him and yelled, "Shut up!"

Dakota looked very sad. I knelt down and asked if he could tell Chante how that made him feel. He turned to her and said, "I felt really, really sad and bad when you yelled at me."

Chante responded, "I'm sorry, Dakota. I didn't mean that, I guess. I was talking to a customer."

I said, "Chante, I think Dakota wants to talk on the telephone with you."

Chante said, "Yeah, but he's not a customer. "

I suggested, "I wonder if Dakota could take the telephone to the house and be a customer?"

"I could call you from the house," Dakota said.

"Yeah, you need lots of stuff," said Chante (getting into it). "Go over and tell me what you need."

Dakota, smiling, "phoned" from the house. Chante had the stuff ready for him when he came to pick it up. He gave her some make-believe money, and she even gave him change! (Gartrell 2011b, 359)

Camille's journal reflections indicate how pleased and amazed she was that the children solved the problem. She states, "These kinds of instances just prove to me that these children will solve their own problems. Sometimes all they need is a little guidance."

**Child negotiation** occurs when one or both children in a conflict choose not to retaliate but to negotiate. Although a certain maturity is required for this, what is more important is an encouraging classroom environment in which conflict management is modeled, taught, and practiced.

The following example of child negotiation features two children early in their kindergarten year. Notice how a *peace prop,* in this case a sock puppet known as a

**high-level mediation:** conflict mediation style in which the teacher becomes a firm but friendly mediator, leading the children through each of the steps in the five-finger formula while expecting, encouraging, supporting, and acknowledging each child's participation

**low-level mediation:** conflict mediation style in which, after calming down and having the teacher get them started, the children take over the process and solve the problem themselves

*power sock,* can aid children as they learn the solemnity and turn taking needed in social problem solving. (*Talk-and-listen chairs* are another prop that can be used for this purpose—children exchange chairs as they alternately talk to explain their side of a conflict and listen to the other's viewpoint. A third prop is a *talking stick*—a decorated stick held at each end by the child whose turn it is to speak, while the other child listens. The two exchange the stick when it is the other child's turn.)

**child negotiation:**
conflict mediation style in which one or both children in a conflict choose not to retaliate but to negotiate on their own without a teacher's help

---

Nakisha and Suel Lin were caring for a variety of dolls in the kindergarten housekeeping area. They both reached for the last doll to be fed, bathed, and put to bed. They started yelling that they each had it first, and Suel Lin took Nakisha's arm and started squeezing it.

"Stop, that hurts," exclaimed Nakisha. "Use your words!"

"I don't know them," yelled Suel Lin.

"Then we get Power Sock," Nakisha demanded. Both girls, still holding part of the doll, walked over and got Power Sock. "I will wear him, Suel Lin, and you tell Sock."

Suel Lin said to Sock, "Baby needs a bath, but we both want to do it."

"Both do it," said Sock in a deep Nakisha voice.

The two girls put back Power Sock and returned to the housekeeping area, <u>still</u> both holding the doll. One girl washed the top half, the other the bottom half. Then Suel Lin held the doll and fed it while Nakisha read a story to the other dolls already in bed. Suel Lin said, "Here's Baby; do you want to read another story?"

"Yeah," said Nakisha, who read another story while Suel Lin rubbed the babies' backs as they lay in their beds. (Gartrell 2011b, 360)

---

When children choose to use a peace prop without teacher guidance, as Nakisha and Suel Lin did, they are practicing child negotiation. In her journal, the student teacher who recorded the anecdote reflected, "I couldn't believe how Nakisha and Suel Lin solved the problem. I didn't have to do anything!"

Children who learn conflict management techniques gain in all the democratic life skills. Through successfully participating in high-level mediation, then in low-level mediation, and perhaps child negotiation, even young children

♦ Find that they have a place in the group and are worthy individuals—like the 2-year-old with the truck at the beginning of the chapter

♦ Learn to express strong emotions through the effective use of words—like storekeeper Chante

♦ Manifest an ability to solve problems cooperatively and civilly—like Jeremiah, Chante and Dakota, and Suel Lin and Nakisha

♦ Accommodate the viewpoints of others who are, at least behaviorally, different from them—like all children in the anecdotes

♦ Think intelligently and ethically—like Jeremiah and Nakisha did

The clear, even dramatic benefits of conflict mediation make this intervention the go-to practice when two children, or a small group of children, experience conflict.

## 4. Use Comprehensive Guidance

Anyone is entitled to a Level Three day, such as the type Roland experienced. Children who show atypical, extreme behaviors over more than a day or so, though, likely have problems that are getting the best of them and that they need help to overcome. Teachers who use guidance take a comprehensive approach in these situations. Comprehensive guidance is especially helpful in aiding children to find a place of acceptance in the group and to express strong emotions in non-hurting ways. When teachers have appropriate expectations for children because they use developmentally appropriate practice and they support children in meeting their basic psychological needs for safety, security, and belonging—including during conflicts—the teachers are guiding children to meet DLS 1 and 2. (A series of three Guidance Matters columns (2011a, c, and d) explore how teachers accomplish these challenging tasks.)

A comprehensive guidance approach might well involve all of the intervention strategies already discussed. It certainly involves reliance on the relationship the teacher is building with the child and ongoing communication with families. Often, teachers develop a formal or informal **Individual Guidance Plan,** a coordinated strategy of intervention and assistance, to help a child who is having ongoing classroom conflicts (see Gartrell 2011e).

The more serious a child's mistaken behaviors, the more people, time, and energy must be involved in working for a solution. The resources needed for comprehensive guidance may well stretch the capacities of individual teachers in many programs. As Gilliam (2005) recommends, local resource teams sponsored by states, which could provide specialized staff, consultants, or technical assistance to program staff and families, should be a vital part of a comprehensive guidance system.

The following is the case study excerpted from another Guidance Matters column, "Comprehensive Guidance" (Gartrell 2008). It shows the difference an individual teacher can make, in this case Robin Bakken, a lead teacher at Campus Childcare, Bemidji State University. Robin illustrates how she used comprehensive guidance with an Individual Guidance Plan and in the process practiced liberation teaching.

**Individual Guidance Plan:** a comprehensive and systematic strategy for addressing a child's serious mistaken behavior that is most often developed and implemented with families

---

I met Joe and his mother, Becky, at a Getting to Know You conference before school started. Joe seemed to be a curious 2½-year-old. His mother was young and a full-time college student. I could tell immediately that Becky truly loved her son, and she appeared to be a devoted caregiver.

Two weeks into the program, Joe began to have trouble getting along with other children. His anxiety level, beginning at drop-off time, seemed to be high. When classmates invaded his personal space, often during group activities, Joe responded by pulling children's hair, kicking, or yelling "Shut up!" When teachers intervened, Joe cried and kicked them. After a few weeks of attempting to guide Joe to use kind words and gentle touches, the director, other staff members, and I decided we needed to pursue a more comprehensive approach.

I began holding short weekly conferences with Becky to get to know her better and to offer her encouragement in her parenting. One day, shortly after our meeting I happened to look out the window and notice Becky sitting on the steps, crying. I took my break early and went out to talk with her. Becky shared her frustration over Joe's behavior: "Why does he act this way? I am tired and don't understand. He is so naughty!"

I responded, "Joe is a very sweet and special boy, and his behavior is the way he responds to stress. He feels threatened by many things right now, and he reacts in the only way he knows. It is mistaken behavior, and it is our job to guide him. It isn't an easy job." I reached over and gave her a hug. My friendship with Becky continued to grow and so did her trust in me. Together with other staff members and the director we developed an Individual Guidance Plan for Joe. At one conference, Becky suggested that we implement a reward system. We tried a sticker chart that recorded and rewarded hourly progress. Becky and I decided that we would call her any time three serious conflicts occurred in a day. When Joe and I called, I first explained the situation to Becky and then had Joe talk with her. Becky was firm but loving. Joe loved talking with his mother, and we would generally see a more relaxed Joe after these phone calls. (I kept tabs to make sure the calls didn't become a habit.)

Joe's conflicts with other children continued, and he needed someone nearby at all times to direct him to more appropriate behavior. I would calm Joe by holding and rocking him. Sometimes I sang. After Joe was calm, I used guidance talks, and he talked to me about what happened. These interactions encouraged bonding and a feeling of trust between us.

I also used humor. I gave Joe options of words to use when he was upset. Yelling "Pickle!" became a favorite. I also gave Joe a cushy ball to hold during stressful situations such as circle time, and made sure that a student teacher or I sat next to him. We rubbed Joe's back or arm or held him on our laps. The ball kept his hands busy and the touch calmed him.

Drop-off time was difficult for Joe and set the mood for the day. With the director's assistance, I arranged to meet him in the office or lounge to spend one-on-one time with him, playing a game or reading. The other staff noticed the difference in Joe— and the entire group—on the days I helped ease him into the class.

Eventually Becky agreed with the staff that an outside mental health assessment was needed for Joe's behavior. Dealing with people outside our center made Becky uncomfortable; to ease her stress, I stayed involved during the assessment process. I worked with the director and others to find resources for Becky; these included a family play therapy program and the school district's Early Childhood Family Education classes for young parents.

To keep up communication, the teaching staff that worked the later shift talked daily with Becky, and I left happygrams. Throughout this whole time, the director was a great support to me—and to Becky too.

One day, four months into working with Joe, he was building with LEGOs when a classmate sat down next to him and took a block off Joe's tower. Joe's previous response would have been to pull the child's hair. This time, however, he shouted, "NO, thank you!" We were so proud of Joe for using his words.

Our guidance plan was finally showing success. Joe learned to say what he needed and what he didn't like. Baby steps were all we needed. Joe grew and so did we. (Gartrell 2008, 44)

Robin's partnership with Becky extended to trying Mom's idea of using stickers. Except in very special situations, such as this one, it is more appropriate to use methods other than token rewards to help young children monitor and modify their behavior (Copple & Bredekamp 2009). Items such as tokens express more praise than encouragement and tend to reward achievement rather than acknowledge a child's efforts.

Robin's consistent affirming contact with Joe, even during conflicts, is what helped this very young child move beyond his Level Three mistaken behavior. Guidance interventions are effective only if the teacher is able to form a relationship with a child outside of conflict situations, to build trust for when conflicts occur. This relationship, along with partnerships with family members, provides the foundation that is essential for children to make needed and real social-emotional progress. The matter of building teacher-child attachments brings us to the next chapter.

# Guidance to Include Every Child

A fundamental issue in the use of guidance in developmentally appropriate classrooms is how teachers regard those children whose behaviors pose challenges to the classroom community. In a national study Gilliam (2005) examined the prevalence of expulsion from preschool programs as a means of handling these challenges. Three key findings in the study were these:

- Children are three times more likely to be expelled from preschools than from public schools, grades K through 12.

- Boys are almost five times more likely to be expelled from preschools than girls.

- Additional resources are needed nationwide to support staff in working with young children who show challenging behaviors, including an increase in mental health professionals to work with the children.

Since the release of this study, despite increased emphasis on education nationally, there has been little progress in increasing resources to early childhood programs and in reducing expulsion rates. Chapter 10 explores seven teaching practices that assist teachers to reach and teach *all* young children, particularly those who exhibit challenging behavior. These practices are as follows:

- The teaching team model
- Contact talks
- Private encouragement
- Compliment sandwiches

◆ Friendly touch

◆ Support for children vulnerable for stigma

◆ Techniques that are particularly effective for supporting boys

## The Teaching Team Model

For me, a major advantage of early childhood programs is the widespread use of teaching teams (NAEYC 2007). The teaching team concept means that some adults are lead teachers, some are assistant teachers, some are aides, and often some are regular volunteers. Under the leadership of the teacher, the team works with children and families *together*. Under the teaching team model, the teacher is the *lead* professional: a classroom manager who is overseeing the program, cooperatively managing the adult team, and, at the same time, teaching and learning with the children (Gartrell 2011). Through collaboration, the team accomplishes together what any member (including the lead teacher) cannot alone (Gartrell 2011).

A natural consequence of the teaching team model is that children's learning and interaction takes place more in small groups, each led by a team member, rather than in large groups led only by the lead teacher. Individual, child-selected activities also become an instructional staple, with a team of adults providing leadership. The teaching team allows for healthy adult-child ratios, which means that more individual interactions can occur, teacher-child attachments become easier to form and maintain, and a more inclusive, personalized educational program can result (NAEYC 2009).

When lead teachers see their role in this way, they are more apt to make decisions for the good of all in the classroom (Gartrell 2011). For instance, perhaps a particular child often pushes the lead teacher's buttons, but the assistant teacher works comfortably with the child. The child might be assigned to the daily small group of the assistant teacher, which increases the chances for a positive adult-child relationship, with consequent benefits for all members of the classroom community due to a decrease in mistaken behavior by the child.

The teaching team can also be helpful in building home-school partnerships, particularly if not all team members are from the community of some of the families. Those team members who do represent the community can contribute their cultural and linguistic skills and assist other staff members to build positive relationships with families.

In primary classrooms, there is often only one adult in the room or contract stipulations may limit the potential of the teaching team model. As a result, specialists who come into the classroom, such as special education teachers, often form a team with the classroom teacher to achieve some of these same benefits. Teachers who are fortunate enough to work with an assistant often develop informal teaching team partnerships. Whatever laws and contracts might specify about who may carry out actual instruction in a classroom, with solid leadership by the lead teacher, children clearly benefit from each team member's strengths and the coordinated efforts of the team.

## Contact Talks

Relationships are built on trust, and sustaining children's trust is fundamental to their progression in any of the democratic life skills. Treating children with respect during interactions—including conflicts—is essential. At all times, teachers work to avoid embarrassment, shame, and humiliation to protect children's self-image and enable them to view the classroom environment as trustworthy. A basic guidance principle is that the teacher builds relationships with children outside of conflict situations and sustains the relationship during conflicts. This is especially true with children who demonstrate challenging behavior. The fundamental practice for building relationships with children is the contact talk.

Two basic types of teacher-child discussions are **task talk** and **contact talk.** Task talk represents the necessary language of getting things done: "Let's get the room cleaned up quickly so we have lots of time outside!" "Please open your math books to page 59." There is plenty of task talk every day in every classroom because there are so many everyday tasks to be accomplished.

**task talk:** the necessary language representing everyday tasks that need to be accomplished

In contrast to the language of task talks, there is the language of interpersonal relationships. This language happens during contact talks. The purpose of a contact talk is to share a few moments of quality time with another human being, to learn more about the other person, and (at selected moments) to share a bit about oneself. While task talks arise naturally during the course of the day, teachers have to look for moments in which to have contact talks with children.

**contact talk:** the language of interpersonal relationships

During the teacher's busy day, the willingness to suspend tasks and share a moment with a child allows for a connection that lasts (Gartrell 2011). Sometimes, contact talks last only a few seconds, as in the following example.

---

Louie runs out the door onto the playground, does a circle around his teacher, jumps to a stop in front of her, and pulls his jeans up above his shoes. "Look, Teacher, new ones!"

Mrs. Ramirez smiles. "Your tenny-runners are white and yellow and blue. You sure can run fast in them."

"Not tenny-runners, Mrs. R—'letic shoes," Louie corrects her.

"I bet you can run really fast in those athletic shoes, Louie."

"Yep, watch me!" Louie runs off.

---

An important time to have contact talks is when children arrive in the morning. While this is generally a busy time for teachers, the effort to arrive a bit earlier in order to have the room ready enough to greet children individually can make a difference in teachers' relationships with children and in setting the tone for the day. Here is an example of a morning contact talk.

---

First grade teacher Jason notices that Jeb walks into class more slowly than usual and has his head down.

Jason: You look a bit sad today, Jeb. [He knows Jeb well enough to just say this and then listen.]

Jeb: My dog, Bumpers, got hit by a car last night.

Jason: Oh, Jeb, I am so sorry. [pauses, gives Jeb a shoulder hug and wait time]

Jeb: My mom and me took Bumpers to the vet, but she said he died quickly and didn't feel any pain. The vet gave me his dog collar to remember him. It's small so I'm keeping it in my pocket.

Jason: You may need to take it easy and not push yourself today, Jeb. Remember, I am here if you need me.

Jeb: [pauses for a few seconds] I know.

---

In emotional terms, it might seem like this contact talk took several minutes. But in actuality, it took less than two minutes and only six exchanges. Jason no doubt made Jeb's day less difficult by his willingness to listen to Jeb and to offer support. When later that morning Jeb spilled his glue, Jason was able to take Jeb's perspective and help the boy cope. Otherwise Jeb might have exploded in frustration—and Jason might not have understood why. Contact talks are key in supportive teaching.

Lead teacher Robin (from an anecdote in the previous chapter) wanted to have contact talks with Joe, who was showing Level Three aggression, when he arrived each day. Other staff members were reluctant to have Robin unavailable during this busy time. Robin had to get the director's backing to have her time freed up to have the talks. But when Joe began to have fewer outbursts during the day, the team came to see the contact talks as a wise investment of Robin's time.

As a follow-up project after a guidance workshop, a third grade teacher made a chart of every child in her class of 28, and held contact talks with five different children each day, putting a check by their names as she did. At the end of a month, she felt that she knew the children better and that the atmosphere of the room had changed. When one child, Mia, asked the teacher how her baby was doing, the teacher realized that the

students were also experiencing increased understanding. The teacher had mentioned to Mia that one night she had had to take the baby to an urgent care facility. The teacher responded to Mia with a smile, "Thank you for asking. Our baby is doing much better."

As Copple and Bredekamp state,

Close teacher-child attachments and supportive social environments are important not only for enhancing self-esteem and shaping positive self- concept but also for promoting school adjustment, academic achievement and social skills. . . . Children at risk for behavioral problems and children with developmental delays or disabilities may be especially affected by the quality of the teacher-child relationships. (2009, 265)

Contact talks are vital to creating a supportive social environment and building teacher-child attachments.

## Private Encouragement

Chapter 8 explored the idea of encouragement as a guidance alternative to praise. Two types of teacher encouragement were introduced: *public encouragement*, which is focused not on individuals but on the group, and *private encouragement*, which is supportive and specific feedback given in a private manner to an individual child. Chapter 8 discussed public encouragement at some length; in this section we'll focus on private encouragement.

Because encouragement often recognizes a child's effort, the prime time for giving private encouragement is during a child's effort, not after an action has been completed. This way the comments are truly encouraging. When the situation is right, private encouragement often becomes a contact talk. Teachers do well to think of the encouragement as happening not just in their initial comments to a child, but also in the conversation that can follow.

The basic element of private encouragement is acknowledgment—noticing the details in what the child is doing. With children whose language is emerging, teachers use *information talk,* stating back what a child says and then elaborating to build the child's receptive language, as in the following example:

Child: Bugs!

Teacher: Yes, you see all those brown ants! They are really crawling around.

Child: Big bunch cwawin. [The child watches the ants keenly for about five minutes.]

---

As children age, positive acknowledgment takes the form of *reflective listening*, which means reflecting back to the child what you perceive her doing, saying, and perhaps feeling (Gartrell 2011). There are clear cognitive applications for private encouragement; for example, "Dinee, you are working so hard writing that story about your dad and the bees. Your brain and your hand must be getting a workout!"

Private encouragement also supports children's social-emotional growth, enabling them to gain self-esteem, a sense of place in the group, and the ability to manage strong emotions. Private encouragement can also provide information teachers can use in task-oriented situations, such as resolving a conflict, as in the following example:

Teacher: Joy Lee, you are sitting by yourself and looking sad. I wonder why? [She pauses, knowing wait times are important.]

Joy Lee: Arnold and Laurel wouldn't let me play. Arnold pushed me and Laurel said, "Yeah." I am sad and mad!

Teacher: Sounds like you have reason to feel sad and mad. What can we do to fix this?

Joy Lee: Tell them to let me play.

Teacher: Yes, we let other children play in this classroom. Would you like to go tell them by yourself or have me go with you? [Joy Lee goes over to negotiate by herself, and the teacher watches, standing nearby.]

---

The nonjudgmental nature of the teacher's private encouragement, triggered by an open-ended question, probably gave Joy Lee permission to say what was on her mind. The course of private encouragement can go in many positive directions.

The following anecdote (Gartrell 2007) gives a sense of the nonverbal and verbal warmth inherent in private encouragement through an interaction between a preschooler and a male graduate student. Preschooler Lamar had been showing dramatic outbursts when he experienced even small frustrations in class (Level Three mistaken behavior). Staff members had been trying to make connections with him and build his level of self-acceptance. Notice how Randy, the graduate student, comments on details in Lamar's picture—positive acknowledgment—and turns Lamar's reaction into a contact talk.

**Observation**—The children start arriving at kindergarten at about 8:30 a.m., and I [Randy] greet them as they come in. They seem very receptive to my greeting, and I watch them disperse to the different centers in the room. One boy, Lamar, is interested in striking up a conversation with me about a picture he has colored. Lamar reaches out and hands me his picture.

Randy: Wow! Looks like you used a lot of green.

Lamar: Well, yeah, frogs are green.

Randy: They are green, aren't they?

Lamar: Yeah.

Randy: You used green there for your frog and blue over there and brown over there. [Lamar smiles.]

Lamar: Yep. I have a picture on the back, too.

Randy: What colors did you use?

Lamar: I used different colors!

Randy: I do see different colors! Yellow and pink and black. [Lamar looks at me with a smile, gleaming with pride.]

Lamar: I would like you to have the picture that I colored.

Randy: Thank you! I will put it on my fridge.

[Lamar peers up from his picture and smiles in amazement. He looks so pleased that I would put his picture up in my home.]

**Reflection**—I was really nervous that I might give Lamar praise instead of encouraging him to keep on with his good work. I like to praise people, and sometimes I have to be careful not to embarrass them and make them feel uncomfortable. When teachers begin to use encouragement, they sometimes find it difficult to know just what to say. Especially when children's art is hard to figure out, teachers can find themselves at a loss for words. I found myself feeling this way at first, and I tried to stay away from, "Oh, you are so good at coloring." I tried to look at Lamar's picture in a different way and to pick out things that were unique about it.

The gesture that let me know Lamar felt comfortable with the way the conversation went was when he gave me his picture to take home. I knew then that he was proud of his work, and he seemed excited to show me other pictures he had colored.

---

As Randy did, teachers allow contact talks to happen when the child's responses to private encouragement grow into a conversation. In the anecdote, Lamar took the step toward conversation when he mentioned he had a picture on the back, too. Randy did

not insist that the conversation stay strictly on the topic of the first picture by saying something such as, "We are talking about your frog picture." Instead he asked about the second picture: "What colors did you use?" This permitted the conversation to open up.

Randy commented that after this event Lamar showed him other pictures he had made. When private encouragement becomes a contact talk, children almost always begin to seek out those adults—sitting with them, coming to them when there is a problem, accepting them if they need to intervene. Private encouragement builds relationships and helps children to grow in the democratic life skills.

## Compliment Sandwiches

Communication that occurs in the context of a task is an opportunity to build or sustain a relationship with a child. Private encouragement is a prime example. As mentioned in previous chapters, the compliment sandwich is a positive way to provide feedback when a teacher perceives that a change is needed in a child's behavior. Given individually to a child, the compliment sandwich conveys the teacher's care for the child and faith that the child can get a task done. The positive acknowledgment in a personalized compliment sandwich affirms in children's eyes that their efforts are worthy and so are they (Gartrell 2007).

Let's look at the contrasting comments of two teachers to a child in second grade during a language arts assignment.

First teacher: You are being careless again. Look at how those sentences wander over the page. You forgot your period there. This is messy work. You will need to do it again before recess.

Second teacher: You have written your own story about going to the zoo. You even used sentences that have capital letters. You just need to rewrite these words on the line and put in some periods, and you will be done way before recess. You can do it, Douglass.

The second teacher used a "triple-decker" compliment sandwich (*three* compliments or encouraging statements) in an academic situation. Compliment sandwiches can also be used during other kinds of tasks and at different levels. Here are two examples.

Preschool teacher: Jamie, you have your coat hung up and your boots off. You just need to find your boots and put them under your coat, and you're all set for center time. Roger has saved a truck for you.

Kindergarten teacher: Sondra, you stayed in your seat, worked really hard, and respected your neighbors. Just keep reminding yourself to use that "inside voice." You are *really* making progress.

When teachers first use compliment sandwiches with intentionality, they sometimes find the practice contrived. With usage, however, it becomes more natural. Often, coming up with the second compliment is difficult. One approach is to restate the first compliment in more general terms, as in the example with Sondra. Another is to emphasize the positive results of completing the task, as in the examples with Jamie and Douglass.

Another benefit of using compliment sandwiches is that the teacher thinks not only of what needs to be changed about a behavior but also of the effort or progress the child is making. This can help the teacher maintain a positive frame of mind and convey to the child, "I am working with you and not against you." In this regard, especially with children who are working on DLS 1 and 2, three compliments per request are more effective than two.

DLS 1: Finding acceptance as a member of the group and as a worthy individual

DLS 2: Expressing strong emotions in non hurting ways

DLS 3: Solving problems creatively—independently and in cooperation with others

DLS 4: Accepting unique human qualities in others

DLS 5: Thinking intelligently and ethically

## Friendly Touch

The use of friendly touch conveys the warmth in relationships like no other practice. Physical closeness accomplishes what words cannot in forming healthy attachments with children (Carlson 2006). Most children have a high need for friendly touch—boys as well as girls (King 2004) and older children as well as younger (Curwin & Mendler 1988). As Hendrick points out, children "require the reassurance and comfort of being patted, rocked, held, and hugged from time to time" (2001, 107). Hendrick states,

Research as well as experience supports the value of close physical contact. Montagu (1986) has reviewed numerous studies illustrating the beneficial effect of being touched and the relationship of tactile experience to healthy physical and emotional development. Investigations documenting the link between touching and the development of attachment confirm those findings. (2001, 107)

Brain research reported by Carlson (2006), Cozolino (2006), and Sousa (2011) provides the physiological link to explain the beneficial nature of friendly touch. Tactile calming promotes helpful hormone secretion and harmonious brain functioning, allowing the child to experience acceptance and trust within a nurturing relationship with the teacher.

Unfortunately, the use of warm physical contact (hugs and friendly touches) by teachers, accepted in times past, has become controversial (Carlson 2006). Now in some school districts and other early childhood settings, teachers ask a child's permission before giving the child a pat on a shoulder or a hug. In many situations, teachers must follow specific policies and communicate with fellow staff, administrators, and family members before using friendly touches with children. Sensationalized court cases have made even teachers of younger children "uneasy about touching or cuddling youngsters lest they, too, be accused" (Hendrick 2001, 107).

Nelson (2002), in his study of men in early childhood education, stresses that men as well as women need to use friendly touch. Nelson and Shikwambi (2010) make the case that the benefits of having male teachers in early childhood programs far outweigh mistaken and discredited notions about men using touch.

Every teacher must make personal decisions regarding touch. Given the value of nurturing touches for children, however, teachers should not dismiss the use of friendly physical contact. Rather, teachers should use it within the limits of a reasonable policy and should fully communicate the rationale for the guideline "friendly touches only" to children, family members, and staff members. As Hendrick (2001) and Carlson (2006) point out, educators do well to maintain written policies that allow classroom visitation by family members, require clear understanding among all staff members regarding physical closeness, and conduct criminal background checks for prospective employees. Such practices support the continuation of this important teaching technique as a legitimate expression of human caring. (For more on the use of friendly touch in building healthy teacher-child relationships, see Carlson 2006).

## Support of Children Vulnerable for Stigma

All humans enter any group situation with a combination of strengths and vulnerabilities in terms of gaining acceptance by the group (Goffman 1963). A particular combination of behavioral, physical, and social/cultural characteristics in a new member can result in the group's acceptance or rejection of that individual. A child's atypical physical appearance or aggressive behavior are two examples of characteristics that may invite ridicule and rejection from other children. Rejection means the individual carries a label of **stigma,** disqualification from full participation in the group.

**stigma:** a label that disqualifies an individual from full participation in the group and leads to a tendency in the group for others to reject and even ridicule the individual

York (2003) and others emphasize that teachers cannot be silent when children make stigmatizing comments to or about another child or reject the child through behavior. Unless a teacher intervenes in a firm but friendly way, the children may think that their teacher condones oppressive behavior. What was initially Level One experimentation mistaken behavior can become learned and expressed at Level Two or even Level Three mistaken behavior—as in extreme instances of exclusion and bullying. Vivian Paley's *You Can't Say You Can't Play* (1993) provides a landmark work on taking a stand for inclusion. For many years Paley made that title statement a principle of her early childhood classrooms. Inclusion is an important goal of the encouraging classroom because the encouraging classroom is only so if it is encouraging for *every* child.

Even teachers, whether consciously or unconsciously, may show verbal and/or nonverbal rejection toward a child, particularly if they are uncomfortable with the child's culture, language, ethnicity, or social background. The rejection may be subtle, like avoiding contact with one child while giving positive feedback to others. Or it may be fairly overt, such as a student teacher calling the same child's name 12 times to refocus his attention during a five-minute, large-group story time. As seen with some Level Two mistaken behaviors, other children may be gradually influenced by the teacher's reactions to that child and may reject the child as well.

Teachers need to act in ways that help a child vulnerable for stigma find acceptance—that liberation teaching we talked about in Chapter 9. In using their leadership to build an encouraging classroom for every child, teachers look for vulnerabilities that may cause a child to be stigmatized and for opportunities to affirm the child's status (Watson 2003). An example is the class meeting described in Chapter 9 with Charley, who experienced ridicule from his classmates when his new leg brace squeaked. The class meeting allowed the children to better understand Charley's leg brace, and this understanding helped them develop a new respect for Charley.

The following is a list of teacher practices that are liberating for children vulnerable for stigma (Gartrell 2011). Teachers who use liberating responses

- ◆ Show clear acceptance of the child as a worthwhile individual and member of the group
- ◆ Empower the child's abilities
- ◆ Educate both the child and the class away from rejecting responses and toward accepting responses
- ◆ Adapt the physical and social environment so that all are included
- ◆ Facilitate cooperative and individual activities so that each child can experience success
- ◆ Show appreciation of the child's family background by sensitively incorporating elements of the family's background and language into the program
- ◆ Use forms of classroom management that guide rather than punish and that teach for the democratic life skills
- ◆ Help other members of the class understand and cope with challenging behaviors from the child

The teacher is using liberation teaching effectively when differing human qualities do not polarize the class, but instead become opportunities for personal affirmation and mutual enrichment. The classrooms of liberating teachers are encouraging, caring communities.

## Effective Techniques for Supporting Boys

In the early 1990s, studies showed the existence of an education gap that, beginning in the elementary grades and continuing through college, identified girls as disadvantaged (Webb, Metha, & Jordan 2007). Boys received more attention in classes, scored higher on college exams, and attended postsecondary programs in higher numbers. Now, with the exception of teacher attention, the gender gap has not just been closed, but reversed (Neu & Weinfeld 2007). Boys more than girls face real challenges to their schooling, including preschool expulsions (Gilliam 2005) and severe discipline practices, low test scores, summer school classes, grade retentions, and special education placements (Neu & Weinfeld 2007).

Mounting research is showing that the lag in educational achievement begins for some boys in preschool (Webb, Metha & Jordan 2007) and continues into adulthood. More female than male students now graduate from high school,

### Teachers and the Gap

The "culture clash" of boys with traditional classroom expectations may be contributing to a gender gap among teachers as well as among children. Nelson's study of NAEYC members (2002) showed that most teachers of young children are female; fewer than 5 percent are male. Increasingly, this trend is also holding true for teachers at the K–12 levels (Johnson 2008). One possible explanation is that because more female students than male students succeed in the traditional classroom, more women than men are comfortable becoming teachers.

Male early childhood teachers, however, greatly benefit both young boys and girls (King 2004). Male teachers are often likely to accept young children's high activity levels and to make the classroom more flexible to accommodate active learning styles (Gartrell 2006; Nelson 2002). They also may be intuitively responsive to the needs of young boys when they experience conflicts (Gartrell 2006; Nelson 2002). This is not to say that many female teachers do not relish having a good number of active boys in their classes; they do, and adjust their classroom cultures accordingly (King 2004). That is the point: To help more children succeed in school (particularly many boys), educators need to create a classroom culture that fits all children.

college, and many graduate programs (Neu & Weinfeld 2007). These authors make the case that a key reason for both high preschool expulsion rates and the education gender gap is the poor fit between many boys and the classroom culture.

Perhaps because of increasing emphasis on test scores, teachers even in prekindergarten have tended to bring more structure to their classes. Students able to succeed in a structured setting tend to be those who can remain focused during sit-down, paper-and-pencil, teacher-directed lessons for a large part of each day. For developmental and behavioral reasons, more girls and fewer boys fit this profile of learners (Neu & Weinfeld 2007). In today's education systems, too many boys are being left out.

## Boy-Friendly Classrooms

Two dynamics can help early childhood teachers make their classrooms inclusive of all children, including active boys. The first dynamic has been introduced in previous chapters: the use of developmentally appropriate practice for *all* children. Sometimes boys' limited engagement in the classroom is dismissed by adults with such comments as "they are not ready," "they have short attention spans," or "that's how boys are." However, programs that are boy-friendly respond to the high activity, full-body learning that is characteristic of many boys (Carlson 2011).

King (2004) provides a case study to show how teachers can move beyond stereotyping boy behavior. In "Guidance with Boys in Early Childhood Classrooms," King illustrates how a teacher changes the curriculum, the schedule, and the environment in ways that increase the engagement of all children, especially boys. The teacher reduced the rough-and-tumble off-task play in her class of 14 boys and 4 girls by taking the following actions:

- ◆ The class participated in very active play right away in the morning so that the children (and the teachers) actually worked up a sweat. They used the play yard outside or the activity room inside when no one else was using it. The staff came to see this as "workout time" for themselves as well.

- ◆ The teacher moved the furniture away from all four walls enough to make a walking track with tape. If children needed further exertion when they came back into the classroom for center time, the track was open for them to use.

- ◆ The teacher set up a physical fitness center with equipment purchased at garage sales and adapted for the children. The center was open each day before breakfast and during center time. The group discussed at a class meeting that girls as well as boys would be using the center.

- ◆ The number of large-group and sit-down lessons was reduced, substituting more active individual and small-group activities and projects led by teaching team members.

In short, the teacher made her classroom less like a library and more like summer camp. The girls as well as the boys thrived in the new, more developmentally appropriate learning environment. The benefits of making these types of modifications are striking: unproductive behavior decreases, productive learning behavior increases, girls become more accepting of their bodies (Carlson 2011), and conflicts involving boys decline (NAEYC 2009). Carlson (2011) documents that as programs fundamentally become more active and responsive to children's needs, both cognitive and physical development are stimulated. The active classroom of the twenty-first century can and should contribute to active, healthy lifestyles for all children, girls and boys—and for teachers as well. (See Gartrell 2008.)

## Intervention Considerations with Boys

The second dynamic in a gender-friendly classroom is an intervention approach that is particularly responsive to boys. King (2004) provides guidance considerations for when boys experience conflicts. Many of these considerations have been presented as general conflict-resolution strategies in the preceding chapters of Part Two. Here are summaries of six of the considerations King sets forth.

**Defuse the situation.** Work to downplay a conflict between children. Sometimes the situation is accidental, or at least not totally intentional. Point this out and informally mediate: "Denard, Ephram didn't mean to knock over your tower. He feels badly about it. I wonder how the two of you can fix it?" Acknowledge and accept emotions so the child knows that you care: "Julian, it is all right to cry. That hurt when you fell over Noah's leg. You have a real owie on your knee. Let's get a bandage for that and see how Noah is doing."

**Use humor, the great tension reliever.** Humor suggests that the adult is in charge of his own emotions enough not to get uptight, and so lets boys know that they don't have to get worked up either. You might kneel down to where two boys are quarreling and say with a smile, "You guys sound like gorillas with stomachaches over here. How about taking some tummy medicine and getting your friendly faces back on?" Humor requires thinking on your feet and, for many of us, actual practice. You don't have to be hilarious, and young children may not completely understand the joke, but saying something with a friendly smile instead of showing anger can go a long way toward calming upset children.

**Avoid threats and embarrassment.** Threats set up power struggles that negatively affect both the teacher-child relationship and the likelihood of successful (win-win) resolution of the conflict situation. Instead, request choices that the child must make. In requesting choices, pose the more desirable alternative as positively as possible, but accept the other choice if the boy makes it.

For example, rather than say, "Martin, if you cannot share the counting cards I will move you to another area," ask the child to make a choice: "Martin, you choose: Share the counting cards or find an activity in another area. Which will it be?" Be ready to accept whatever choice the boy makes. Also be prepared to follow up with him, perhaps with a guidance talk after emotions have cooled. Avoiding embarrassment by keeping your conversation as private as possible helps the boy retain pride in himself, an important ingredient in self-acceptance.

**Follow through.** It is important to follow through when responding to a boy's mistaken behavior. Boys seem to be sensitive to whether or not adults do what they say they will do. When adults do not follow through, they lose boys' respect (Kindlon & Thompson 1999). Boys may feel that they do not have to listen because the adult appears powerless or doesn't really care. As an example, don't shout across the room for Mitchell to behave and then go on to something else. Walk over to him, establish your presence, and interact with him. Give him choices. Follow through on the decided course of action. Stay with it.

**Talk with boys about their emotions.** It is important for adults to talk with boys about their emotions (Kindlon & Thompson 1999; Polce-Lynch 2002; Pollack 2001;). Sometimes when boys appear to be angry, they are masking feelings of pain, embarrassment, or fear. Encourage boys to develop a large repertoire of labels for the emotions they are feeling (Newberger 1997). Clearly, teaching about emotions and their expression goes beyond conflict interventions by teachers. Social-emotional intelligence—basic to learning democratic life skills—must be addressed as an educational priority in the curriculum.

**Nurture boys.** Boys want and need emotional connectiveness (Kindlon & Thompson 1999; Newberger 1997; Pollack 2001). Boys need to be cuddled, held, and responded to with kind words. They need your unconditional personal regard. When they fall or when a friend uses unkind words, boys need you to respond in a warm, caring, and nurturing manner. Even when a boy is defiant or has hurt another child, let that child know he is still a fully accepted and valued member of the class. He just needs to work to on a few things, and it is up to you to help him.

Teachers must make it a priority to develop their programs and their interpersonal relationships in a way that is friendly to both genders. In classrooms where teachers do so, girls as well as boys respond to the active programming and positive leadership (Gurian & Stevens 2004). Teachers and families can work together to better understand all that boys accomplish in the classroom, which will lead to equalization of the education gender gap (King 2004). It starts with early childhood programs that are inclusive of boys as well as girls.

# PART THREE

# Teaching for the Democratic Life Skills

# Prelude to Part Three

## The Democratic Life Skills

DLS 1: Finding acceptance as a member of the group and as a worthy individual

DLS 2: Expressing strong emotions in non-hurting ways

DLS 3: Solving problems creatively—independently and in cooperation with others

DLS 4: Accepting unique human qualities in others

DLS 5: Thinking intelligently and ethically

I see the democratic life skills in developmental rather than instructional terms. By this I mean adults do not first "teach" DLS 1, then DLS 2, and then DLS 3 chronologically using set curriculum, methods, and testing. Rather, teachers foster children's development of the democratic life skills through experiences that children's brains transcribe into enhanced (though beginning) executive functioning and perspective taking. Teachers intentionally guide this development by using practices (and adjustments) similar to those shown in the following illustration:

Five-year-old Samantha, new in the classroom, leaves a complicated puzzle to do a quick task requested by the teacher. When she returns, Andrew is in her chair working on her puzzle. Samantha gets upset. The teacher helps Samantha first calm down and then explain the situation to Andrew, which she does. With the teacher's prompting, Samantha tells Andrew he can have the puzzle as soon as she is finished with it. Andrew looks at

Samantha and the teacher and says he hopes it will be soon. Samantha pauses, looks at the complicated puzzle, and asks Andrew if he wants to help. The two work on the puzzle together. The teacher thanks Samantha and Andrew for working things out and walks away relieved that they were able to solve a problem not entirely of their own making. Samantha and Andrew finish the puzzle together.

To turn the conflict into a learning opportunity, the teacher intentionally worked with Samantha, a new student, to increase her feelings of acceptance within the group (DLS 1) and to help her express her frustration in a potentially effective yet non-hurting manner (DLS 2). The situation also allowed the teacher to give both children practice with solving a problem cooperatively and creatively (DLS 3). Young children learn to accept human differences by discussing and resolving everyday conflicts. That Samantha and Andrew were able to overcome their differences and work together on the puzzle indicates progress toward acceptance of unique human qualities in each other (DLS 4).

One could make the case that when Samantha invited Andrew to help her finish the puzzle, she was acting intelligently and ethically in the situation (DLS 5). As evidenced in the example, even young children can act at DLS 5, the highest and most abstract of the democratic life skills, with concrete, if intuitive, autonomous acts (respecting the need of another person and sharing what both want). As children mature, they will gain a more generalized, reflective capacity to think globally and act locally. This is supported by the continuation of a nurturing environment. Each time early childhood professionals assist children to manage conflicts, they are modeling DLS 5.

Often in the classroom, the teacher focuses intentionally on a particular skill she believes a child is ready to work on. In fact, in the Samantha and Andrew anecdote, the teacher's goal in asking Samantha to assist with a task was to help the child feel part of her own new classroom community, DLS 1. What often happens, though, especially when conflicts arise, is that the teacher ends up working with children on additional skills beyond what she originally intended. Instead, the teacher often provides guidance on a combination of skills. In turn, the child's learning is usually a "combo platter," too, as it is usual to gain experience with more than one life skill at a time.

A "logical" stair-step approach would focus too much on the order of the skills and unrealistically restrict teachers' scaffolding efforts to focus on one skill or another. In the human relations laboratory of the classroom, early childhood professionals take more of a psychological approach. They direct their teaching toward a skill they believe the child is ready to work on, but through reciprocal interactions, they also accommodate the full educational potential of any experience in the developmentally appropriate program (Gartrell 2011). The demarcation that is qualitative, I believe, is between the first two steps, which constitutes the child's ability to meet needs for safety, belonging, and acceptance, and the second three steps concerning growth needs. The latter set constitutes the capacity for creative, intelligent, and ethical encounters with the everyday situations of life.

The chapters that follow in Part Three explore each democratic life skill and follow a similar format: First, there is an explanation of the specified skill; second, anecdotes bring classroom realities into the discussion; third, I give comments about challenges children face and signs of children's progress in relation to the skill; and fourth, a guide highlights teaching practices that encourage development of the skill.

# Democratic Life Skill 1:
# Finding Acceptance as a
# Member of the Group and as
# a Worthy Individual

A dults use guidance to teach for the democratic life skills. Guidance is vital for families to use as well, of course. At a *practical* level, teachers encourage families to use guidance through establishing and maintaining reciprocal partnerships.

Early childhood professionals begin by guiding children toward DLS 1: finding acceptance as a member of the group and as a worthy individual. The first component of DLS 1 has to do with the children's social-psychological process of finding acceptance in their reference groups—first and foremost in the family, and then, for a large number of children, in early care and education communities outside of the home. Beginning with the initial parent-child attachment, young children must experience unconditional acceptance before they can build self-acceptance as worthy individuals (Ainsworth et al. 1978). Only with the trust, low stress levels, and sense of belonging that comes with secure attachments can children engage in the neuro-psychological process of positive identity formation.

**DSL 1: Finding acceptance as a member of the group and as a worthy individual**

**DSL 2: Expressing strong emotions in non-hurting ways**

**DSL 3: Solving problems creatively—independently and in cooperation with others**

**DSL 4: Accepting unique human qualities in others**

**DSL 5: Thinking intelligently and ethically**

However, the realities of modern family life and child care are that by kindergarten, most young children will have been in several care settings or classrooms and maybe even more than one family environment (Gestwicki 2013). Depending on the nature of the adult-child attachment and the child's temperament, each of the possibly many transitions can be an experience that ranges from mildly anxious to an ordeal. This is why teachers need to be unconditionally accepting and friendly: the young child's basic need for trust in the world is met through acceptance in each new group. With the feeling that one has a place in the group, the young child gains in self-acceptance and can forge ahead with the mentally healthy process of progress with the other democratic life skills. Outside of the home, this dynamic of group acceptance empowering self-acceptance is mediated by the teacher.

## Finding a Place in the Group

Positive group affiliation precedes the young child's ability to form positive self-identity—which encompasses both self-image (one's feelings about self) and self-concept (the ideas about self garnered from perceptions) (Ladd & Ettekal 2009). How teachers handle relationships with each child in the classroom community is, of course, crucial. With new children, teachers especially need to be welcoming.

Helping young children transition into group settings often gets complicated, and working together as a teaching team can really help. In the following anecdote, Jeri, as a new lead teacher in a class of 32- to 48-month-olds, tells of an experience in which she welcomes and accepts a parent and child despite an assistant's missed opportunity to help with a difficult transition.

Carlos, age 3, is an only child. He has begun to attend the center five full days each week. On this particular day, I hear Carlos several moments before he enters our classroom. His mother lives on campus and has given him a sled ride to the center, as well as right into our classroom! I hear Carlos's exclamations, "No, no, no Mommy, no go today; no, stay here Mommy." Upon Carlos's entrance, I notice one staff member giving another a look like, "Uh-oh, here comes trouble." Carlos's friends are anxious to say hello and greet both him and his mother. Before taking his coat off, Carlos unzips his backpack and starts sorting out his toys from home—a tractor, loader, grader, and bulldozer. One toddler, Trish, immediately grabs the bulldozer, and Damien runs off with the tractor, which leaves Carlos with only two of his vehicles.

I am engaged in conversation with Carlos's mother at the time, helping her with the transition, and notice that the other staff member steps in and takes control of Carlos's situation. She raises her voice and says, "Trish, Damien, and Carlos. Come here, all of you, over here!" The toddlers continue their play with Carlos's prized possessions. Carlos continues to be upset and begins to cry. After a few more tries, the staff member realizes that Trish and Damien aren't going to give Carlos his belongings back. The staff member takes Carlos aside and tells him, "You're going to have to share, I guess, because your friends want to see them, too, and you know you aren't supposed to have home toys in the class."

About then, I tell Carlos's mother goodbye and step over to where Carlos is shaking and sobbing uncontrollably. He sits clutching the two toys that are left. I speak in a calm voice as I put my arm around Carlos's shoulders, saying, "Carlos, I know that these toys are very special to you and they are your favorite. Sometimes you don't want to share with your friends, and that is okay because the toys belong to you. I can walk with you over to your friends to tell them you'd like your toys back." Carlos looks me square in the eye and hollers, "NO!" So I leave Carlos and proceed to the two children, getting down next to them. I explain that Carlos has brought these toys from home and that they aren't for sharing unless Carlos decides he'd like to share them. Trish and Damien are quick to understand this, as they both have brought toys from home on occasion as well. The vehicles are returned to Carlos, and he quickly secures them in his backpack. He continues to sit by the door and grip his belongings for five minutes following this interaction. I eventually get him playing with the other children. Later on in the day, I talk with the staff about working together as a team to help children work through difficult transitions. (Adapted from Gartrell 2000, 10–12)

Teachers who use guidance balance the needs of the child and expectations of the program in ways that help the child find a place in the group. Jeri showed this ability in four ways.

First, she helped Carlos through a transition made more difficult by the reactions of other staff members. Jeri demonstrated that she appreciated the boy's feelings and enabled him to get through the crisis of his mom leaving and the other children taking his toys at the same time. She intervened to help Carlos retrieve his "security objects" and regain self-esteem.

Second, Jeri guided the other children to consider Carlos's feelings and helped to make it easier for him to transition from his mother to the classroom. Separation situations impact other children in the class, not just the child experiencing strong feelings. Jeri helped Trish and Damien be contributing community members—with DLS 3—and recover from "being in trouble" with the other teacher.

Third, Jeri made a solid point in her reflection about the no-toys-from-home rule. When children cannot understand rules, enforcing them "because children need to learn to follow rules" tends to make problems worse. Teachers do need to enforce established limits, but sensibly, in ways that guide children toward the full group membership and healthy self-esteem.

Fourth, Jeri later had a *staff guidance talk* with the assistant about the need to place higher importance on providing welcoming responses to a new child than on less important "property rules." Jeri had been working for a while on helping this assistant to be more positive with the children, and she took the opportunity after the children had left for the day to reinforce this need. (During the meeting, I am sure Jeri used more than one compliment sandwich.)

A teaching team that collaborates effectively builds an encouraging classroom for every child in ways that a single teacher—even a skilled teacher like Jeri—cannot alone. In many classrooms, the adults are assigned to a small group of children. They do activities and routines, including eating, together (NAEYC 2007). (Reading together in a small group is so different than a story read in a large group.) Assigned small groups within a class allow adults to form a primary

caregiver relationship with each child, adding to the reliability of this new out-of-home experience.

## An Ongoing Effort

Over time some young children show patterns of atypical Level Three mistaken behaviors. As a result, these children can become vulnerable for rejection by peers and even teachers. Unless helped to overcome their vulnerabilities and find a place in the group, the resulting negative self-labeling can have a long-term negative impact on school success and personal development (Ladd & Ettekal 2009). Notice in the following anecdote how lead teacher Jen works very hard with two 3-year-olds who are vulnerable for stigma to help each find successful membership in the group.

Jen is lead teacher for a group of young preschoolers, most of whom are younger than age 4, including Atreyu and Wyatt. She leads the group in a welcoming song, asking the children how they each feel today. She asks Atreyu how he is feeling. He looks at her, then puts his head down. The adult behind him rubs his back. Since it was Atreyu's turn, she asks the children, "Do you think Atreyu is feeling happy or sad today?" When a few children say sad, Jen asks, "Why do you think he is feeling sad?"

Someone suggests Atreyu is sick. Jen responds, "That would make me feel sad. I don't think he is sick. I think Atreyu is missing his mom today. So he is feeling sad. He might need a little extra friendliness today." Gail, a volunteer, rubs Atreyu's shoulders. He looks down the whole time, but does not object to being the focus of attention.

After singing the greeting song for Wyatt, Jen asks, "Wyatt, how do you feel today?" Smiling, Wyatt says, "I got a blanket." Jen acknowledges, "Yes. Does that make you feel happy?" Wyatt exclaims, "Yeah!" He holds the blanket to his face and smiles.

A bit later, Jen and Atreyu stand by a horizontal time line that shows the daily schedule of activities. She is holding his hand and rings a bell: "It's cleanup time. Please put your toys away." Wyatt, also near Jen, is using two four-foot cardboard strips as ramps for his car. Wyatt falls to the floor, kicking and screaming.

Jen kneels down to Wyatt, keeping Atreyu close. "Wyatt, are you upset because it's cleanup time?" Wyatt continues to scream but stops kicking.

Jen helps Wyatt up: "My goodness, you have some deep feelings today." Again holding Atreyu's hand, she points to the time line: "Wyatt, I was just showing Atreyu that first we have circle and breakfast, and then we will play outside." Jen shows Atreyu the end activity. "That's when your mom is coming to pick you up." Pointing to work time on the chart, Jen adds, "Look, Wyatt. At work time, you can use the ramps again." Wyatt has quieted, listening to Jen, but cries again.

Jen says to Wyatt, "It looks like you aren't done with the ramps. Do you want to put them someplace where you can get them at work time?" Wyatt walks away carrying one ramp. Still holding Atreyu's hand, Jen takes the other ramp and says, "Let's go with Wyatt to help him find a place for the ramps." Jen and Atreyu walk together, holding the second ramp. The three put the ramps in a special place until work time. Atreyu still looks sad. Wyatt goes on to the next activity.

Later, during work time, both Wyatt and Atreyu play with the ramps, using first cars then balls. Wyatt enjoys the activity nonstop for 40 minutes. Atreyu smiles for the first time that morning when his car goes down the ramp. When a third child, Mark, later takes Atreyu's ball, Jen coaches Atreyu to say, "That's my ball." Mark gives Atreyu his ball back, and Jen asks Atreyu if he can help Mark find his own ball. Atreyu nods and goes with Mark to find a second ball.

Jen helped these 3-year-old boys feel welcome, accepted, and worthy. She used a morning greeting song, teaching from a time line, and supportive responses during conflicts to ensure that the boys felt they belonged in the classroom. She used educational materials appropriate for their age and interests to nudge them toward growth, changing the plans for work time to do so. In this early childhood classroom Atreyu and Wyatt likely found themselves to be fully accepted members of the group.

## Toward Positive Self-Identity

To support the first part of DLS 1 teachers guide children so that the children find acceptance in the group. To address the second part of DLS 1 they help children accept themselves as worthy individuals.

When preschoolers come from family situations that are overwhelming for the parent, the child is also likely to be overwhelmed. Parent-child attachments in these situations are likely to be anxious ones, which puts children on edge and makes it difficult for them to be accepted in new groups, undermining their growth toward self-acceptance.

In the following anecdote, which originally appeared as the November 2011 Guidance Matters column in *Young Children*, notice how Rena makes difficult decisions regarding Harrison's behavior. The feedback children receive during conflicts directly affect the messages they internalize about who they are and how they should behave (Gunnar, Herrera, & Hostinar 2009; Lowenthal 1999). Rena's use of guidance helped Harrison in his difficult tasks of gaining group acceptance and progressing toward positive personal identity.

Harrison is 27 months old when he joins the toddler room. After a few days, Harrison begins to have conflicts just after arriving in the morning. He will not wash his hands or come to the breakfast table. When teacher Rena invites him, he works himself into a rage, yelling the F word (with his own particular pronunciation) and throwing things. Because his behavior distresses the other toddlers, Rena has to physically move him to a far corner of the room and hold him until he calms down.

When Harrison repeats this behavior over the following days, Rena talks with Betty, his mom, whom she had met only a few days earlier. Rena says she enjoys having Harrison in her group. But, she tells Betty, he is having a problem, especially after he arrives, and she wants to work together with her to help Harrison. Betty shares that their house is small, and the activities of some family members often keep Harrison from settling down and getting to sleep. From their conversation, Rena believes that the toddler's aggressive behavior probably is due to lack of sleep related to conditions at home.

Rena works out a strategy with Betty and the other staff. When Harrison arrives in the morning, she approaches him in a low-key way and gives him the choice of getting ready for breakfast or snuggling. Harrison usually chooses snuggling and occasionally falls asleep. During the day, Rena gives him choices between two activities. Harrison begins making choices and participating more. Rena and the two assistant teachers also seek out opportunities for one-on-one snuggling and contact talks—a few minutes of shared quality time—with him throughout each day.

Over that first month, Rena develops a relationship with Betty, who discloses a bit more about the family's home situation. Rena learns that two male members of the family are particularly affected by poverty and clinical depression. This leads Rena to refer the family to Early Head Start, where they could receive family assistance; however, there is a waiting list and therefore no opening for Harrison.

Sometimes Harrison eats breakfast. He tends to eat late and eat little, but at least he starts eating. Gradually Harrison accepts the routine in the toddler classroom. Rena remains open to his need for a morning snuggle, but Harrison needs closeness on arrival only some days. The staff realize that while they cannot change Harrison's home environment, they can help him feel safe and welcome in the toddler room and maintain a positive relationship with his mother. (Gartrell 2011, 62)

The 27-month-old was clearly bringing a high stress level into the toddler classroom. Rena guessed that the stress was due to Harrison's having to transition from one kind of chaotic situation at home to another perceived kind in the classroom. When he was tired and stressed by his family situation, Harrison's fear of getting on with the day with a bunch of strangers totally occupied his mind.

"Teacher, I am stressed by my home life and overwhelmed by the prospect of having to function in the classroom today. I need immediate cuddling to allay my stress," is not a sentiment that a toddler is capable of communicating. Harrison expressed his fear, frustration, and anger by swearing and throwing things. The conflict, with immediate personal reaction by the teacher, resulted in an adrenalin rush that temporarily masked the stress he was feeling. The toddler concluded pre-consciously that (in the toddler classroom anyway) a tantrum was a powerful behavior.

Harrison's *reactive aggression* (using force as a mistaken survival reaction to protect himself) was becoming *instrumental aggression* (using physical and/or psychological force to impose one's will on another or get one's way). Beginning with the real possibility of rejection by teachers and peers, mistaken coping strategies involving aggression pose long-term risks for children's development and well-being (Ettekal & Ladd 2009). With the dangers to Harrison's future development that a mistaken coping strategy involving aggression entails, Harrison's long-term ability to see himself as worthy person was at risk (Shonkoff & Garner 2011).

Rena's response to Harrison provides a key for helping toddlers begin to figure out who they are. Her strategy of giving Harrison a choice of going to breakfast or cuddling

was to lower his stress level through building a relationship. With the trust that accompanied the relationship, Harrison was able to begin learning coping skills other than acting out (Gartrell 2011). Rena was able to further affirm the toddler's self-worth by empowering Harrison to directly participate in the resolution of his problems (and sustain him as a member of the group).

Rena and the assistant teachers recognized that building teacher-child attachments involves one-on-one time outside of conflict situations. Because arrival is such a busy time of day, teachers often find it challenging to have a *personal contact talk* (quality one-on-one time; see Chapter 10) when a child first enters the room. But I have found that contact talks upon arrival can be a wise time investment that frequently benefits the entire group. (The talks often can be fairly brief, but teachers do need to give the child undivided attention.)

Effective use of the teaching team to allow such moments is crucial. Only through the relationship could Harrison find a place in the group and work on a self-identity not tinged by an emerging negative self-fulfilling prophecy. When Harrison had fewer conflicts during the day because he had personal contact upon arrival, the entire staff came to realize that the early morning contact time was a wise investment.

The trend in his behavior—having fewer tantrums, needing fewer pre-breakfast cuddles, making choices about activities during the day, becoming engaged—indicates that Harrison was adjusting to the routines of group membership. Moving from a self-image defined by acting out to an emerging self-identity as a worthy group member indicates the progress Harrison was making toward attainment of DLS 1. Harrison's situation illustrates well how the two parts of DLS 1 are so intertwined in the lives of young children and how the responses of an early childhood teacher can be so important in a young child's life.

## Teaching Practices That Help Young Children Find Acceptance

1. Use the teaching team to build primary caregiver relationships with each child through the structured (daily) use of small groups.

2. Arrange for team members who get along well with vulnerable children to work with those children in their small groups.

3. Use intentionally welcoming responses when each child (and family member) arrives.

4. Hold regular contact talks with every child each day.

5. Try contact talks upon arrival when children are showing Level Three mistaken behaviors (see Chapter 9).

6. Adapt curriculum and instruction to be inclusive of children vulnerable for stigma; often this means offering more physically active experiences (see Chapter 10).

7. Be intentionally supportive of children vulnerable for stigma during guidance interventions.

8. Build and maintain positive relationships with children and their families.

# Democratic Life Skill 2: Expressing Strong Emotions in Non-Hurting Ways

Current interpretations of brain research emphasize "the neuroscience of self-regulation" (Blair & Diamond 2008; Florez 2011; Galinsky 2010). Self-regulation refers to the ability to control thoughts, feelings, and impulses "to appropriately respond to the environment" (Florez 2011, 46).

Among many others who have researched this topic, Blair and Diamond's (2008) research indicates (in the apt wording of Florez) that "children who engage in intentional self-regulation learn more and go further in their education" (Florez 2011, 46). They cite the famous "marshmallow study" (Blair 2002), in which a tester put a marshmallow in front of individual preschoolers and told them that when the tester left, they could choose to eat the one marshmallow, or wait 15 minutes and they would get two marshmallows. According to the research, the children who regulated their impulses and waited for two marshmallows did better educationally in the long term than those who did not wait.

## Management, Not Regulation

So why didn't I phrase this democratic life skill "self-regulating strong emotions"? After all, the term does have an established tradition, going back to the notion of "self-discipline" in pre-neuroscientific times. The developers of Tools of the Mind, a research-based early childhood curriculum, argue that a part of self-regulation parallels Vygotsky's notion of self-talk becoming intentional thought as the child develops and is helped with social-emotional scaffolding (Bodrova & Leong 2007). Galinsky (2010) explains that self-regulation is an essential function of developing executive functions.

From the millisecond a child perceives harm, threat, or an opportunity for personal gain, the neuropsychological response is not simply to either give into or to suppress negative impulses. From my standpoint, in agreement with Elliot (2003), the term "self-regulation" is too basic to describe the myriad of perceptions, emotional interpretations, reaction formulations, response decisions, behavioral manifestations, and resulting self-evaluative messages that occur within the mind and body of the still-developing child.

To illustrate, Florez mentions a child who sits on her hands rather than hit another child who has pinched her (2011). In my experience, children rarely react to harm by simply sitting on their hands. Angry children who might *want* to hit another child, but do not, find another way to express their turmoil: They may complain loudly, call for the teacher to help, bury their head in their arms, bang on a box with blocks, or exhibit any combination of such responses. (Twice in the last few years I have observed older preschoolers invoke negotiation: "You're not supposed to pinch; you're supposed to use your words!") In an instantaneous mental process, their brains channel the strong emotions into other actions; they *manage* the expression of the impulse—deciding what to do instead—rather than simply control the impulse.

For me the issue is deeper than what one child does when another takes his marker or pinches. The issue goes back to the legendary dispute between Freud and Adler that resulted in Adler breaking from orthodox Freudian psychology (Ansbacher & Ansbacher 1956). Freud argued that human behavior is largely the product of an ongoing, mostly subconscious struggle between the "id," the strong motivation of the pleasure principle, and the "super-ego," the moralistic mental regulator of pleasure-seeking impulses.

On the other hand, Adler's thinking was that human behavior happens as a developing self with prosocial potential comes into conflict with external, sometimes oppressive social pressures to direct and control that development. Adler's position was similar to Froebel's ([1826] 1887), who maintained it is other people in children's lives who misinterpret children's mostly innocent behaviors as inappropriate and therefore convince a child that he is bad.

In the Adlerian perspective, mental health isn't about continuous self-regulation to repress internal negative impulses (Ansbacher & Ansbacher 1956). Mental health is the ability to manage ever-changing thoughts and feelings in order to figure out what is the best thing to do, given the influence of significant others and one's own developing self. Living well is the constant process of managing feelings and thoughts in the face of increasingly complex social influences, which any growing individual can only partially understand.

## Teaching for DLS 2

In guiding for the democratic life skills, teachers work to assist children toward redirecting hurtful impulses into more reflective courses of action, a brain process not so much focused on regulation—stifling the impulse—as managing the impulse amidst a mix of possible responses.

In education for democracy, it comes down to helping children express strong emotions in ways that don't harm others and don't harm themselves. Through the relationship with the child, the teacher understands something of the child's circumstances. She respects the child enough to believe he will learn not just what *not* to do, but what to do *instead*. Through being "unrelentingly positive" (a term I once heard renowned educator Marian Marion use in a presentation), the teacher helps the child learn alternatives to stress-caused/stress-producing mistaken behavior. Management of feelings, rather than regulation of impulses, remains for me the path to civil functioning in democratic society.

## Charlane and Jamal

The following study and discussion, which are adapted from a Guidance Matters column in *Young Children* (Gartrell 2011a), illustrate a teacher who works hard to assist a young child learn to express strong emotions in non-hurting ways.

During the first week of a Head Start program in September, Jamal, almost 5 years old, punched another child in the stomach. An assistant teacher looked after the hurt child. Charlane, the teacher, approached Jamal, saying, "There is no hurting children in this class." She marched him to a time-out chair where Jamal sat with his head down. After about 10 minutes, the teacher explained to Jamal how serious it was to hit another child and told him to use his words next time. She then had him return to work time. Jamal hung back, not joining the other children.

The following Monday Jamal again punched a child in the stomach. As the teacher walked toward him, Jamal stood up and walked to the chair on his own, muttering, "Goin' to the chair 'cause I'm no good."

Wincing when she heard this, Charlane got down on Jamal's level and put her arm around him. After a minute she whispered, "Jamal, everyone in this class is a good kid. But I can't let you hurt other kids, and I can't let them hurt you." She stayed with Jamal, and then they read a book together.

Later that day, the teacher asked the home visitor about Jamal. The home visitor had found out that just before the program year began, Jamal's mother had been sent to mandatory drug treatment. Jamal and his sisters were split among different relatives. Over the weekend, his mom had visited the children in a central location. After she returned to treatment the children were again split up.

Charlane discussed with her center supervisor the guidance approach she planned to take with Jamal, and then Charlane met with the two assistant teachers to talk with them about what she planned to do and why.

Charlane went out of her way to spend quality time (have contact talks) with Jamal during the next few weeks. She noticed that he had problems transitioning during the opening group activity, so she began spending 10 minutes alone with him each day when he first arrived. After a few days everyone saw a change in Jamal's morning behavior. Over time, the two assistants also had daily contact talks with Jamal.

One morning in December, I entered the classroom as Charlane was speaking quietly to Jamal: "You didn't hit or kick. You came and told me, 'I am angry.' You did it, guy! Why don't you go into the restroom and spit in the sink as long as you want. Then we will talk." (Charlane later told me that spitting in the sink was a temporary way on this day for Jamal to work through his anger without hurting anyone.) The boy walked into the restroom and a minute later went right to the water fountain. While he was getting a drink, Charlane, who had disinfectant ready, wiped out the sink, and then they had a guidance talk. Charlane then quietly and informally followed the steps of social problem solving. Charlane helped Jamal rejoin the group by using the blocks with another child, and the two played and then cleaned up.

It is not surprising that Charlane reacted to Jamal's first conflict the way she did. She judged the conflict as misbehavior and—not knowing what else to do—disciplined him through temporary expulsion on a time-out chair. There is a centuries-old moral attitude that people are either good or bad. This attitude leads some teachers to punish a child who causes conflicts because they think that the child, even if young, should know better (Greenberg 1988). Often these teachers do so because they have been taught or in their experience acquired the common belief that punishment is an effective guidance strategy and will shame the child into being good.

This misbehavior-punishment attitude is problematic. It is a *technician reaction*—an automatic response to a situation during which a teacher uses a traditional approach without reflecting on its usefulness. Noted educators and psychologists of the last 100 years—ranging from Montessori and Piaget to Maslow and Erikson (see Chapters 2 and 3)—have found the misbehavior-punishment technician reaction to conflicts to be fundamentally unhealthy. Recent research on brain development confirms the foresightedness of these respected authorities: When conflicts occur, teachers should teach, not punish (Gartrell 2011b).

As stated in Chapter 4, in the early years, the child's brain has *plasticity* (the ready ability to build neuron networks in response to experience). During this time, the young child is just beginning to form the neuroarchitecture in the thinking centers of the brain that allow for *executive functioning*. Executive functions include the child's abilities to manage impulses and stay on task, engage in memory processes and learning, solve problems, and resolve issues.

According to research summaries by Gunnar, Herrera, and Hostinar (2009) and Shonkoff and Garner (2012), chronic "toxic" stress during a child's early life is detrimental to the development of healthy executive functioning. Stress causes a chemical reaction that short-circuits the thinking centers and hyperstimulates the *amygdala* and related parts of the brain that regulate the fight-or-flight reaction.

When the amygdala is hyperstimulated by stress, a child tends to regard situations as threatening and often acts aggressively in self-defense. Using punishment in an attempt to stop this *reactive aggression* (see Chapter 9) keeps the child's stress levels high and makes it more difficult for the child to develop healthy executive functioning. Without adult guidance, this disruptive cycle can affect the child into adulthood, degrading that individual's learning, behavior, and relationships along the way (Gunnar, Herrera, & Hostinar 2009; Shonkoff & Garner 2012).

## Restoring Calm

We now know that because of the sensitivity of brain development in young children, post-traumatic stress reactions can be caused by less severe trauma than previously thought (Gunnar, Herrera, & Hostinar 2009; Lowenthal 1999; Lubit 2006). With young children, it is helpful to think of post-traumatic stress reactions in terms of degrees. A child dealing with post-traumatic stress may exhibit, at varying levels of intensity, behaviors such as the inability to stay focused, frequent emotional outbursts, and the rejection of relationship overtures (Lowenthal 1999).

Sometimes it *is* difficult to find out exactly what is going on with a child who is experiencing serious conflicts. However, proactive efforts to understand and offer active support are crucial toward reducing the detrimental effects of high stress in the child's life to that child's brain development. A good starting point for teachers is to simply view a child who shows frequent reactive aggression as a likely victim of difficult circumstances rather than a bully.

Teachers should always start an intervention for handling reactive aggression by restoring calm. Perform a quick triage—separate the children and check for injuries—then calm everyone down, including yourself. Use deep breathing or give the child time and space, a cooling-down time. Once calm is restored, conduct conflict mediation and/or a guidance talk and follow up by learning more about the child exhibiting the reactive aggression and the details of the situation.

Charlane's interventions, at the beginning of the year and thereafter, illustrate the difference between a time-out—removing a child for something he has done as a punishment—and a cooling-down time, after which a follow-up guidance talk can begin to solve the problem (Gartrell 2011b). It is sometimes appropriate to have an upset child leave the place of a conflict, but only when the teacher is an active partner in the calming process and follows up with guidance. To give a child a time-out and expect him to "think about what he has done" (which is developmentally difficult for young children) is an inappropriate and unhelpful practice (Readdick & Chapman 2000). To teach a child to express strong feelings in non-hurting ways requires more.

## Reaching the Child Beyond the Aggression

In my view, Jamal was showing reactive aggression: When he punched the other children, his brain told him he was protecting himself. At first, his teacher saw him as a bad child who was misbehaving; she initially reacted as a technician (Readdick & Chapman 2000). However, with the second conflict she recognized that her technician reaction had not worked. In this moment, she changed from a technician to a *guidance professional*, becoming open to understanding and responding to Jamal more constructively.

When aggressive conflicts occur, the reaction of the technician is to run out of patience and punish. Working as a guidance professional, though, Charlane became open to understanding what was really going on with Jamal (Weber 1987). This attitude change gave her more tools to work with than just temporary expulsion.

First, Charlane realized that to help Jamal, she had to build a relationship with him. She decided to spend quality time with Jamal outside of the conflicts he was having. Regular morning contact talks were an important part of her approach (Gartrell 2011b). *Contact talks* between a teacher and child constitute quality times that allow the parties to learn more about each other and build trust. Charlane encouraged other classroom staff to have these talks with Jamal as well, and explained that the talks don't have to be long, but they do need to happen.

Second, Charlane found out more about Jamal's life and family. In talking with the home visitor, Charlane learned about his mom's drug treatment and the separation of the children among other relatives. Charlane and the staff reached out to the family, including a sister the mother was close to, and worked hard to build relations when the mother returned home.

Third, Charlane worked with Jamal in a firm but friendly way to manage his reactive aggression. In the anecdote, Charlane guided Jamal to use self-removal when his emotions grew strong. She had him try calming techniques (sometimes unconventional). The two engaged in guidance talks, and Charlane helped Jamal make amends and rejoin classmates after conflicts. The teacher accepted slow progress. It took three months before Jamal could consistently monitor his strong feelings and come to her for help. Learning from that first encounter, Charlane was always there. Jamal built trust in his teacher and himself as a result of their relationship. His home situation improved, too. Over time the child's stress level went down and he made clear progress with DLS 2.

## Long-Term Lessons

Marlys, a 20-year veteran early childhood teacher, once recounted a meeting she had with Cheryl, a young adult who had been in her class years before. Cheryl greeted her former teacher with a hug and shared that she was an early childhood major in college because of this teacher. Marlys shed a tear and thought, "This is the reason I am a preschool teacher." After Cheryl left, the veteran teacher thought more and said to herself, "That kid?!" Cheryl had driven Marlys bonkers the whole year the child was in her room. But Cheryl never knew it.

Teachers are only human: they cannot like every child equally. But as professionals, they *can* figure out how to build and maintain a positive relationship with each child, even during conflicts. This step leads to positive outcomes for a child who otherwise might tumble into a cycle of stress, reactive aggression, punishment, and more stress. No one would wish such a future on any child, and educators can help to steer the child on another course.

With good teaching in the social-emotional domains, the child gains DLS 1 and 2—motivated by the brain's deep-seated need for safety, security, and belonging. The child then becomes able to work on growth needs. Jamal showed that progress in a way that should make us smile—as Charlane revealed: "You didn't hit or kick. You came and told me, 'I am mad.' You did it, guy!" Jamal's self-removal, an example of progress in managing strong emotions in non-hurting ways, should not be regarded as an end in itself. But in this case self-removal does mark a transition in progress from DLS 2 to 3.

To the extent that teachers help a child to express strong emotions in non-hurting ways, they empower the child to progress from safety skills to growth skills. In doing so, the early childhood professional is teaching for more than self-regulation. By using guidance to teach for the democratic life skills, the teacher is preparing young children to think and act intelligently and ethically, and is truly educating for democracy.

## Teaching Practices That Help Young Children Express Strong Emotions in Non-Hurting Ways

1. Consider children to be months old rather than years old. Think of classroom conflicts as mistaken behavior anyone can make in the difficult process of learning the democratic life skills.

2. Rise above value judgments about either children or their behavior when conflicts occur. Look at classroom conflicts as teaching and learning opportunities in relation to the democratic life skills.

3. Build relationships and trust levels with children outside of conflict situations.

4. During conflicts, sustain trust levels by not embarrassing children and being intentionally supportive of children's self-esteem—firm, but also friendly.

5. Make sure the use of developmentally appropriate practice is inclusive and supports the abilities and needs of every child in the group. Regard off-task behavior as a sign the program needs review and possible modification.

6. Use your knowledge about young children to recognize the sources of conflicts—property disputes, territory disagreements, and privilege conflicts being the most common sources.

7. Use your knowledge of the child to head off serious conflicts, ease children through conflicts that occur, and facilitate mutually satisfactory resolutions to conflicts.

8. After triaging for injuries, use calming techniques as a first step in guidance interventions for resolving conflicts.

9. Decide whether an intervention calls for a guidance talk, conflict mediation, or a class meeting.

10. Use the five-finger formula for social problem solving, more formally in conflict mediation situations, less formally in guidance talks and class meetings.

11. Teach children conflict management skills by intentionally moving from high-level mediation to low-level mediation to child negotiation.

12. With children who experience continuing conflicts, use comprehensive guidance, including the relationships already being built with family members.

# 14

# Democratic Life Skill 3: Solving Problems Creatively— Independently and in Cooperation with Others

Carla, an older 4-year-old (4 years, 11 months), is no longer challenged by any of the five puzzles in the table toys area of her child care classroom. She takes out all five at once, dumps the pieces face down on the table, and mixes them up. She then selects a piece, decides which puzzle frame it goes in, places the piece, and selects another. The impressed adult watches as Carla completes all five puzzles, placing each piece in the correct puzzle frame on the first try. The next day the adult brings in a 30-piece puzzle. Carla completes it with minimal help in about 15 minutes.

Six-year-olds Delmon and Renilda are working together to complete a 50-piece puzzle that is a new addition to the math/manipulatives center in their kindergarten. They have the pieces sorted into three groups on the table, two by predominant color and one of "border" pieces that have one or two straight edges. Tucson, newly 5 years old, wants to join. The two older children think he will need some guidance so they give him the group of border pieces to work with. Renilda monitors Tucson's efforts and helps him when he gets stuck. The three complete the puzzle and do a three-way high five when they are done.

**DLS 1: Finding acceptance as a member of the group and as a worthy individual**

**DLS 2: Expressing strong emotions in non-hurting ways**

**DLS 3: Solving problems creatively—independently and in cooperation with others**

**DLS 4: Accepting unique human qualities in others**

**DLS 5: Thinking intelligently and ethically**

Creative problem solving is an active, even proactive, process in the face of situations encountered. To engage in creative problem solving, the individual must withstand the uncertainty of what is to be decided, the urge to leave the task if it gets hard, and often other people's expectations about how to proceed. This is why I reiterate Maslow's (1962) observation that young children must have basic needs met for safety and security before they can venture into the unknown. In the practical terms of the democratic life skills, children must have observable gains in DLS 1 and 2 in order to make the crucial transition to working on DLS 3.

This is also why children must be intrigued by new learning experiences but not challenged to the point of anxiety. Unless adequate support accompanies the high expectations of the challenge, children's stress levels go up, and creativity goes down (Jensen 2009). Too often frustration rather than successful closure is the outcome. Let's put the discussion in terms that followers of the psychologist Vygotsky might especially appreciate.

The teacher is always working to help children move from what they know on their own to what they can learn with perceptive teaching (Vygotsky [1935] 1978). On any given day for any child, the teacher has a sense of the child's **zone of proximal development** (the psychological distance between what a child can learn on her own and what she can learn with nudging and encouragement). Vygotsky's term, *scaffolding,* defines the assistance that helps the child move through the zone—and engage in the psychological experience of finding new meaning (Gartrell 2011). Classmates, as well as teachers, can assist with scaffolding.

To refer to the second example, Renilda and Delmon concluded that Tucson could not have contributed to completing the 50-piece puzzle without assistance. But they did not dismiss Tucson as "too little to do this puzzle." They, in particular Renilda, provided Tucson with the necessary scaffolding cues that allowed this young kindergartner to contribute. The three felt a sense of accomplishment together.

The two anecdotes at the beginning of this chapter illustrate children creatively solving problems—independently and in cooperation with others. The key step is a child's willingness to engage in an activity, the hallmark of the transition from working on a need for safety to a need for growth. Carla took the creative action of defining her own problem that she was intrigued to solve. The problem solving for Renilda and Delmon was not just in completing the puzzle, but also in engaging Tucson in a way so that all three could solve the puzzle. Both dimensions of problem solving, individual and cooperative, constitute DLS 3.

## Independent Problem Solving

Learning how to learn is perhaps the chief contribution of early childhood education to the child (Smilkstein 2011; Thomas & Seely Brown 2011). The process involves children overcoming fears of the new, intuitively or consciously defining problems, and solving them in their own way. When teachers need to be most careful in scaffolding is when the young child engages with "first time" learning experiences. If the curriculum is developmentally appropriate, the learner successfully engages in such firsts every day. An important task of the teacher is to plan and implement curriculum so that every young child has a reasonable chance of success in tasks, which builds the learner's confidence and competence relative to further learning (Smilkstein 2011).

Teachers often know when a child has gained from first experiences and is ready to encounter new, perhaps related, situations on her own. Teachers in these cases have kindled the child's *mastery motivation* (see Chapter 5), the intrinsic motivation to do and to learn (Reineke, Sonsteng, & Gartrell 2008). Notice in the following anecdote 4-year-old

**zone of proximal development:** the psychological distance between what a child can learn on her own and what she can learn with nudging and encouragement

Vera's progress with DLS 3 through her eventual but lengthy engagement in the activity. Note how family child care provider Kali's subtle scaffolding allows Vera's mastery motivation to engage.

---

**OBSERVATION:** On this day, the sensory table was filled with shaving cream and toy people and animals. Vera watched closely for a while as two other children put on their aprons and dipped their hands into the cream. I approached Vera and asked her if she wanted an apron, and she nodded her head. She quickly put one on and started playing with the figures. She made quiet animal noises while she played with them. After about 15 minutes, Vera went into the bathroom and washed her hands. When she came out, I asked her if she wanted some help taking her apron off. She hesitated for a moment and then said, "I'm not done in there yet," with a bashful grin. Vera joined the others at the table and played for quite some time.

**REFLECTION:** I was very pleased to see how involved Vera was in the sensory table. She tends to be shy and quiet, and I rarely see her fully engaged in an activity. I was happy to see that she did not shy away from the other children, as she often does. I feel like she is really making some progress. By watching Vera interact with this particular activity, I became even more convinced that it is extremely important to have a variety of different activities, because you never know when you will spark something in any child. (Adapted from Gartrell 2000, 58–59)

---

Vera made outstanding progress here, from bystander to sensory scientist. In this one activity, she had to figure out how to get started, how to engage in the sensory play, which animal sounds to make, whether she was really finished, and how to ask to continue. These are not easy tasks for a child who finds it difficult to initiate conversations and engage in activities. Through this successful experience, the child gains the motivation to take initiative in other things in the future (Thomas & Seely Brown 2011).

The main attribute of sustained self-directed activity—continuing on task—is essential in independent problem solving (Lehrer 2012). This attribute was clear in Vera's response, "I'm not done in there yet"—Vera stuck with the activity, showing what Lehrer refers to as "grit" (2012). Successful problem solving through play can give rise to long-term interests—like animal study—and to executive function competencies like initiating and persisting in activities (Honig 2007; Thomas & Seely Brown 2011).

## Cooperative Problem Solving

Solving problems in cooperation with others requires not only the skills previously discussed, but also the ongoing requirement of accommodating the viewpoints of others. The following anecdote illustrates the cooperative/competitive dynamic in many group endeavors (and certainly found in the emerging cooperative problem-solving abilities of many young boys). Jackie, a student teacher, recorded an observation and reflection regarding the merging of parallel activities for two boys in kindergarten.

---

**OBSERVATION:** During choice time today, Dylan and Caleb were sitting at the art table making pictures. Caleb drew a box with a dot in the middle.

Caleb (to Dylan): Look, this is a fly trap and I caught a fly.

Dylan: I am going to draw a spider trap and catch a spider; then my spider is going to eat your fly.

Caleb: It can't eat my fly because it can fly away and spiders can't fly.

Dylan: If I draw wings on my spider, it will be able to fly and then it can catch your fly and eat it up!

---

Their conversation continued for about six more turns. After they had finished, they put away their drawings and together went to find something else to do.

**Reflection:** Dylan and Caleb were able to use their imaginations and be creative in the pictures they were drawing. If they were given a coloring book, this freedom to be creative and imaginative would not have happened. Caleb and Dylan were also problem solving. They figured out that if they drew wings on the spider, it could catch the fly. They were certainly practicing their scientific understanding about spiders and flies. They were also working on the development of their social and verbal skills by the way they communicated with each other. Although their game had some rivalry to it, they left the table as friends. (Adapted from Gartrell 2000, 60)

The spider and fly study illustrates the tensions and accommodations that are necessary for young children as they merge, for the moment, their individual worlds. Vygotsky ([1935]1978) argued that scaffolding, almost by definition, needed to be accomplished by more capable others. In contrast, with developmentally appropriate practice, *peer scaffolding* happens all of the time. This social aspect of learning is natural because young children are social beings. Much in developmentally appropriate practice speaks to this reality of humankind, beginning with infants and toddlers (Copple & Bredekamp 2009).

As Jackie noted, when an activity involves more than completion of a teacher-prescribed task, collective creativity kicks in. An amazing feature of early childhood education (and for teachers, an enduring benefit) is that for young children at DLS 3, limited real-life experience serves as an opportunity for innovative, cooperative problem solving—through which their life experiences are expanded.

In the following anecdote, Rachel describes her conversation with three preschoolers, two girls and a boy, who live in a rural area and who had visited Minneapolis/St. Paul (the Twin Cities) but never lived there.

It was choice time, and the children were engaged in various activities (dramatic play, computers, reading corner, writing corner, and block area). Two girls and a boy were playing with blocks. They were stacking the blocks one on top of the other. I went over and asked them what they were building. "A skyscraper," said Maggie. I then asked them where they would usually find a skyscraper. "In the [Twin] Cities," said David.

I wondered how they might make a city with their blocks. "By making a bunch of skyscrapers," said Maggie. Kathleen nodded and kept working. I could see they were really involved in building their city so I acknowledged the comment, smiled, and walked to another group. The children proceeded to stack the blocks, but now they had about six to eight separate stacks. I went over to the three children and asked them if they could tell me what they made with the blocks.

"Minneapolis," said Maggie.

"See, here's the stadium, the post office, and the grocery store," said David.

When children are engaged in a developmentally appropriate activity—as these children were—they integrate what they know and creatively hypothesize about the rest. With brief scaffolding by the teacher, the trio took on the problem of how to construct an "actual" city, a concept on the fringe of their actual experience. This mixed-gender group worked to accommodate each other's viewpoints and engaged in (noncompetitive) cooperative problem solving.

## Cooperative Problem Solving Involving Interpersonal Conflicts

In terms of democratic life skills, the highest form of cooperative problem solving is when children fall into conflicts and climb out together. Young children face real challenges in working through conflicts, including having strong feelings and developmental difficulty in understanding others' points of view. However, most also have some real strengths, such as a relative absence of abiding pride and the ability to forgive and forget.

In early childhood education settings, children who are transitioning from DLS 2 to 3 experience two kinds of interpersonal conflicts: directly with a teacher and with other children. Ben, a prekindergarten student teacher, provides illustrations of both types of conflicts and how he helped the children with problem solving in each.

### Conflicts with the Teacher

The following anecdote is an interesting example of a child-teacher conflict. Ben wasn't the adult who had the initial conflict with the child, but with the teacher's nod, Ben did step in to help the child work the problem through.

> After an incident Jonathan was brought to his cubby by one of the teachers to cool off. After a minute I walk over to Jonathan, kneel down a short distance from him, and begin a conversation.
>
> Ben: How are you feeling?
>
> Jonathan: I'm mad.
>
> Ben: You're mad?
>
> Jonathan: Yeah, I'm mad at you, and I hate you.
>
> Ben: Oh, I am sorry I made you mad. [Not quite sure how. Another teacher had put him by his cubby.]
>
> Jonathan: [pauses and starts thinking] And I hate this. [pulls out a small piece of paper with blue crayon on it, rips it and throws the pieces on the floor] And I hate my name.
>
> Ben: You hate your name? How it is written?
>
> Jonathan: Yeah, I hate it, and I want to make a different one.
>
> Ben: You want to make a new name?
>
> Jonathan: Yeah. [He stops and thinks for about five seconds and I wait for him to add more.] I hate this. [points at the paper on the floor] I want to make a new name. [stands up and walks over to the paper picks it up and rips it again]
>
> Ben: You want to make a new name?
>
> Jonathan: Yeah.

Ben: What color do you want to make it?

Jonathan: Blue.

Ben: You're going to make your name blue? Do you like blue?

Jonathan: Yeah. [stops and thinks] NO! I hate blue.

Ben: You hate blue?

Jonathan: Yeah, I hate blue.

Ben: [I think about asking why he hates blue but decide to ask something else.] What color do you want to make it?

Jonathan: Red.

Ben: Oh? Do you like red?

Jonathan: Yeah, I like red.

Ben: Red like your shirt?

Jonathan: Yeah, like my shirt. And like Mario. Mario is red, and Luigi is green.

Ben: Mario is red.

Jonathan: And I am going to make a new name.

Ben: So you will make your new name red?

Jonathan: Yeah, and it will have an "A."

Ben: An "A"?

Jonathan: Yeah, do you know what else starts with "A"?

Ben: What?

Jonathan: [beckons me closer and whispers in my ear] Aburane. [digital game character's name]

Ben: Aburane? You're right, that does start with an "A."

Jonathan: Yeah. [He starts looking intently at the other children, who are in circle dancing to the chicken dance.]

Ben: Do you want to join in with the other children?

Jonathan: Yeah.

Ben: Where is your spot?

Jonathan: It's the purple one. I can show you.

[Brings me to his spot and we sit down. Jonathan joins in the circle activity.]

---

Ben accepted Jonathan's strong emotions without judgment. Tuning in to Jonathan's cues, Ben used reflective listening and intentional pauses as communication techniques while Jonathan put his feelings into words. He also got to Jonathan's eye level, made friendly eye contact (a cultural norm for Jonathan), and smiled now and then.

Ben was really helping Jonathan transition from DLS 2 to 3. Jonathan was learning he could work with a teacher to resolve conflicts that he had somehow fallen into. (This contact talk around a conflict illustrates why it takes teachers with perspective-taking abilities [empathy] to work with children.)

## Conflicts with Other Children

Playdough provides so many learning opportunities, not the least of which is helping children learn democratic life skills. Notice in the following anecdote how Ben stays calm and focused. The student teacher stays with the children to find a solution to their problem: their solution together and not Ben's alone.

Note also that Ben's use of the **five-finger formula** is not perfect here. However, conflict mediation, as with any guidance technique, does not have to be perfectly done. With caring leadership from the early childhood professional, the mediation (like teaching in general) just has to be good enough to bring the children along.

Four children are playing with playdough at the art center during choice time. Will comes to the table and wants to play with the playdough also. He walks to the table, looks at Nouri's playdough for a moment, and proceeds to grab a chunk from her without asking.

Nouri: Hey that's mine! [Nouri tries to grab the playdough back.]

Will: [pulls away and screams] No, I want to play, too.

Ben: Okay kids, hang on a second. I see that you are a little upset, so could you both take some good deep breaths for me? [They look at me; they are both really unhappy. I start by taking a deep breath myself, and they follow my example.] Okay, let's talk about this. Will, can you tell me what happened? And then Nouri can tell me what happened.

Will: I want to play playdough, but there is none in the box.

Ben: So you wanted to play with some playdough but there was no more left in the playdough box.

Will: [nods head]

Ben: OK, Nouri can you tell me what happened?

Nouri: I was playing with the playdough, and then Will came and took my playdough, and I said it was mine.

Ben: So you were playing with the playdough, and Will came up and took some of your playdough.

Nouri: Yeah.

Ben: So the problem is that Will wants to play with playdough also but there is no more left?

Both: [nod heads]

Ben: OK, let's think for a second. How can we solve this? [The children sit for a few seconds.]

Will: I could ask.

Nouri: Yeah! And I can share because you are a good buddy.

Ben: So Will should ask if he can have some playdough, and Nouri you are going to share some. Is that right?

Both: Yeah!

Will sits down, and Nouri shares some of her playdough. A few seconds later one of the other children comes over with a piece of playdough and gives it to Will. It seems like the other children were listening closely and wanted to make sure Will got enough playdough.

Merilee: You can have some of mine. [gives playdough to Will]

Will: Thanks!

Ben: Thank you for sharing, Merilee.

The rest of the playdough time goes well. When the students are putting it away I go to Will.

Ben: Thanks for asking if Nouri could share her playdough. Using words helps kids stay friends. It works better than grabbing, right?

Will: Yeah, Nouri would share if I asked!

## Five-Finger Formula for Social Problem Solving

1. Thumb: Calm everyone down—yourself, too.

2. Pointer: Help the parties to accept how each person sees the conflict. (This may not be what happened as you saw it.)

3. Tall guy: Brainstorm possible resolutions. (Provide suggestions for children with limited language ability or who are dual language learners. Respect nonverbal signs of agreement or disagreement.)

4. Ringer: Agree to one solution and try it. (This is not your imposed solution but one that all agree to.)

5. Pinky: Monitor the solution and provide follow-up feedback to individuals. (Talk especially with children who need to manage emotions more effectively during conflicts. Use compliment sandwiches in these follow-up guidance talks.)

Ben: [I also take a second to talk to Nouri.] Thanks for sharing your playdough with Will; that helped you two to be friends again.

Nouri: Yeah, we are going to play outside, too.

In Ben's Head Start class the adults had been teaching conflict management to the children through mediation and guidance talks, all year. Ben's successful (albeit not perfect) mediation helped Will and Nouri move past the conflict to a solution that allowed them to be friendly again. Children may not be "best buddies" before or after a conflict. Still, after calming down, they generally appreciate being assisted to resolve the matter so that they can get along.

When teachers see children going with the agreed-to solution, and then often playing together, they should smile: On this day the children have successfully experienced, and hopefully gained in, the skills of cooperative problem solving.

## Teaching Practices That Help Young Children Solve Problems Creatively—Independently and in Cooperation with Others

1. Provide an active learning environment in which children can engage in problem solving, independently and in cooperation with others, on a continuous basis.

2. Modify the learning environment as necessary to include every child in an ongoing problem-solving activity. (This often means increasing activity levels in the program.)

3. Recognize that young children are motivated by self-defined products and achievements. Minimize models and teacher-defined products to maximize children's confidence and competence in creative activity.

4. Plan intentional opportunities for children to engage in cooperative as well as individual creative endeavors.

5. Respond to the principle that for cognitive experiences to have lasting significance, the child's affect (emotional set) during these experiences needs to be positive.

6. Respect children's individual attention spans as indicators of the level of their engagement in creative activities. Remember that lifelong interests and skill sets begin in early childhood.

7. Remember that the limits of children's creativity should not be defined by adult expectations, but by the creative acts of children themselves.

8. Provide for a developmental range in materials and experiences that go beyond the usual expectations of what children at a particular age can and cannot accomplish.

9. Use private encouragement—acknowledgment, reflective feedback, guiding questions, and open suggestions—to support children in their creative learning activity.

10. Delight in the creative accomplishments of children, even if they are not completely in line with your expectations.

# Democratic Life Skill 4: Accepting Unique Human Qualities in Others

I n their unique way, young children are amazingly perceptive. If you have a spot of peanut butter on your cheek, if you are wearing your older, more comfortable shoes, or if the back of your jeans has a bit of glue mixed with glitter on it (or in my case, if I forgot to shave), they will tell you about it.

The theme of this chapter is how to help children interpret their perceptions of others in ways that are appreciative rather than rejecting. Calm, clear, and nonjudgmental explanations given by the teacher to the child are absolutely key. As teachers guide a child toward interpretations that balance impulse with reflection, they help the child progress with DLS 4. Teachers begin this guidance by being open to what the perception-interpretation process actually is like during early childhood.

Children reach literal, categorical, and sometimes fanciful conclusions based on their experiences and perceptions. For instance, a child who has a male physician and sees only pictures of male doctors thinks that all doctors are male. An early childhood professional who asks a female physician to visit the program fundamentally changes this preoperational stage perception.

The wonder and charm in how children perceive things keeps many early childhood teachers in the field. Accepting the developmentally determined thinking processes of young children, the teacher builds upon children's perceptiveness to gently expand their vision.

**DLS 1: Finding acceptance as a member of the group and as a worthy individual**

**DLS 2: Expressing strong emotions in non-hurting ways**

**DLS 3: Solving problems creatively—independently and in cooperation with others**

**DLS 4: Accepting unique human qualities in others**

**DLS 5: Thinking intelligently and ethically**

A preschooler riding a trike on the playground tells his teacher, "Me and my shadow are riding all over the place. We are getting a workout."

Grinning, the teacher responds, "You and your shadow better get drinks of water, Thomas, so you both don't get all dried out."

Thomas replies, "My shadow doesn't drink water, Teacher, just me."

## Interpreting Human Differences

**social identity:** the sum total of perceptions of oneself (self-concept) and feelings about oneself (self-esteem) relative to others who are similar to and different from oneself

Infants as young as 6 months notice differences in skin color (Katz & Kofklin 1997). By age 2, children can comment on differences in gender and skin color. By age 3, "children begin asking questions about their own and others' attributes, including racial identity, language, gender, and physical disabilities" (Derman-Sparks & Olsen Edwards 2010, 12). By age 5, children are well underway with the formation of **social identity,** the sum total of perceptions of oneself (self-concept) and feelings about oneself (self-esteem) *relative to others who are similar to and different from themselves* (Derman-Sparks & Olsen Edwards 2010). Children make these conscious and preconscious judgments about themselves relative to their perceptions of others based on gender, racial, ethnic, cultural, religious, and economic class criteria.

Children's social identities are influenced by the messages, *direct* and *indirect*, that they receive from others (Derman-Sparks & Olsen Edwards 2010). The initial source of social feedback is family members, but friends, media sources, and early childhood programs also soon become contributing influences. Messages like "boys don't cry" and "you look like a princess in that dress" are examples of *direct* messages that influence social identities.

One source of *indirect* messages is from environments that lack diversity, where children miss opportunities to extend principles of social give-and-take to people who are unlike themselves. A second source of indirect messages is double, contradictory meanings that children experience, such as "skin color doesn't matter" when the message from media and other social entities may be that skin color does matter (Derman-Sparks & Olsen Edwards 2010).

Young children pick up on the fundamental message of who is and who is not important in their social world. If a teacher shows unambiguous favoritism or unambiguous correction, criticism, and psychological distancing toward some children—due to their behavior, gender, race, religion, disability, and so on—other children notice and resonate with this message (Ladd 2006). Young children tend to record experiences of discrimination as emotional memories. These memories can become "pre-prejudices"—the beginning of a tendency to show discrimination (York 2003).

# Anti-Bias Education and Liberation Teaching

*Anti-bias education* means that adults intentionally teach children accepting responses toward others whatever their unique human qualities (Derman-Sparks & Olsen Edwards 2010). Teachers, in particular, need to model accepting responses toward children and families who are vulnerable for stigma (negative social separation from the group) (see Chapter 10). In anti-bias education, teachers reject the "power of silence"—the tendency to remain quiet in the face of oppressive interactions out of fear of "not saying the right thing" (York 2003). Instead, when children interpret human qualities in rejecting terms, these early childhood professionals show leadership that guides children away from settling into pre-prejudices—and instead leads them toward inclusive social identities.

---

A new child in a kindergarten group has thick glasses that magnify the appearance of her eyes. The children notice. Anne says, "I'm not playing with Lucy. Her eyes are funny." To which her teacher Marcie replies, "It's just fine to play with Lucy, Anne. Those glasses help her see so she can do fun things as school." The teacher starts Anne, Lucy, and another child on the task of sorting through a big box of markers to find and toss out the dry ones. When they are done, the three girls create story pictures of a class trip to a petting zoo. They laugh together about a "cute" lamb they saw, so young that it was still wobbly on its feet. All three draw pictures of the lamb, talking while they work.

---

With any children who are vulnerable for stigma, the teacher practices *liberation teaching*, a term that means never giving up on anyone in her charge and helping each child to overcome whatever vulnerabilities for stigma he may face (Gartrell 2011). In the sections that follow, we look at the potentially stigmatizing reactions by some young children toward others due to the factors of race, hygiene, disability, and gender, and how teachers can help guide children toward interpreting their perceptions of others in ways that are appreciative rather than rejecting and ultimately aid in their development of DLS 4. (Children rejecting other children on the basis of their mistaken behavior has been addressed in Chapters 12 and 13.)

## Skin Colors and Young Children

Young children are adept at noticing details of physical appearance and wondering about the differences they see. In terms of differences in skin color, the organic antidote to children's forthright questions, which are only embarrassing if the presiding adult makes them so, is including families with a variety of skin tones together in the classroom community.

But many classrooms in programs and schools across the country have limited racial diversity. Because children notice and ask questions about any new child or adult in the class, teachers should take the opportunity to discuss skin color differences in terms that build inclusive social identities. Teachers encounter—and counter—still-forming pre-prejudice about race every day.

In the following anecdote, a preschool teacher discusses Becca, a student teacher "who showed more moxie than I would have had" in a difficult situation.

---

Becca was a student teacher in the group of 4s and 5s at our child care center, and I was her cooperating teacher. One day at lunch, Martin, who is European American, came to the table reluctantly, I think because he saw he would be sitting next to Brandon, who is American Indian. Becca, who was eating at that table, greeted Martin warmly. Martin said quietly but distinctly, "I'm not sitting next to Brandon. He got dirty skin."

---

Becca gave Brandon a hug and whispered something in his ear. Then she went over to Martin, knelt down and told him, "Brandon's not dirty, Martin. He just has more color in his skin than you do. Lots of people have different skin colors, and that's fine. What's important in our class is that everyone is friendly to everyone." As she said this, she guided Martin to his chair and continued, "Brandon, could you pass the milk to our friend Martin?" Brandon did, and Martin half-heartedly thanked him.

Later that day, I noticed that Martin and Brandon were playing together. I complimented Becca for how she handled the situation and mentioned that Martin's dad had showed what I thought was racial prejudice when I had met with him and his wife during parent conferences.

When Martin's dad picked him up that evening, I noticed Becca talking to him. Afterward, I asked her what the conversation was about. Becca smiled and said, "Only that Martin had commented that another child who was American Indian had dirty skin. I thought Dad would want to know, so he could reinforce what we tell the children in our class: People have different skin colors, but what's important is that we are all friends and get along."

Becca did something that I am not sure I could have done. The dad left with skin color a bit redder than when he came in! I was quite relieved to see Martin in school the next day. Becca, to her credit, acted like nothing unusual had happened. (Adapted from Gartrell 2000, 82–83)

Becca's leadership here (with the father as well as the son) demonstrates liberation teaching. That Martin and Brandon played together later says a lot about both boys' progress toward DLS 4. Often all it takes is teachers who show democratic leadership.

The matter-of-fact explanation that teachers give to children to explain racial differences makes even children's comments that show pre-prejudice sound like requests to better understand human differences. Young children simply have not learned yet how to ask such questions politely. For a teacher using guidance, these are ultimate teaching moments. In the following anecdote, notice how teacher Rosalynn helps Tom come away with a new idea about the meaning of skin color.

In a suburban first grade, Tom, a member of an all–European American class, approached his teacher, who is African American. Without looking directly at her, but with some emotion, Tom declared, "Teacher, somebody's different in here."

Rosalynn responded, "Do you mean me, Tom? My skin is a darker color than yours and that's one of the special things that makes me who I am." Tom frowned and shook his head, but the teacher thought that her skin color was probably what Tom had on his mind.

The next day Tom's mother, an occasional classroom volunteer, called the teacher and said, "Rosalynn, I just have to tell you what happened last night. Tom and I were in the supermarket when an African American woman went by with a shopping cart. Tom turned to me and said, "Look, Mom, there goes a teacher!" (Adapted from Gartrell 2011, 485)

Young children are just beginning to learn about human differences. Teachers who see human differences as rich opportunities for teaching and learning proactively assist young children to make progress with DLS 4.

## Young Children and Hygiene

An olfactory memory takes me back to one February day when Stanley arrived at the Head Start program in a stinky state.

I knew that the plumbing in Stanley's house was a hand-pump in the kitchen sink, and the water heater was a big pot on a propane gas stove. A metal bathtub, somewhat bigger than a laundry basket, sat right next to the stove; it had a drain spout attached to a hose. For heat, the family used a very old woodstove. After a snow, the first walkway the family shoveled was to the outdoor privy. There was too much snow on this particular weekend to drive to the Laundromat in town.

On that Monday it didn't take long for the Level Two mistaken behavior to start, the catchy kind; alliteration was in the air. "Stinky Stanley," still more whispered than said, was beginning to catch on. So Stan sat on my lap while the other children arrived, and we read books before breakfast. I sat next to Stan at breakfast and put my arm around his shoulder. Stan sat on my lap during circle time, while I read the book of the day.

By choice time, a health care worker was able to get Stan cleaned up and in a change of clothes. (We had worked out this arrangement at the beginning of the year with all the families—whatever the cause of a stink, stain, or soak.)

While Stan was gone, the rest of us had a quick class meeting. We discussed that what they said had hurt a child's feelings, and it should stop. Besides, Stan was a valued member of our classroom community, and we needed to be friendly to him. (I worked hard to model that fact throughout the day.) I reminded them that it is sometimes hard to get cleaned up in the winter. Stan smelled great when he got back. We all noticed the difference. The name-calling stopped.

For young children, the growing ability to accept unique human characteristics (including those related to bodily functions) comes down to what teachers do when they hear oppressive remarks. As in the preceding anecdote, teachers who help children understand how the other child feels—what Galinsky (2010) calls "perspective taking"—make all the difference for progress in DLS 4.

## Including Children Who Have Disabilities

We have seen how a teacher helped kindergartner Anne to join in play with Lucy, who wore special glasses. Monica, the teacher in the following anecdote, took preparatory steps before Darcy, a child with a physical disability, joined the kindergarten class. Building a positive sense of anticipation in the group is a useful practice in working for DLS 4. In this case notice how Maria, a classmate, helped the teacher figure out how to include the new student in a vigorous physical activity.

The day before Darcy, a child with a physical disability, joined the group, Monica held a class meeting. The teacher provided sample crutches like Darcy's for the children to look at and try later in the dramatic play area. Monica read a picture book about a young child who uses crutches. They talked about how to be friendly with their new classmate, Darcy. The next day the children intentionally included Darcy in their play, checking with her about what she could and could not do.

When the class was getting ready to play a cooperative game of Red Light-Green Light, 5-year-old Maria asked Darcy if she would rather move with the other children or help the teacher with the red and green signs. Amazed, the teacher stood there and listened. Darcy decided to help with the signs—a plan the teacher herself had not yet formed, but it worked out well.

This one scenario shows how the democratic life skills come together in effective guidance teaching. Monica was guiding Darcy in meeting DLS 1 and the rest of the class in making progress with DLS 4. Maria was showing skill at levels 3, 4, *and* 5. From my perspective, to the teacher's credit, Monica did not tell Maria to "only take care of Maria"— she used Maria's idea. Perhaps teachers need to be at DLS 5 themselves to nurture this quality in others? We will return to this matter in Chapter 16.

## Toward a Gender-Friendly Classroom

Gender issues generate frequent roadblocks to children in progressing toward DSL 4. Teaching teams in which men and women work together, of course, is the organic solution to this dilemma (Nelson & Shikwambi 2010). Visitors working in non-gender stereotyped roles—stay-at-home dads, male nurses, female doctors, female fire-fighters—certainly can help to increase children's thinking about the way men and women are in society. Regardless of gender, the teacher shows positive leadership to make activities, routines, and interactions gender-inclusive. In this anecdote notice how the teacher works with three boys playing "firemen."

In a kindergarten classroom three boys are playing "firemen," using the climber for their station and the dramatic play areas for the "house on fire." Charlene asks to play but is told, "You can't 'cause you're a girl. Only boys can be firemen." Charlene tries to get on the climber anyway, but the boys block her way and begin yelling.

The teacher intervenes: "Hey, guys, do you remember our book about firefighters? Men and women can both be firefighters. That's why we call them firefighters instead of firemen. How can Charlene help you as a firefighter?"

The other boys don't object when Steve says, "Okay, Charlene, you can steer on the back." The teacher watches as the four get on their wooden bench "fire truck" and "speed off" to the fire. Charlene helps fight the fire, and it is she who thinks to save the two babies. The fire crew rides back to the station with Charlene sitting in the middle proudly holding the dolls. Charlene continued to play with the boys—she no longer sits only on the back of the "fire truck." And no one commented the next week when Charlene and Della played firefighter with two boys. (Adapted from Gartrell 2011, 488)

I have visited early childhood classrooms where boys and girls work and play comfortably in mixed groups, don't think to complain if they hold hands in line, and just plain live together well in the classroom. Gender differences are no big deal.

However, in other classrooms, I have seen a different ethos operating. Boys and girls have their own groups, activities, and priorities. The teachers in the second kind of classroom are not necessarily actively promoting gender pre-prejudice, but my personal view is that perhaps these teachers let their own conscious or unconscious gender stereotypes filter down to the children.

It seems to me that gender-stereotyped schooling practices typically reveal themselves in the adult's view of what is appropriate behavior in the classroom. The notion of classrooms being quiet, orderly places, even in early childhood, seems to influence these teachers' views (Carlson 2011). Boys and what some may call "boy behavior" typically are challenging for teachers who value a "sit down and follow directions" classroom regimen. In this kind of classroom, teachers might well favor those students who are able to comply with their schooling expectations, which often are most girls and only some boys. Other boys in these classrooms may feel teachers' rejection (Gilliam 2005).

Mullins argues that it is time for single-sex schools to "improve education" (2009, 120). In my view, this argument comes about because schools have failed to teach girls and boys to appreciate the unique human qualities in each other beginning at an early age.

Carlson (2011) makes the case, also supported in Gartrell and Sonsteng (2008), that physically active classrooms are developmentally appropriate for all young children. Sustained physical activity empowers healthy brain and physical development in girls as well as boys. In friendly, active classrooms, happy brain hormones prevail. All children find engagement in activity that is intriguing and interact together without pressures toward social identities encumbered by gender stereotypes. With sanctioned vigorous play and generally active programs, what some term "boy behaviors"—inattentiveness, rowdiness, rambunctiousness—do not become issues (Carlson 2011; King 2004). Boys as well as girls—as with the firefighters in the anecdote—make progress with DLS 4.

## Gaining DLS 4

The following anecdote comes from my recent observation in a family child care program, which the provider operates under a contract with the local Head Start agency.

During work time, 5-year-old Derrick, the one child of color, was working on a computer. Knowing that Cindy, their teacher, encouraged children working together when the computer station was open, Derrick invited four different children to come join him. The next oldest child, a young 4-year-old, spent 10 minutes with Derrick. He knew the game and the two played together.

Then Alayna, 23 months old, joined him. Derrick patiently taught her the basics and for five minutes helped her play the game. Then Alayna stopped, and I thought she was going to leave. Instead, she sat and watched Derrick play for another 10 minutes, with Derrick smiling and talking with her throughout. She only left when it was time to clean up and go outside. The two of them stood up together, Alayna just barely coming up to Derrick's waist.

When adults model and teach for inclusive social identities, when they practice liberation teaching with children vulnerable for stigma, and when they use developmentally appropriate, anti-bias practices, children become accepting of unique human qualities and think of human differences as a natural part of life.

## Teaching Practices That Help Young Children Accept Unique Human Qualities in Others

1. Model friendly relations and accepting relationships with every child in the class.
2. Model friendly relations and accepting relationships with all other adults in the class, in particular children's family members who visit.
3. Model and teach conflict management techniques that show understanding and respect for all parties involved.
4. Plan and implement cooperative activities that involve children and adults in the classroom across different diversities—gender, age, race, language ability, and so on—in order to promote inclusive group spirit.
5. Use private acknowledgment and encouragement with individuals and groups showing inclusive social relations across different diversities within the class.
6. On an interactive basis, invite families to share aspects of their linguistic, ethnic, interest, and activity micro-cultures with the class, and build an inclusive social studies program around features of family and community life. (Micro-cultures refer to the mix of cultural, linguistic, ethnic, religious, social, and personality variables in any family that define the values, beliefs, interests, activities, and behavior tendencies of that family.)
7. Practice anti-bias and liberation teaching to make discriminatory, excluding comments and incidents into teaching and learning opportunities in relation to the worthiness of each individual as a full member of the group.

# 16

# Democratic Life Skill 5: Thinking Intelligently and Ethically

D LS 5, the ability to think intelligently and ethically, or *autonomy* in Piaget's terms, is the highest of the democratic life skills. Because young children are so dependent on others for continuing development, children who demonstrate the democratic life skills—including DLS 5—cannot be expected to be "at" this level in an enduring and consistent way. The complexities of coming of age indicate to me that only if children continue with secure attachments at home and developmentally appropriate education at school will they have the relationships and the environments that support the continuing development of all the democratic life skills.

Still, 30-plus years of brain research (Cozolino 2006; Galinsky 2010; Sousa 2012) suggest that children who reach DLS 5 in early childhood have a higher likelihood of continuing with this skill than children who do not. My rationale for this statement comes down to the viable neuroarchitecture that children build during early childhood as a result of secure attachments and developmentally appropriate education. The long-term studies on high-quality early childhood education, cited in Chapter 5, suggest that the social-emotional benefits last into adulthood (Public Policy Forum 2008; RAND Corporation 2005). However, research on topics related to the democratic life skills still needs to be done. I wrote this book to bring this subject into focus.

## Toward DLS 5

In the previous chapter, 5-year-old Maria asked Darcy (the new child who used crutches) if she would rather move with the children during Red Light-Green Light or help the teacher with the two colored signs for the game. Maria's question was an indication that she was progressing toward DLS 5. Maria was working from a growing relationship with Darcy, and her question was sincere. The teacher recognized Maria's intent to be inclusive with her new friend Darcy and followed the child's lead. In learning any high-level skill, children, like all of us, are going to make mistakes. With a child struggling to gain DLS 1 and 2, teachers who practice guidance work hard to understand the mistakes and help children learn from them. They should do the same for a child progressing toward DLS 5.

The encouraging classroom, in which guidance works in concert with developmentally appropriate practice, belongs to the entire community of learners—including both adults and children. The teacher who accepted Maria's assistance as a helpful suggestion from a fellow community member (and not as a remark by a child who does not know her place) is fostering that child's progress toward DLS 5.

To sustain efforts by children to act at DLS 5, we need to remember both a developmental limitation and a vulnerability of early childhood. The limitation is that acting with autonomy is a high-level skill for everyone, even more so for young children who are just starting this skill. Young children's perspective-taking abilities and executive functions are just beginning to develop.

However, unkind responses by adults to young children's early efforts with this skill may well undermine their continuing efforts. Long ago Froebel recognized that adults can negatively influence children by misinterpreting sincere and innocent motivations in their enthusiastic behaviors (Froebel [1826] 1887). His remark still holds true today, especially in relation to actions that show budding autonomy. For example, consider the following anecdote.

> Four-year-old Sylvia notices that a visiting parent has sat in some white glue with glitter in it. Trying to be helpful she says to the parent, "You have glitter on your butt." The parent gives the child a "how dare you" look. Before she says something to the child, however, the teacher, who was right there, comments, "What Sylvia means is that you may have sat in a bit of glue and glitter. You can hardly notice it, and it will wash out. Thanks for caring about our guests, Sylvia, and for trying to help out."

The teacher could have said "Sylvia, you need to be more respectful to adults. This is not something that you need to point out. You just worry about the glue and glitter that is sticking to your hand. I am sorry, Mrs. Badasch. It is just a tiny bit of glue, and it will wash out." Instead she chose to model and teach DLS 5. Lesson: Children progress with DLS 5 when they see their teachers using it and when teachers support children in their beginning efforts.

### Months Old, Not Years Old

The developmental difference between a child who acts at DLS 5 and an adult who does is significant. A child like Maria successfully completes an act of autonomy in a way that makes things better. The child's still plastic neuroarchitecture changes as a result of this experience (Cozolino 2006; Sousa 2012) (see Chapter 4). This neurological change contributes to emerging executive functions, which strengthens the child's capacity to act similarly in the future. Experiential success engenders healthy neurological development across the frontal lobes, prefrontal cortex, thalamus, and hippocampus that sustains the likelihood of future prosocial acts.

Of course not all adults consistently muster DLS 5 responses in social situations, but overall older individuals have more experience and neural architecture to help them with prosocial interactions. Adults also communicate from a position of less dependence on other members of the group—though rarely with total independence. The pressure is always there to "go along to get along." Children, and adults in groups where they must answer to others (like in the workplace), always face a dilemma in deciding whether to share what is in their minds and hearts. This challenge pertains especially to situations when a person witnesses a hurting behavior. The danger of not speaking up is that silence lends tacit approval to oppressive ideas and actions. When oppression happens and people turn their heads, the downward slide of the group, away from autonomous considerations, becomes more likely (York 2003).

So many of us look to the work and character of Jesus, Mahatma Gandhi, Mother Teresa, the Dalai Lama, and Martin Luther King Jr. and conclude . . . the principled life is way too hard! But education for democracy is about "everyday heroes," people doing little things that are right, frequently in cooperation with others. And if children are educated toward autonomy from the beginning, conflicts over time become more civil, and people become better able to work together to figure things out.

First attempts at autonomy are going to be faulty, shaky, or both. If teachers remember that they are assisting the child to begin building lifelong skills, their perspective will allow them to be supportive of first efforts. When the child moves on to the next grade level, where their skill building goes the teacher cannot say. But due to the course of healthy brain development, being a force for good guidance early in life can only help children into the future.

I know what I am asking here—the only thing harder than learning and practicing democratic life skills is teaching them to others. Flat out in my view, early childhood professionals are the most important teachers in the child's life.

# Three Anecdotes

The following three anecdotes illustrate the progress children make toward DLS 5.

## The Tricycle

The first anecdote illustrates the developmental egocentrism of early childhood—the fact that young children are just beginning to develop social perspective. Notice teacher Julia's response to Dimitri as the boy tries to make things better after taking advantage of his younger cousin. (In helping young children make progress toward DLS 5, the glass is always half full.)

> When the temperature hits minus 20 with wind-chill, the preschool class usually stays inside. Raul is happily riding his favorite trike in the active playroom. He was at the right place at the right time when an older 4-year-old got off. However, his cousin Dimitri, almost 5 years old, had signed up for the trike at the beginning of the time-block. He, not Raul, is next on the list.
>
> Dimitri catches up to Raul and stands facing him with one leg on either side of the front wheel. He tries to persuade Raul it is his turn. Raul yells, "No," and then screams as Dimitri grabs one arm and forces Raul off the trike. As Dimitri rides off, he looks over his shoulder and sees their teacher Julia tending to Raul, whose screams have become howls.
>
> Dimitri makes a U-turn and rides over to Raul and Julia. He gets off the trike and offers it to Raul, explaining to the teacher, "He was crying loud and he needed it more."
>
> The teacher asks Raul if he wants to ride. Giving his cousin a wary stare, Raul nods and gets on the trike. The teacher says, "It's Dimitri's turn when you are done, remember?" Raul nods as he rides away.
>
> Julia has seen the whole thing. She has Dimitri sit by her on the floor and the two have a guidance talk. Dimitri explains what happened as he saw it. The two converse about how the younger preschoolers are still learning the routines, and they brainstorm ideas about what Dimitri could do next time instead of taking the trike. Julia then tells Dimitri that his coming back and giving the trike to Raul was a considerate and helpful thing to do.
>
> Julia had already decided that Dimitri should still get his turn and oversees the transition when Raul gets tired of riding. She asks Dimitri if there is something he can say to Raul. Dimitri tells him sorry and thanks.

Seems like at the beginning Dimitri was at DLS 3 here—he did solve the problem creatively!—but he didn't express his strong emotions considerately, and he didn't appreciate Raul's unique human qualities. One could make the case that Dimitri was thinking mostly about himself until he heard his cousin's wails. He tried then to make the situation "right," which Julia saw as opportunity to teach for autonomy.

The teacher knew Dimitri well enough to guess that he felt bad about taking the trike (helped to this feeling by Raul's protestations). She also recognized that his attempt to make restitution showed progress toward DLS 5 and acknowledged his intent and his effort.

Julia's decision to let Dimitri ride the trike when Raul was done reflects her guidance perspective on the situation. The outcome of Dimitri's causing the conflict was not the "logical consequence" of losing the privilege of riding. The *guidance consequence* was that he looked honestly at the conflict and learned a better way to handle it next time. Julia wanted to convey to Dimitri that she believed in his progress toward autonomy. She built on her relationship with the boy to encourage him to keep making progress. With her leadership, Julia helped Dimitri move toward thinking intelligently and ethically. Perhaps next time he might do so from the beginning of a conflict.

## Peaches

A 3-year-old, Oliver, in a mixed-age classroom loved canned peaches and was excited to have them for dessert at lunch. He loved them so much that he declared his affinity to the whole room with a sweeping arm gesture—that knocked his peach onto the floor. Oliver wailed and thunked his head down on the table. Teacher Catara said, "It's all right, Oliver, it was an accident. We'll get this one cleaned up and get you another one." As Catara was on the floor with Oliver trying to help, she realized that this was the last peach! They had just enough for each child to have one.

Catara knew what was coming next, and they took a very long time cleaning up the spill. As she slowly got Oliver to the table, he looked down at his place and there was a peach in a bowl! Catara looked at the peach and looked up at Hilda, the almost-5-year-old sitting next to the boy.

"He needed it more than me," she said. "He was very sad." The teacher asked Oliver if there were something he could say to Hilda. He said, "Thank you, Hilda." The teacher thanked Hilda, too, then and again later when the two were reading a book.

This is one of my favorite anecdotes. After sharing it at a training once, a participant said to me, "The teacher should not have let Hilda do this. A natural consequence of spilling your peach, if that's the last one, is that you don't get any. By letting Hilda give him hers, the teacher was not letting him learn to face reality."

By permitting Hilda to give Oliver her peach, I thought the teacher was letting the lesson be learned that there is compassion in life, that people can care about each other and show this caring. Maybe if both kids were 5, the teacher might have stressed the reality lesson. My guess is that Oliver would have reacted differently if he were two years older when he spilled his peach. But he was not, and Hilda acted intelligently and ethically by empathizing with this distraught younger classmate.

A teacher might develop emergent curriculum from an experience like this by reading a book about generosity such as *The Rainbow Fish* or *The Giving Tree* and holding a class meeting about decisions to give to others: when to give and perhaps when not to. (No child, in this case Hilda and Oliver, should be singled out in such a discussion.) People should perhaps have this conversation more than once in their lives; the conversation might as well start in preschool with what caring is and why it is important to show to others.

Hilda certainly modeled perspective taking in her action. On this day, pure and simple, she was at DLS 5.

## The Haircut

Do you remember your first friendship? Most likely it was with a child you met during the preschool years. Maybe you are still friends, maybe not, but you probably still have warm feelings toward that person. Just as lifelong interests get started in the early years, I believe friendships do, too (Gartrell 2011), some of which we are lucky enough to continue throughout our lives.

Note I am not talking here about, "We are all friends in this classroom." I believe it is presumptuous of teachers to think they should define for children who their friends are. A little guy nailed this one for me once. He replied to a teacher who made a remark about all children in the class being friends by saying, "Gil's not my friend. He's my mate," as in classmate. We do need to encourage children to be friendly with all of their classmates, but children, like the rest of us, should have the right to decide their friendships for themselves.

In the following anecdote, related by Head Start student teacher Krista, Ansha and Lena had definitely decided that they were fast friends.

---

Ansha and Lena, both nearly 5 years old, hugged each other when they arrived in the morning and hugged each other goodbye when they left in the afternoon. They played together whenever the teachers did not have them in different groups. The two lived in different parts of town, and the teachers were not sure if they ever got together outside of school. This knowledge may have made the staff more tolerant about the two hanging together so much.

Lena's hair was so long it almost came to her waist. Her mom kept it immaculately brushed and sometimes braided. On one Friday afternoon, the two girls hugged goodbye, and Lena went home to her sister who was in her late teens—their mom had gone out of town for the weekend and older sister was in charge. Lena's sister had just begun cosmetology school, and on Monday Lena arrived with a blue buzz cut!

The teaching team saw Lena arrive and stood there with their mouths open. They had no idea what to say. Lena walked over to Ansha, hugged her hello, and asked, "What do you think of my new haircut?" "Ansha started to say something, then changed her mind. She said, 'I'm still getting used to it.'"

"Me too," said Lena, and the two went off to play. The teaching team already knew Ansha was a child who had it together, but they found out how together she was during this exchange. That morning Ansha taught all of us in the room what to say!

---

Lena's long hair was so established in everyone's mind that a blue buzz cut shocked this veteran staff. Ansha knew a lot was riding on her response, decided against her initial impulse, and said something that showed both honest smarts and an appreciation for her friend's feelings. At age 4, Ansha was thinking intelligently and ethically—she was responding at DLS 5. That's what friends are for, at any age.

My contention is that it is going to be easier for children who are encouraged toward DLS 5 in their younger years to attain and sustain this democratic life skill. I say this because progress toward DLS 5 signifies the presence of the healthy attachments that young children need with their families, caregivers, and teachers. The resulting empowerment toward healthy executive functioning (including perspective taking) gets imprinted neurologically in key structures of the still-plastic brain (Cozolino 2006; Sousa 2012).

Not to encourage young children to respond intelligently and ethically in social situations is to pose long-term roadblocks for them along the more and less traveled roads of life. Caring adults need to be sensitive to children's efforts in relation to DLS 5, even when their behaviors may be outside of typical adult comfort zones. The goal of education for democracy is DLS 5, enabled by the attainment of DLS 1 through 4, which provides the foundation.

## Teaching Practices That Help Young Children Progress with Thinking Intelligently and Ethically

1. Plan for and be alert to situations in which children can show prosocial behaviors, including sharing, taking turns, cooperating, perspective-taking, guiding, helping, and resolving situations in which others and the child both can gain.

2. Recognize the difficulty in using the above behaviors successfully through use of friendly guidance and support with imperfect attempts.

3. Encourage and privately acknowledge children's efforts at prosocial behavior, including beginning efforts.

4. Avoid putting undue pressures on young children by bringing public attention to individual attempts at intelligent and ethical behaviors.

5. Help children see prosocial acts as positive reflections on self-identity, rather than as social or moral obligations.

6. Support children beyond the high self-expectation for "good" behavior some bring with them into the classroom.

7. Work with family members to help them see and accept the capacities of their children for prosocial acts.

8. Recognize that early childhood professionals help children to build the *foundations* for intelligent and ethical decision making through a grounding in DLS 1 through 4. It is easier for the child to build if the foundation is strong.

# 17

# Next Steps: Development, Demonstration, and Practice

I n order to hand over the concept of an education for a civil society to readers, I have shared the foundations for this approach—historical, educational, psychological, and neuropsychological. I have explained what I believe to be key classroom dynamics—developmentally appropriate practice that includes family-teacher partnerships, developmentally appropriate methods and content, and the use of guidance with individuals and groups. I have explored each of the democratic life skills and what they can look like when applied in early childhood education settings. Still, literally and figuratively, my approach has been anecdotal.

For education for a civil society to have an impact beyond this book, the construct of the democratic life skills has to be quantified: Models must be developed, field-tested, researched, discussed, and further developed. I've reached two conclusions about the democratic life skills: 1) Teaching for these skills inherently dovetails with developmentally appropriate practice at all levels of education, early childhood and beyond; and 2) teaching and assessing for the democratic life skills can be done in conjunction with existing broad-scale preschool curriculum models, such as HighScope (Epstein & Hohmann 2012) and Creative Curriculum® (Dodge et al. 2010), and with intentionally designed models that reflect a local community's goals for children. By intent if not design, teaching for the democratic life skills is also compatible with the CLASS teacher assessment system (Pianta et al. 2008).

An assessment system developed for the democratic life skills should focus on each skill separately, using authentic assessment methods such as checklists, observational samples, and portfolio entries (in perhaps both paper and digital formats). The Appendix in this book provides an initial analysis of elements of each democratic life skill, suggesting the direction an assessment system might take. I see this system making intrapersonal and interpersonal intelligences—healthy social-emotional development—a central dimension in schooling that intends to educate children for our modern, diverse, democratic society.

Three dimensions of teaching for the democratic life skills that have been developed in this book are pivotal. First, partnerships between families and educators should be reciprocal, expressed in the concept and operation of community-centered schools and programs that provide comprehensive education services. Second, teachers should be empowered to use developmentally appropriate practice, inclusive of all members of the community of learners, and should be held educationally accountable for the effectiveness of their teaching. Third, the management system of the encouraging classroom, in which education for civil democracy occurs, should be guidance, the goals of which are the democratic life skills.

In operationalizing teaching and learning systems that focus on the democratic life skills, it is important to find a way for individuals and groups to interact cooperatively and respectfully (ethically). It is the modeling and teaching of the democratic life skills in American classrooms that will allow us to sustain a promising future for society in the twenty-first century and beyond.

# Appendix

## Initial Operationalization Charts of the Democratic Life Skills

To begin to quantify elements of the democratic life skills, I have provided the following charts with information regarding typical challenges children face in relation to gaining each skill, children's typical behaviors at the beginning point in relation to the skill, and teacher practices that empower children to make progress to develop the skill. This initial operationalization chart provides a focus for additional study, discussion, development, and demonstration of education practices regarding teaching for the democratic life skills.

### DLS 1: Finding acceptance as a member of the group and as a worthy individual

**Children** working on this skill may be new to the program, may feel they are in danger of being stigmatized (excluded from the group), and/or may be dealing with high stress levels (due to neurological, environmental, or a combination of factors). Children who are young and inexperienced in situations that older children are comfortable in are particularly susceptible to environmental stressors.

**Typical child behaviors**
—Observes interactions and experiences but does not join in
—Experiences pronounced stress in what others regard as routine adjustments, minor tasks, and small frustrations
—Resists teacher efforts to be included in class routines and activities
—Loses emotional control easily
—Shows lack of confidence when engaged in activities
—Has difficulty regaining composure

**Teachers** work to create relationships with children outside of conflict situations, sustain relationships during conflicts, and build trust levels in children.

### DLS 2: Expressing strong emotions in non-hurting ways

**Children** working on this skill have progressed enough in DLS 1 to initiate interactions with peers and adults. Conflicts occur because children are just beginning to learn skills to prevent and resolve problems and to express strong emotions in ways that do not make conflicts worse.

**Typical child behaviors**
—Continues to work on the ability to share, take turns, cooperate; has conflicts in these situations
—Shows frequent, sometimes dramatic frustration and/or aggression during conflicts
—May show instrumental aggression (such as bullying) toward younger/smaller children
—Reacts to adult intervention with sometimes intense emotional expressions, such as aggression and/or psychological distancing
—Is able to recover some self-esteem after guidance interventions (more so than children at DLS 1)

**Teachers** build relationships with children outside of conflict situations and build trust levels to make guidance interventions effective. Teachers use what they have learned about what works with these children to ease them through, and help them resolve, conflicts. Teachers use calming techniques (different from time-outs), guidance talks, conflict mediation, and sometimes class meetings when children at DLS 2 have conflicts. To sustain relationships with children, teachers avoid embarrassing and shaming them and teach them alternatives to hurting behaviors. When children experience continuing serious conflicts, teachers use comprehensive guidance, usually involving family members.

## DLS 3: Solving problems creatively—independently and in cooperation with others

**Children** work on this skill *in two dimensions:* as individuals and together with others.

*Individually,* the child summons the capacity to engage, focus, persevere, and resolve the matter she is working on, in the child's own way. Examples include a child's willingness and ability to engage in open-ended activities, such as with art and building materials, and confidently arrive at self-defined products, such as giving the reindeer Rudolph a yellow nose instead of a red one "so Santa can see better."

*Together with others,* there is the give and take of cooperation in completing tasks, with each child engaging, focusing, persevering, and with others solving the problem. An example is three kindergarten children who build a three-story apartment building or castle with blocks, put miniature figures in "windows" on each level, and identify each figure. The three may argue about figure identities and placement, but they work it all out. Resolving conflicts with minimal adult assistance is characteristic of children working at DLS 3.

### Typical child behaviors

**INDIVIDUALLY:**

—Accesses and engages with open-ended learning activities

—Stays with problems and tasks

—Solves problems, obtains results, and creates products in own way

—Finds personal gratification in creations and the problem-solving process

**IN COOPERATION WITH OTHERS:**

Through give and take with others,

—Accesses and engages with open-ended learning activities

—Stays with problems and tasks until completion

—Solves problems and creates products in unique ways

—Finds personal gratification in mutual creations and the problem-solving process

**Teachers** provide a learning environment in which children can actively engage in problem solving, independently and in cooperation with others. Teachers provide a variety of learning opportunities so that every child is engaged. Teachers recognize that the process is more important than the product and do not compel children to make predetermined products. They give enough, but only as much, assistance as children need to feel ownership of the problem solving. Teachers use private encouragement—acknowledgment, reflective feedback, guiding questions, and suggestions—to support children in their problem-solving efforts.

## DLS 4: Accepting unique human qualities in others

**Children** work on this skill by going out of their usual peer-group comfort zones to initiate friendly interactions with others. Examples include an older child playing with a younger child; a girl and boy playing together; children who have different racial or linguistic characteristics playing together; a child who does not have special needs playing with a child who does; a child who is a veteran in the group playing with a new child; a child who is seen as popular playing with a child who may be vulnerable for stigma; and a child interacting with a new adult, such as a parent or other volunteer, who is unfamiliar.

**Typical child behaviors**

—Joins in spontaneous groupings with children who may differ in age, gender, or racial characteristics

—Initiates cooperative activity with children who may have differing human qualities

—Initiates interactions with children and adults in the classroom who may be new

—Shows inclusiveness and even support for children who may be vulnerable for stigma

—Discusses differences in human qualities, including behaviors and viewpoints, in a matter-of-fact way, with apparent intent to understand, not judge

**Teachers** set the scene by modeling friendly relations and accepting relationships with every child in the class, and with all other adults in the room. Teachers apply friendly leadership to prevent and resolve excluding acts by individuals (children and other adults) toward others in the classroom. Teachers set up learning situations where children can have positive interactions with others different from themselves. Teachers positively acknowledge inclusive pairings and groupings within the class. Teachers use private acknowledgment with individual children who show acceptance of others across differences in viewpoints as well as differing human qualities.

## DLS 5: Thinking intelligently and ethically

**Children** work on this skill when they respond to another child's needs and perspectives as much as their own. For example, a child gives up a turn, like riding a trike, to another child; a child offers to help another child or a teacher with a task; a child offers to share materials with others; or after being hurt or yelled at by another, a child does not retaliate but negotiates a resolution. An important component of this skill is that the child does not feel pressured to show prosocial behavior; he chooses to do so.

**Typical child behaviors**

—Gives up turn or materials for child who "needs it more"

—Comforts another child who might be sad or upset

—Invites another child to join in an activity or offers joint use of a material

—Offers to help another child or an adult

—Expresses how another child might be feeling

—Leads others in cooperative problem solving, even when other children in the group have strong opinions

—Chooses not to take advantage of situations or another child for her own gain

—Suggests a solution to a problem that shows thought and takes others' views into consideration—even if the other is showing signs of aggression

**Teachers** set the scene by modeling friendly relations and building positive relationships with every child in the class and with all adults in the room. Teachers set up learning situations where children can have positive interactions with others different from themselves. Teachers are accepting of etiquette mistakes children may show in beginning efforts to think intelligently and ethically. Teachers use appropriate private acknowledgment with individual children who show prosocial behaviors.

# Glossary

**achievement gap:** The disparity in academic performance among different groups of students, as determined by standardized tests.

**attachment:** A lasting psychological connectedness between human beings, particularly between a child and parent or other meaningful adult.

**authentic assessment:** A type of assessment that uses tasks that are as close as possible to real-life practical and intellectual challenges. It is based on observations and samples of children's classroom work.

**child negotiation:** Conflict mediation style in which one or more children in a conflict choose not to retaliate but to negotiate on their own without a teacher's help.

**community schools:** Schools that serve as community centers with close ties to families.

**compliment sandwich:** An encouragement technique that provides at least two positive statements about a child's effort and progress and one suggestion for growth.

**comprehensive education services:** Family and child support services incorporated into schools, such as child care, parent education, and health and nutrition support.

**contact talk:** The language of interpersonal relationships.

**democratic life skills (DLS):** The emotional and social capacities individuals need to function civilly in modern, diverse, and complex democratic society.

**developmentally appropriate practice (DAP):** An approach to teaching that is grounded in how young children develop and learn and in what is known about effective early education.

**education gap:** The disparity in the quality of education experienced by different groups of learners due to an inadequacy of targeted, coordinated resources.

**encouragement:** Specific, supportive statements that acknowledge effort and progress.

**encouraging classroom:** The physical and social-emotional environment of a community of learners that empowers all children to develop and learn.

**executive function:** The coordinated abilities to stay on task in attending and thinking, plan and organize thoughts as in problem solving, and utilize short- and long-term memory to facilitate thought processing.

**guidance:** A way of teaching that nurtures each child's potential through consistently positive (sometimes firm, but always friendly) interactions; classroom management that teaches rather than punishes.

**high-level mediation:** Conflict mediation style in which the teacher becomes a firm but friendly mediator, leading the children through each of the steps in the five-finger formula while expecting, encouraging, supporting, and acknowledging each child's participation.

**Individual Guidance Plan:** A comprehensive and systematic strategy for addressing a child's serious mistaken behavior that is most often developed and implemented with families.

**instrumental aggression:** The use of force to get what one wants.

**liberation teaching:** Helping children who are vulnerable for stigma (exclusion from the group) overcome their vulnerabilities and find a place of acceptance, perhaps even leadership, with their peers.

**low-level mediation:** Conflict mediation style in which, after calming down and having the teacher get them started, the children take over the process and solve the problem themselves.

**mastery motivation:** The intrinsic drive for learning within the child.

**mistaken behavior:** An intentional or unintentional action that causes a conflict or contributes to complications in getting the conflict resolved; error in judgment.

**praise:** General, evaluative statements given to recognize an accomplishment.

**progressive education:** Forward-looking education that respects diversity and educates the whole child; that balances the needs of the developing child with academics; and that focuses on development that advances children's ability to learn in the context of a democratic community.

**reactive aggression:** Behaviors used in self-defense when a child perceives a situation as threatening.

**reflective listening:** Repeating back the thoughts and feelings the other person is expressing.

**self:** The sum of the feelings and thoughts one has about who one is (self-identity), along with the mental processes—conscious, preconscious, and unconscious—that together write, direct, and produce those feelings and thoughts.

**social identity:** The sum total of perceptions of oneself (self-concept) and feelings about oneself (self-esteem) relative to others who are similar to and different from oneself.

**stigma:** A label that disqualifies an individual from full participation in the group and leads to a tendency in the group for others to reject and even ridicule the individual.

**task talk:** The necessary language representing everyday tasks that need to be accomplished.

**template function:** The working of genes to build the basic structure of the brain

**toxic stress:** High levels of stress not ameliorated through a secure attachment; causes neurochemical reactions that overwhelm the hypothalamus, the center for maintaining the normal state of functioning, and hyperstimulate the child's fight-or-flight reactions.

**transcription function:** The working of genes to continue brain development by converting the individual's perceived experiences into brain matter.

**windows of opportunity:** Important periods in which the young brain responds to certain types of input from its environment to create or consolidate neural networks.

**zone of proximal development:** The psychological distance between what a child can learn on her own and what she can learn with nudging and encouragement.

# References

## Chapter 1

Copple, C. & S. Bredekamp, eds. 2009. *Developmentally Appropriate Practice in Early Childhood Programs Serving Children from Birth through Age 8.* 3rd ed. Washington, DC: NAEYC.

Cozolino, L. 2006. *The Neuroscience of Human Relationships.* New York: W.W. Norton and Company.

Gardner, H.E. 2006. *Multiple Intelligences: New Horizons in Theory and Practice.* New York: Basic Books.

Gartrell, D. forthcoming. *A Guidance Approach for the Encouraging Classroom.* 6th ed. Belmont, CA: Wadsworth/Cengage Learning.

Piaget, J. [1932] 1960. *The Moral Judgment of the Child.* Glencoe, IL: The Free Press.

## Chapter 2

Baker, M.C. 1966. *Foundation of John Dewey's Educational Theory.* New York: Atherton Press.

Blow, S. 1908. *Educational Issues in the Kindergarten.* New York: D. Appleton and Company.

Brickman, W.W., & S. Lehrer. 1959. *John Dewey: Master Educator.* New York: Society for the Advancement of Education.

Children's Defense Fund. 2011, July. "Moments in America for Children." In *The State of America's Children.* Washington, DC: Author. www.childrensdefense.org/child-research-data-publications/moments-in-america-for-children.html.

Comenius, J. [1638] 1896. *The Great Didactic.* Trans. M.W. Keatinge. London: Adam and Charles Black.

Dewey, J. *The School and Society and The Child and the Curriculum.* Digireads.com Publishing [1897; 1902] 2010. Kindle edition.

Dewey, J. [1916] 1966. *Democracy and Education: An Introduction to the Philosophy of Education.* New York: The Free Press.

Dewey, J. [1938] 1997. *Experience and Education.* New York: Touchstone.

Froebel, F. [1826] 1887. *Education of Man.* Trans. W.N. Hailmann. New York: D. Appleton and Company.

Khadaroo, S.T. 2010, June. "Graduation Rate for US High-Schoolers Falls for Second Straight Year." *Christian Science Monitor.* www.csmonitor.com/USA/Education/2010/0610/Graduation-rate-for-US-high-schoolers-falls-for-second-straight-year.

Kramer, R. 1988. *Maria Montessori: A Biography.* New York: Da Capo Press.

Lillard, P.P. 1998. *Montessori: A Modern Approach.* New York: Shocken Books.

Montessori Australia. 2011. "A Biography of Dr. Maria Montessori." Author. http://montessori.org.au/montessori/biography.htm.

Montessori, M. [1912] 1964. *The Montessori Method.* New York: Shocken Books.

Montessori, M. [1949] 2007. *The Absorbent Mind.* Radford, VA: Wilder Publications.

Neill, A.S. 1995. *Summerhill School: A New View of Childhood.* Rev. ed. New York: St. Martin's Griffin.

NNDB. 2012. "Maria Montessori." Soylent Communications. http://www.nndb.com/people/189/000108862/.

Osborn, D.K. 1991. *Early Childhood Education in Historical Perspective.* 3rd ed. Athens, GA: Daye Press.

Progressive Education Network. 2012. "About PEN: History and Purpose." Author. www.progressiveed.org/about_pen.php.

Ross, E.D. 1976. *The Kindergarten Crusade: The Establishment of Preschool Education in the United States.* Athens, Ohio: Ohio University Press.

Shapiro, M.S. 1983. *Child's Garden: The Kindergarten Movement from Froebel to Dewey.* University Park, PA: The Pennsylvania State University Press.

Standing, E.M. [1959] 1998. *Maria Montessori: Her Life and Work.* New York: Plume/Penguin Group.

Weber, E. 1969. *The Kindergarten: Its Encounter with Educational Thought in America.* New York: Teachers College Press.

Westbrook, R.B. 1995. *John Dewey and American Education.* Ithaca, NY: Cornell University Press.

# Chapter 3

Ansbacher, H.L., & R.R. Ansbacher, eds. 1956. *The Individual Psychology of Alfred Adler: A Systematic Presentation in Selections from His Writings*. New York: Harper Torchbooks.

Bettelheim, B. 1987. *Good Enough Parenting: A Book on Child Rearing*. New York: Random House.

Charlesworth, R. 2010. *Understanding Child Development*. 8th ed. Clifton Park, NY: Thomson Delmar Learning.

Children's Defense Fund. 2011. "Moments in America for Children." In *The State of America's Children*. Washington, DC: Author. www.childrensdefense.org/child-research-data-publications/moments-in-america-for-children.html.

Cloud, J. 2010. "Educating for a Sustainable Future." In *Curriculum 21: Essential Education for a Changing World*, ed. H.H. Jacobs, 168–185. Alexandria, VA: ASCD.

Combs, A.W. ed. 1962. *Perceiving, Behaving, Becoming: A New Focus for Education*. Washington, DC: ASCD.

Copple, C., & S. Bredekamp, eds. 2009. *Developmentally Appropriate Practice in Early Childhood Programs Serving Young Children from Birth through Age Eight*. 3rd ed. Washington, DC: NAEYC.

Dewey, J. *The Child and the Curriculum*. Digireads.com Publishing [1899] 2010. Kindle edition.

Elkind, D. [1981] 2006. *The Hurried Child*. Cambridge, MA: Da Capo Press/Perseus Books Group.

Erikson, E.H. 1963. *Childhood and Society*. New York: W.W. Norton and Company.

Froebel, F. [1826] 1887. *Education of Man*. Trans. W.N. Hailmann. New York: D. Appleton and Company.

Galinsky, E. 2010. *Mind in the Making: The Seven Essential Life Skills Every Child Needs*. New York: HarperCollins.

Gardner, H.E. 1993a. *Frames of Mind: The Theory of Multiple Intelligences*. New York: Basic Books/Perseus Book Group.

Gardner, H.E. 1993b. *Multiple Intelligences: The Theory in Practice*. New York: Basic Books/Perseus Book Group.

Gardner, H.E. 1995. *The Unschooled Mind: How Children Think and How Schools Should Teach*. New York: Basic Books/Perseus Book Group.

Gardner, H.E. 1999. *Intelligence Reframed: Multiple Intelligences for the 21st Century*. New York: Basic Books/Perseus Book Group.

Gardner, H.E. 2006. *Multiple Intelligences: New Horizons in Theory and Practice*. New York: Basic Books.

Gardner, H.E. 2010. "Howard Gardner." Harvard University. http://pzweb.harvard.edu/pis/hg.htm.

Gardner, H.E., M. Csikszentmihalyi, & W. Damon. 2001. *Good Work: When Excellence and Ethics Meet*. New York: Basic Books/Perseus Book Group.

Gartrell, D. forthcoming. *A Guidance Approach for the Encouraging Classroom*. 6th ed. Belmont, CA: Wadsworth/Cengage Learning.

Hirsh-Pasek, K, & R.M. Golinkoff. 2011. "The Great Balancing Act: Optimizing Core Curricula through Playful Pedagogy." In *The Pre-K Debates: Current Controversies & Issues*, eds. E. Zigler, W.S. Gilliam, & W.S. Barnett, 110–116. Baltimore, MD: Paul H. Brookes Publishing.

Hofstater, R. [1944] 1992. *Social Darwinism in American Thought*. Boston: Beacon Press.

Hoghughi, M., & A.N.P. Speight. 1998. "Good Enough Parenting for All Children: A Strategy for a Healthier Society." *Archives of Disease in Childhood* 78:293–300. www.ncbi.nlm.nih.gov/pmc/articles/PMC1717536/pdf/v078p00293.pdf.

Jensen, E. 2009. *Teaching with Poverty in Mind: What Being Poor Does to Kids' Brains and What Schools Can Do About It*. Alexandria, VA: ASCD.

Katz, L.G. 1995. *Talks with Teachers of Young Children*. Norwood, NJ: Ablex Publishing.

Khadaroo, S.T. 2010. "Graduation Rate for US High-Schoolers Falls for Second Straight Year." *Christian Science Monitor*. www.csmonitor.com/USA/Education/2010/0610/Graduation-rate-for-US-high-schoolers-falls-for-second-straight-year.

Kirschenbaum, H. 1989. *Carl Rogers: Dialogs: Conversations with Martin Buber, Paul Tillich, B.F. Skinner . . . and Others*. New York: Houghton Mifflin.

Maslow, A.H. 1962. *Toward a Psychology of Being*. Princeton, NJ: D. Van Nostrand Company.

Montessori, M. [1949] 2007. *The Absorbent Mind*. Radford, VA: Wilder Publications.

Piaget , J. [1932] 1960. *The Moral Judgment of the Child*. Glencoe, IL: The Free Press.

Purkey, W.W. [1970] 2006. *Self Concept and School Achievement*. Englewood Cliffs, NJ: Prentice-Hall.

Purkey, W.W. [1978] 1996. *Inviting School Success: A Self-Concept Approach to Teaching and Learning*. Belmont, CA: Wadsworth.

Rogers, C.R. 1961. *On Becoming a Person.* Boston: Houghton Mifflin.

Rose, L.C. 2004. "No Child Left Behind: The Mathematics of Guaranteed Failure." *Educational Horizons.* 82 (2): 121–130.

Schickedanz, J.A., & D.I. Schickedanz. 1981. *Toward Understanding Children.* Boston: Little, Brown.

Winner, E. 2012. "The History of Howard Gardner." Author. Accessed July 18, www.howardgardner.com/bio/lerner_winner.htm.

Winnicott, D. 1953. "Transitional Objects and Transitional Phenomena." *International Journal of Psychoanalysis,* 34: 89–97.

Wolk, S. 2008. "Joy in School." *Educator Leadership* 66 (1): 8–14.

World Corporal Punishment Research. 2010. "Corporal Punishment in US Schools." Author. Accessed July 18, 2012. www.corpun.com/counuss.htm.

# Chapter 4

Ainsworth, M., M. Blehar, E. Waters, & S. Wall. 1978. *Patterns of Attachment.* Hillsdale, NJ: Erlbaum.

Baker, A., & L. Manfredi/Petitt. 2004. *Relationships, the Heart of Quality Care: Creating Community Among Adults in Early Care Settings.* Washington, DC: NAEYC.

Bowlby, J. [1969] 1982. *Attachment and Loss, Vol. 1: Attachment.* New York: Basic Books.

Copple, C., & S. Bredekamp. 2009. *Developmentally Appropriate Practice in Early Childhood Programs Serving Children from Birth through Age 8.* 3rd ed. Washington, DC: NAEYC.

Cozolino, L. 2006. *The Neuroscience of Human Relationships.* New York: W.W. Norton and Company.

Davis, C., & A. Yang. 2005. *Parents and Teachers Working Together.* Turner Falls, MA: Northeast Foundation for Children.

Fisher, P., M.R. Gunnar, M. Dozier, J. Bruce, & K. Pears. 2006. "Effects of Therapeutic Interventions for Foster Children on Behavior Problems, Caregiver Attachment, and Stress Regulatory Neural Systems." *Annals of the New York Academy of Science,* 1094, 215–225.

Friedman, S.L., & D.E. Boyle. 2008. "Attachment in US Children Experiencing Nonmaternal Care in the Early 1990s." *Attachment & Human Development* 10 (3): 225–261.

Galinsky, E. 2010. *Mind in the Making: The Seven Essential Life Skills Every Child Needs.* New York: HarperCollins.

Gartrell, D. 2011a. "Reactive Aggression." *Young Children* 66 (1): 58–60.

Gartrell, D. 2011b. "Aggression, the Prequel: Preventing the Need." *Young Children* 66 (6): 62–64.

Gunnar, M.R., A. Herrera, & C.E. Hostinar. 2009. "Stress and Early Brain Development." In *Encyclopedia on Early Childhood Development* [online], eds. R.E. Tremblay, R.G. Barr, R. Peters, & M. Boivin, 1–8. Montreal, Quebec: Centre of Excellence for Early Childhood Development. www.child-encyclopedia.com/documents/Gunnar-Herrera-HostinarANGxp.pdf.

Gunnar, M., & K. Quevedo. 2007. "The Neurobiology of Stress and Development." *Annual Review of Psychology* 58:145–173.

Hoghughi, M., & A.N.P. Speight. 1998. "Good Enough Parenting for All Children: A Strategy for a Healthier Society." *Archives of Disease in Childhood* 78: 293–300. http://www.ncbi.nlm.nih.gov/pmc/articles/PMC1717536/pdf/v078p00293.pdf.

Ladd, G.W., & L.M. Dinella. 2009. "Continuity and Change in Early School Engagement: Predictive of Children's Achievement Trajectories from First to Eighth Grade?" *Journal of Educational Psychology* 101 (1): 190–206.

Ladd, G.W., & I. Ettekal. 2009. "Classroom Peer Acceptance and Rejection and Children's Psychological and School Adjustment." *Interpersonal Acceptance* 3 (1): 1–3.

LeDoux, J. 1996. *The Emotional Brain.* New York: Simon and Schuster.

Lowenthal, B. 1999. "Effects of Maltreatment and Ways to Promote Children's Resiliency." *Young Children* 75 (4): 204–209.

Lubit, R.H. 2010. "Post-Traumatic Stress Disorder in Children." http://emedicine.medscape.com/article/918844-overview.

Main, M., & J. Solomon. 1986. "Discovery of an Insecure-Disorganized/Disoriented Attachment Pattern: Procedures, Findings and Implications for the Classification of Behavior." In *Affective Development in Infancy,* eds. T.B. Brazelton & M. Yogman, 95–124. Norwood, NJ: Ablex.

Ostrowsky, M.M., & E.Y. Jung. "Building Positive Teacher-Child Relationships." Center on the Social and Emotional Foundations for Early Learning. Accessed July 23, 2012. http://csefel.vanderbilt.edu/briefs/wwb12.pdf.

Reineke, J., K. Sonsteng, & D. Gartrell. 2008. "Nurturing Mastery Motivation: No Need for Rewards." *Young Children* 63 (6): 89–97.

Shonkoff, J. P., & A.S. Garner. 2012. "The Lifelong Effects of Early Childhood Adversity and Toxic Stress." *Pediatrics* 129 (1): 232–246. http://pediatrics.aappublications.org/content/early/2011/12/21/peds.2011-2663.full.pdf.

Shonkoff, J.P., & D.A. Phillips, eds. 2000. *From Neurons to Neighborhoods: The Science of Childhood Development.* Washington, DC: National Academies Press.

Siegel, D. 2001. *The Developing Mind.* New York: Guilford.

Sousa, D.A. 2011. *How the Brain Learns.* Thousand Oaks, CA: Corwin.

Vygotsky, L.S. [1930–35] 1978. *Mind in Society: The Development of Higher Psychological Processes.* Ed. and trans. M. Cole, V. John-Steiner, S. Scribner, & E. Souberman. Cambridge, MA: Harvard University Press.

Warren, R. 1977. *Caring, Supporting Children's Growth.* Washington, DC: NAEYC.

# Chapter 5

Barnett, W.S. 1995. "Long-Term Effects of Early Childhood Programs on Cognitive and School Outcomes." *The Future of Children Project* 5 (3): 25–50. www.princeton.edu/futureofchildren/publications/docs/05_03_01.pdf.

Barton, P.E., & R.J. Coley. 2009. "Those Persistent Gaps." *Educational Leadership* 67 (4): 18–23.

Boyd-Zaharias, J., & H. Pate-Bain. 2008. "Class Matters—In and Out of School." *Phi Delta Kappan,* 90 (1): 40–44.

Cohen, P. 2010. " 'Culture of Poverty' Makes a Comeback." *New York Times,* October 17. www.nytimes.com/2010/10/18/us/18poverty.html?pagewanted=all.

Copple, C. ed. 2012. *Growing Minds: Building Strong Cognitive Foundations in Early Childhood.* Washington, DC: NAEYC.

Copple, C., & S. Bredekamp. 2006. *Basics of Developmentally Appropriate Practice: An Introduction for Teachers of Children 3 to 6.* Washington, DC: NAEYC.

Daggett, W.R. "Successful Schools: From Research to Action Plans." Paper presented at the Model Schools Conference, Nashville, TN, June 2005. http://www.leadered.com/pdf/Successful%20 Schools%206-05.pdf.

Diefendorf, M., & S. Goode, eds. 2005. *The Long Term Economic Benefits of High Quality Early Childhood Intervention Programs.* Chapel Hill, NC: National Early Childhood Technical Assistance Center (NECTAC) Clearinghouse on Early Intervention and Early Childhood Special Education. www.nectac.org/~pdfs/pubs/econbene.pdf.

Finn-Stevenson, M., & E. Zigler. 1999. *Schools of the 21st Century: Linking Child Care and Education.* New York: Random House Publishing/Trade Paperbacks.

Goodman, P. 1966. *Compulsory Mis-Education and the Community of Scholars.* New York: Random House.

Harlem Children's Zone. 2009. "Promise Academy Charter Schools: Going Beyond the Walls of the Classroom." Author. Accessed July 22, 2012. http://www.hcz.org/programs/promise-academy-charter-schools.

Hyson, M. 2012. "Becoming Enthusiastic and Engaged." In *Growing Minds: Building Strong Cognitive Foundations in Early Childhood*, ed. C. Copple, 41–61. Washington, DC: NAEYC.

Jensen, E. 2009. *Teaching with Poverty in Mind: What Being Poor Does to Kids' Brains and What Schools Can Do About It.* Alexandria, VA: ASCD.

Kohl, H. 1967. *36 Children.* New York: New American Library.

Kozol, J. 1967. *Death at an Early Age: The Destruction of the Hearts and Minds of Negro Children in the Boston Public Schools.* Boston: Houghton Mifflin Harcourt.

Kozol, J. 1991. *Savage Inequalities: Children in America's Schools.* New York: Random House.

National Head Start Association. 2012. "NHSA History." Author. www.nhsa.org/about_nhsa/nhsa_history.

Promising Practices Network. 2011a. "The Abecedarian Project." Author. www.promisingpractices.net/program.asp?programid=132.

Promising Practices Network. 2011b. "Child-Parent Centers." Author. www.promisingpractices.net/program.asp?programid=98.

Promising Practices Network. 2011c. "HighScope Perry Preschool Program." Author. www.promisingpractices.net/program.asp?programid=128.

Public Policy Forum. 2008. "Research on Early Childhood Education Outcomes."
Author. www.publicpolicyforum.org/Matrix.htm.

RAND Corporation. 2005. "Proven Benefits of Early Childhood Interventions: Labor and Population
Research Brief." Excerpted from *Early Childhood Interventions: Proven Results, Future Promise*,
L.A.Karoly, M.R.Kilburn, & J.S. Cannon. Santa Monica, CA: RAND Corporation. www.rand.org/
content/dam/rand/pubs/research_briefs/2005/RAND_RB9145.pdf.

Reineke, J., K. Sonsteng, & D. Gartrell. 2008. "Nurturing Mastery Motivation: No Need for Rewards."
*Young Children* 63 (6): 89–97.

Rogers, C.R. 1962. "The Interpersonal Relationship: The Core of Guidance." *Harvard Educational
Review* 32 (4): 416–429.

Rose, L.C. 2004. "No Child Left Behind: The Mathematics of Guaranteed Failure." *Educational Horizons* 82 (2): 121–130.

Siegel, D. 2001. *The Developing Mind.* New York: Guilford.

Tough, P. 2008. *Whatever It Takes: Geoffrey Canada's Quest to Change Harlem and America.* New
York: Houghton Mifflin Harcourt.

## Chapter 6

Crawford, P.A., & V. Zygouris-Coe. 2006. "All in the Family: Connecting Home and School with
Family Literacy." *Early Childhood Education Journal* 33 (4): 261–267.

Gartrell, D. 2000. *What the Kids Said Today: Using Conversations with Children to Become a Better
Teacher.* St. Paul, MN: Redleaf Press.

Gartrell, D. 2004. *The Power of Guidance: Teaching Social-Emotional Skills in Early Childhood Classrooms.* Washington, DC: NAEYC/Cengage Learning.

Gartrell, D. 2011. *A Guidance Approach for the Encouraging Classroom.* 5th ed. Belmont, CA: Wad-
sworth/Cengage Learning.

Gartrell, D. 2012. "'Goodest' Guidance: Teachers and Families Together." Guidance Matters. *Young
Children* 67 (3) 66–68.

Genishi, C., & A.H. Dyson. 2009. *Children, language, and literacy.* New York: Teachers College Press,
Columbia University.

Gestwicki, C. 2013. *Home, School and Community Relations.* 8th ed. Belmont, CA: Wadsworth/
Cengage Learning.

Gonzalez-Mena, J. 2006. *Diversity in Early Care and Education: Honoring Differences.* Boston:
McGraw-Hill.

Gonzalez-Mena, J. 2008. *50 Strategies for Communicating and Working with Diverse Families.* Boston:
Pearson.

Gonzalez, N., L.C. Moll, & C. Amanti, eds. 2005. *Funds of Knowledge: Theorizing Practices in Households and Classrooms.* Hillsdale, NJ: Lawrence Erlbaum Associates.

Halgunseth, L.C., A. Peterson, D.R. Stark, & S. Moodie. 2009. *Family Engagement, Diverse Families,
and Early Childhood Education Programs: An Integrated Review of the Literature.* Washington, DC:
NAEYC and the Pew Charitable Trusts.

Hymes, J.L. [1953] 1974. *Effective Home-School Relations.* Sierra Madre, CA: Southern California Association for the Education of Young Children.

Kersey, K.C., & M.L. Masterson. 2009. "Teachers Connecting with Families—In the Best Interest of
Children." *Young Children* 64 (6): 34–38.

Locke, B. 1919, July. "Manufacturers Indorse [sic] the Kindergarten." *Kindergarten Circular* 4. Washington, DC: Department of the Interior, Bureau of Education.

Marian, V., Y. Faroqui-Shah, M. Kaushanskaya, H.K. Blemenfeld, & S. Li. 2009. "Bilingualism: Consequences for Language, Cognition, Development, and the Brain." *The Asha Leader.* www.asha.org/
Publications/leader/2009/091013/f091013a.htm.

NAEYC. 2009. "Developmentally Appropriate Practice in Early Childhood Programs Serving Children from Birth through Age 8." Position statement. Washington, DC: Author. www.naeyc.org/
positionstatments/dap.

Nemeth, K. 2012. "Enhancing Practice with Infants and Toddlers from Diverse Language and Cultural Backgrounds." *Young Children* 67 (4): 49–57.

Pappano, L. 2007. "Meeting of the Minds." *Harvard Education Letter* 23 (4): 1–3.

Shin, H.B.., & Kominksi, R.A. 2010. *Language Use in the United States: 2007.* American Community
Survey Reports, United States Census Bureau.

# Chapter 7

Copple, C., & S. Bredekamp, eds. 2009. *Developmentally Appropriate Practice in Early Childhood Programs Serving Children from Birth through Age 8.* 3rd ed. Washington, DC: NAEYC.

Combs, A.W., & D.M. Gonzales. 2008. *Helping Relationships: Basic Concepts for the Helping Professions.* Boston: Allyn &Bacon.

Department of Natural Resources. 2003. "Managing for Results." http://files.dnr.state.mn.us/aboutdnr/budget/budgetpres0303.pdf.

Dewey, J. [1916] 1997. *Democracy and Education: An Introduction to the Philosophy of Education.* New York: Free Press.

Elkind, D. 2006. *Miseducation: Preschoolers at Risk.* New York: Knopf.

Galinsky, E. 2010. *Mind in the Making: The Seven Essential Life Skills Every Child Needs.* New York: HarperCollins.

HighScope Educational Research Foundation. 2003. *Preschool Child Observation Record* (COR). 2nd ed. Ypsilanti, MI: HighScope Press.

Hyson, M. 2008. *Enthusiastic and Engaged Learners: Approaches to Learning in the Early Childhood Classroom.* New York: Teachers College Press; Washington DC: NAEYC.

Jacobs, H.H. 2010. *Curriculum 21: Essential Education for a Changing World.* Alexandria, VA: ASCD.

Kagan, S.L., E. Moore, & S. Bredekamp, eds. 1995. *Reconsidering Children's Early Development and Learning: Toward Common Views and Vocabulary.* National Education Goals Panel, Goal 1 Technical Planning Group on Readiness for School. Washington, DC: US Government Printing Office. www.negp.gov/reports/child-ea.htm.

Minnesota Department of Natural Resources. 2008. "Lakes, Rivers, and Wetlands Facts." www.dnr.state.mn.us/faq/mnfacts/water.html.

NAEYC. 2009. "Developmentally Appropriate Practice in Early Childhood Programs Serving from Children Birth through Age 8." Position statement. Washington, DC: Author. www.naeyc.org/positionstatements/dap.

Reineke, J., K. Sonsteng, & D. Gartrell. 2008. "Nurturing Mastery Motivation: No Need for Rewards." *Young Children,* 63 (6): 89–97.

Rogers, C.R. 1962. "The Interpersonal Relationship: The Core of Guidance." *Harvard Educational Review* 32 (4): 416–429.

Rose, L.C. 2004. "No Child Left Behind: The Mathematics of Guaranteed Failure." *Educational Horizons* 82 (2): 121–130.

Smilkstein, R. 2011. *We're Born to Learn: Using the Brain's Natural Learning Process to Create Today's Curriculum.* New York: Corwin.

Thomas, D., & J. Seely Brown. 2011. *A New Culture of Learning: Cultivating the Imagination for a World of Constant Change.* Self-published. Printed by CreateSpace.


# Chapter 8

Charles, C.M. 2005. *Building Classroom Discipline.* New York: Longman.

Copple, C., & S. Bredekamp, eds. 2009. *Developmentally Appropriate Practice in Early Childhood Programs Serving Children from Birth through Age 8.* 3rd ed. Washington, DC: NAEYC.

DeVries, R., & B. Zan. 2003. "When Children Make Rules." *Educational Leadership* 61 (1): 22–29.

Dreikurs, R. 1968. *Psychology in the Classroom.* 2nd ed. New York: Harper and Row Publishers.

Ettekal, I., & G.W. Ladd. 2009. "The Stability of Aggressive Behavior toward Peers as a Predictor of Externalizing Problems from Childhood through Adolescence." In *Handbook of Aggressive Behavior Research,* eds. C. Quin & S. Tawse. Hauppauge, NY: Nova Science Publishers, 115–147.

Gartrell, D. 2004. *The Power of Guidance: Teaching Social-Emotional Skills in Early Childhood Classrooms.* Washington, DC: NAEYC/Cengage Learning.

Gartrell, D. 2006. "The Beauty of Class Meetings." Guidance Matters. *Young Children* 61 (6): 54–55.

Gartrell, D. 2007. "'You Really Worked Hard on Your Picture!' Guiding with Encouragement." Guidance Matters. *Young Children* 62 (3): 1–4.

Gartrell, D. 2010. "Beyond Rules to Guidelines." *Exchange* (July/August): 52–56.

Gartrell, D. 2011. *A Guidance Approach for the Encouraging Classroom.* 5th ed. Belmont, CA: Wadsworth/Cengage Learning.

Gartrell, D. 2012. "From Rules to Guidelines: Moving to the Positive." *Young Children* 67 (1): 56–58.

Ginott, H. 1972. *Teacher and Child.* New York: Avon Books.

Glasser, W. 1969. *Schools without Failure*. New York: Harper and Row.

Harris, T.T., & J.D. Fuqua. 2000. "What Goes Around Comes Around: Building a Community of Learners through Circle Times." *Young Children 55* (1): 44–47.

Hitz, R., & A. Driscoll. 1988. "Praise or Encouragement? New Insights into Praise: Implications for Early Childhood Teachers." *Young Children 43* (5): 6–13.

Kelly, F.D., & J.G. Daniels. 1997. "The Effects of Praise versus Encouragement on Children's Perceptions of Teachers." *The Journal of Individual Psychology* 53: 1–11.

Kohn, A. 1993. *Punished by Rewards: The Trouble with Gold Stars, Incentive Plans, A's, Praise, and Other Bribes*. New York: Houghton Mifflin.

Ladd, G.W. 2008. "Social Competence and Peer Relations: Significance for Young Children and Their Service Providers." *Early Childhood Services* 2 (3): 129–148.

McClurg, L.G. 1998. "Building an Ethical Community in the Classroom: Community Meeting." *Young Children 53* (2): 30–35.

NAEYC. 2009. "Developmentally Appropriate Practice in Early Childhood Programs Serving Children Birth through Age 8." Position statement. Washington, DC: Author. www.naeyc.org/positionstatements/dap.

Piaget, J. [1932] 1960. *The Moral Judgment of the Child*. Glencoe, IL: The Free Press.

Readdick, C.A., & P.L. Chapman. 2000. "Young Children's Perceptions of Time Out." *Journal of Research in Childhood Education* 15 (1): 81–87.

Reineke, J., K. Sonsteng, & D. Gartrell. 2008. "Nurturing Mastery Motivation: No Need for Rewards." *Young Children* 63 (6): 89–97.

Vance, E., & P.J. Weaver. 2002. *Class Meetings: Young Children Solving Problems Together*. Washington, DC: NAEYC.

Watson, M. 2003. "Attachment Theory and Challenging Behaviors: Reconstructing the Nature of Relationships." *Young Children* 58 (4): 12–20.

Wien, C.A. 2004. "From Policy to Participation: Overturning the Rules and Creating Amiable Classrooms." *Young Children 59* (1): 34–40.

Wolfgang, C.H. 1999. *Solving Discipline Problems*. New York: John Wiley & Sons.

# Chapter 9

Copple, C., & S. Bredekamp, eds. 2009. *Developmentally Appropriate Practice in Early Childhood Programs Serving Children from Birth through Age 8*. 3rd ed. Washington, DC: NAEYC.

Cozolino, L. 2006. *The Neuroscience of Human Relationships*. New York: W.W. Norton.

Dodge, K.A. 1991. "The Structure and Function of Reactive and Proactive Aggression." In *The Development and Treatment of Childhood Aggression,* eds. D.J Pepler & K.H. Rubin, 201–218. Hillsdale, NJ: Erlbaum.

Galinsky, E. 2010. *Mind in the Making: The Seven Essential Life Skills Every Child Needs*. New York: HarperCollins.

Gartrell, D. 1987. "More Thoughts. Punishment or Guidance?" *Young Children* 42 (3): 55–61.

Gartrell, D. 2004. *The Power of Guidance: Teaching Social-Emotional Skills in Early Childhood Classrooms*. Clifton Park, NY/Washington, DC: Thomson Delmar Learning/NAEYC.

Gartrell, D. 2006a. "Conflict Mediation." Guidance Matters. *Young Children* 61 (2): 88–89.

Gartrell, D. 2006b. Guidance Matters. *Young Children* 61 (1): 105–106.

Gartrell, D. 2008. "Comprehensive Guidance." *Young Children*, 63 (1): 44–45.

Gartrell, D. 2011a. "Aggression, the Prequel: Preventing the Need." Guidance Matters. *Young Children* 66 (6): 62–64.

Gartrell, D. 2011b. *A Guidance Approach for the Encouraging Classroom*. 5th ed. Belmont, CA: Wadsworth/Cengage Learning.

Gartrell, D. 2011c. "Children Who Have Serious Conflicts: Part One, Reactive Aggression." Guidance Matters. *Young Children,* 66 (1): 58–60.

Gartrell, D. 2011d. "Children Who Have Serious Conflicts: Part Two, Instrumental Aggression." Guidance Matters. *Young Children* 66 (4): 60–62.

Gartrell, D. 2011e. "Handout 1: The Individual Guidance Plan." *NEXT for TYC: An NAEYC Professional Development Source* 4 (3).

Gilliam, W.S. 2005. "Prekindergarteners Left Behind: Expulsion Rates in State Prekindergarten Systems." FCD Policy Brief Series 3. New York: Foundation for Child Development. www.challenging-behavior.org/explore/policy_docs/prek_expulsion.pdf.

Gunnar, M.R., A. Herrera, & C.E. Hostinar. 2009. "Stress and Early Brain Development." In *Encyclopedia on Early Childhood Development* [online], eds. R.E. Tremblay, R.G. Barr, R. Peters, & M. Boivin, 1–8. Montreal, Quebec: Centre of Excellence for Early Childhood Development. www.child-encyclopedia.com/documents/Gunnar-Herrera-HostinarANGxp.pdf.

Kaiser, B., & J. Sklar-Rasminsky, J. 2012. *Challenging Behavior in Young Children.* 3rd ed. Boston: Allyn & Bacon.

Ladd, G.W., & L.M. Dinella. 2009. "Continuity and Change in Early School Engagement: Predictive of Children's Achievement Trajectories from First to Eighth Grade?" *Journal of Educational Psychology* 101: 190–206.

Ladd, G.W., & Ettekal, I. 2009. "Classroom Peer Acceptance and Rejection and Children's Psychological and School Adjustment." *Interpersonal Acceptance* 3 (1): 1–3.

*Merriam-Webster Online*, sv "punishment," accessed August 1, 2012, www.merriam-webster.com/dictionary/punishment.

Nansel, T.R., M. Overpeck, R.S. Pilla, W.J. Ruan, B. Simons-Morton, & P. Scheidt. 2001. "Bullying Behaviors Among U.S. Youth: Prevalence and Association with Psychosocial Adjustment." *Journal of the American Medical Association* 285 (16): 2094–2100.

Ostrowsky, M.M., & E.Y. Jung. "Building Positive Teacher-Child Relationships." Center on the Social and Emotional Foundations for Early Learning. Accessed July 23, 2012. http://csefel.vanderbilt.edu/briefs/wwwb12.pdf.

Readdick, C.A., & P.L. Chapman. 2000. "Young Children's Perceptions of Time Out." *Journal of Research in Childhood Education* 15 (1): 81–87.

Reynolds, E. 2006. *Guiding Young Children.* Mountain View, CA: Mayfield Publishing Company.

Surgeon General. 1999. *Surgeon General's Report on Violence.* Washington, DC: Department of Health and Human Services.

# Chapter 10

Carlson, F.M. 2006. *Essential Touch: Meeting the Needs of Young Children.* Washington, DC: NAEYC.

Carlson, F.M. 2011. *Big Body Play: Why Boisterous, Vigorous, and Very Physical Play Is Essential to Children's Development and Learning.* Washington, DC: NAEYC.

Copple, C., & S. Bredekamp, eds. 2009. *Developmentally Appropriate Practice in Early Childhood Programs Serving Children from Birth through Age 8.* 3rd ed. Washington, DC: NAEYC.

Cozolino, L. 2006. *The Neuroscience of Human Relationships.* New York: W.W. Norton.

Curwin, R.L., & A.N. Mendler. 1988. *Discipline with Dignity.* Alexandria, VA: ASCD.

Gartrell, D. 2006. "Boys and Men Teachers." Guidance Matters. *Young Children* 61 (3): 92–93.

Gartrell, D. 2007. "'You Really Worked Hard on Your Picture!' Guiding with Encouragement." Guidance Matters. *Young Children* 62 (3): 58–59.

Gartrell, D. 2008. "Promoting Physical Activity: It's Proactive Guidance." Guidance Matters. *Young Children* 63 (2): 51–53.

Gartrell, D. 2011. *A Guidance Approach for the Encouraging Classroom.* 5th ed. Belmont, CA: Wadsworth/Cengage Learning.

Gilliam, W.S. 2005. "Prekindergarteners Left Behind: Expulsion Rates in State Prekindergarten Systems." FCD Policy Brief Series 3. New York: Foundation for Child Development. www.challenging-behavior.org/explore/policy_docs/prek_expulsion.pdf.

Goffman, E. 1963. *Stigma: Notes on the Management of Spoiled Identity.* Englewood Cliffs, NJ: Prentice-Hall.

Gurian, M., & K. Stevens. 2004. "Closing Achievement Gaps: With Boys and Girls in Mind." *Educational Leadership* 62 (3): 21–26.

Hendrick, J. 2001. *The Whole Child.* Englewood Cliffs, NJ: Merrill/Prentice Hall.

Johnson, S.P. 2008. "The Status of Male Teachers in Public Education Today." *Education Policy Brief* 6 (4): 1–5, 8–11.

Kindlon, D., & M. Thompson. 1999. *Raising Cain: Protecting the Emotional Lives of Boys.* New York: Ballantine Books.

King, M. 2004. "Guidance with Boys in Early Childhood Classrooms." In *The Power of Guidance: Teaching Social-Emotional Skills in Early Childhood Classrooms*, D. Gartrell, 106–124. Washington, DC: NAEYC/Cengage Learning.

NAEYC. 2007. *NAEYC Early Childhood Program Standards and Accreditation Criteria: The Mark of Quality in Early Childhood Education*. Washington, DC: Author.

NAEYC. 2009. "Developmentally Appropriate Practice in Early Childhood Programs Serving Children from Birth through Age 8." Position statement. Washington, DC: Author. www.naeyc.org/positionstatements/dap.

Nelson, B.G. 2002. *The Importance of Men Teachers and Why There Are So Few*. Minneapolis, MN: Men in Child Care and Elementary Education Project. www.menteach.org.

Nelson, B.G., & S.J. Shikwambi. 2010. "Men in Your Teacher-Preparation Program: Five Strategies to Recruit and Retain Them." *Young Children* 65 (3): 36–41.

Neu, T.W., & R. Weinfeld. 2007. *Helping Boys Succeed in School: A Practical Guide for Parents and Teachers*. Waco, TX: Prufrock Press.

Newberger, J.J. 1997. "New Brain Development Research—A Wonderful Window of Opportunity to Build Public Support for Early Childhood Education." *Young Children* 52 (4): 4–9.

Paley, V.G. 1993. *You Can't Say You Can't Play*. Cambridge, MA: Harvard University Press.

Polce-Lynch, M. 2002. *Boy Talk: How You Can Help Your Son Express His Emotions*. Oakland, CA: New Harbinger Publications.

Pollack, W. 2001. *Real Boys Workbook: The Definitive Guide to Understanding and Interacting with Boys of All Ages*. New York: Villard Books.

Sousa, D.A. 2011. *How the Brain Learns*. Thousand Oaks, CA: Corwin.

Watson, M. 2003. "Attachment Theory and Challenging Behaviors: Reconstructing the Nature of Relationships." *Young Children* 58 (4): 12–20.

Webb, L.D., A. Metha. & K.F. Jordan. 2007. *Foundations of American Education*. Upper Saddle River, NJ: Merrill.

York, S. 2003. *Roots and Wings: Affirming Culture in Early Childhood Programs*. St. Paul, MN: Redleaf Press.

## Chapter 11

Gartrell, D. 2011. *A Guidance Approach for the Encouraging Classroom*. 5th ed. Belmont, CA: Wadsworth/Cengage.

## Chapter 12

Ainsworth, M., M. Blehar, E. Waters, & S. Wall. 1978. *Patterns of Attachment*. Hillsdale, NJ: Erlbaum.

Ettekal, I., & G.W. Ladd. 2009. "The Stability of Aggressive Behavior toward Peers as a Predictor of Externalizing Problems from Childhood through Adolescence." In *Handbook of Aggressive Behavior Research*, eds. C. Quinn & S. Tawse, 115–147. Hauppauge, NY: Nova Science Publishers.

Gartrell, D. 2000. *What the Kids Said Today: Using Classroom Conversations to Become a Better Teacher*. St. Paul, MN: Redleaf Press.

Gartrell, D. 2011. "Aggression, the Prequel: Preventing the Need." Guidance Matters. *Young Children* 66 (6): 62–64.

Gestwicki, C. 2013. *Home, School, and Community Relations*. 8th ed. Belmont, CA: Wadsworth/Cengage Learning.

Gunnar M.R., A. Herrera, & C.E. Hostinar. 2009. "Stress and Early Brain Development." In *Encyclopedia on Early Childhood Development* [online], eds. R.E. Tremblay, R.G. Barr, R. Peters, & M. Boivin, 1–8. Montreal, Quebec: Centre of Excellence for Early Childhood Development. www.child-encyclopedia.com/documents/Gunnar-Herrera-HostinarANGxp.pdf.

Ladd, G.W., & Ettekal, I. 2009. "Classroom Peer Acceptance and Rejection and Children's Psychological and School Adjustment." *Interpersonal Acceptance* 3 (1): 1–3.

Lowenthal, B. 1999. "Effects of Maltreatment and Ways to Promote Children's Resiliency." *Young Children* 75 (4): 204–209.

NAEYC. 2007. *NAEYC Early Childhood Program Standards and Accreditation Criteria: The Mark of Quality in Early Childhood Education*. Washington, DC: Author.

Education for a Civil Society

Shonkoff, J.P., & A.S. Garner. 2011. "The Lifelong Effects of Early Childhood Adversity and Toxic Stress." *Pediatrics* 129 (1): 232–47. http://pediatrics.aappublications.org/content/early/2011/12/21/peds.2011-2663.full.pdf.


## Chapter 13

Ansbacher, H.L., & R.R. Ansbacher, eds. 1956. *The Individual Psychology of Alfred Adler: A Systematic Presentation in Selections from His Writings.* New York: Basic Books.

Blair, C. 2002. "School Readiness: Integrating Cognition and Emotion in a Neurobiological Conceptualization of Children's Functioning at School Entry." *American Psychologist* 57 (2): 111–127.

Blair, C., & A. Diamond. 2008. "Biological Processes in Prevention and Intervention: The Promotion of Self-Regulation as a Means of Preventing School Failure." *Development and Psychotherapy* 20 (3): 899–911.

Bodrova, E., & D.L. Leong. 2007. *Tools of the Mind: The Vygotskian Approach to Early Childhood Education.* 2nd ed. Upper Saddle River, NJ: Merrill/Prentice Hall.

Elliot, R. 2003. "Executive Functions and Their Disorders." *British Medical Bulletin* 65 (1): 49–59.

Florez, I.R. 2011. "Developing Young Children's Self-Regulation through Everyday Experiences." *Young Children* 66 (4): 46–51.

Froebel, F. [1826] 1887. *Education of Man.* Trans. W.N. Hailmann. New York: D. Appleton and Company.

Galinsky, E. 2010. *Mind in the Making: The Seven Essential Life Skills Every Child Needs.* New York: HarperCollins.

Gartrell, D. 2011a. "Children Who Have Serious Conflicts, Part 1: Reactive Aggression." *Young Children* 66 (2): 58–60.

Gartrell, D. 2011b. *A Guidance Approach for the Encouraging Classroom.* 5th ed. Belmont, CA: Wadsworth/Cengage Learning.

Greenberg, P. 1988. "Avoiding 'Me against You' Discipline." *Young Children* 43 (1): 24–25.

Gunnar M.R., A. Herrera, & C.E. Hostinar. 2009. "Stress and Early Brain Development." In *Encyclopedia on Early Childhood Development* [online], eds. R.E. Tremblay, R.G. Barr, R. Peters, & M. Boivin, 1 8. Montreal, Quebec: Centre of Excellence for Early Childhood Development. www.child-encyclopedia.com/documents/Gunnar-Herrera-HostinarANGxp.pdf.

Lowenthal, B. 1999. "Effects of Maltreatment and Ways to Promote Children's Resiliency." *Childhood Education* 75 (4): 204–209.

Lubit, R. 2006. "Posttraumatic Stress Disorder in Children." Last modified April 20, 2011. www.emedicine.com/ped/topic3026.htm.

Readdick, C.A., & P.L. Chapman. 2000. "Young Children's Perceptions of Time Out." *Journal of Research in Childhood Education* 15 (1): 81–87.

Shonkoff, J.P., & A.S. Garner. 2012. "The Lifelong Effects of Early Childhood Adversity and Toxic Stress." *Pediatrics* 129 (1): 232–246.
http://pediatrics.aappublications.org/content/early/2011/12/21/peds.2011-2663.full.pdf.

Weber, N. 1987. "Patience or Understanding." *Young Children* 42 (3): 52–54.


## Chapter 14

Copple, C., & S. Bredekamp, eds. 2009. *Developmentally Appropriate Practices in Early Childhood Programs Serving Children from Birth through Age 8.* 3rd ed. Washington, DC: NAEYC.

Gartrell, D. 2000. *What the Kids Said Today: Using Classroom Conversations to Become a Better Teacher.* St. Paul, MN: Redleaf Press.

Gartrell, D. 2011. *A Guidance Approach for the Encouraging Classroom.* 5th ed. Belmont, CA: Wadsworth/Cengage Learning.

Honig, A.S. 2007. "Play: Ten Power Boosts for Children's Early Learning." *Young Children* 62 (5): 72–78.

Jensen, E. 2009. *Teaching with Poverty in Mind: What Being Poor Does to Kids' Brains and What Schools Can Do about It.* Alexandria, VA: ASCD.

Lehrer, J. 2012. *Imagine: How Creativity Works.* Boston, MA: Houghton Mifflin, Harcourt.

Maslow, A.H. 1962. *Toward a Psychology of Being.* Princeton, NJ: D. Van Nostrand Company.

Reineke, J., K. Sonsteng, & D.J.Gartrell. 2008. "Nurturing Mastery Motivation: No Need for Rewards." *Young Children* 63 (6): 89–97.

Smilkstein, R. 2011. *We're Born to Learn: Using the Brain's Natural Learning Process to Create Today's Curriculum.* 2nd ed. New York: Corwin.

Thomas, D. & J. Seely Brown. 2011. *A New Culture of Learning: Cultivating the Imagination for a World of Constant Change.* Self-published. Printed by CreateSpace.

Vygotsky, L.S. [1930–35] 1978. *Mind in Society: The Development of Higher Psychological Processes.* Ed. and trans. M. Cole, V. John-Steiner, S. Scribner, & E. Souberman. Cambridge, MA: Harvard University Press.

## Chapter 15

Carlson, F.M. 2011. *Big Body Play: Why Boisterous, Vigorous, and Very Physical Play Is Essential to Children's Development and Learning.* Washington, DC: NAEYC.

Derman-Sparks, L., & J. Olsen Edwards. 2010. *Anti-Bias Education for Young Children and Ourselves.* Washington, DC: NAEYC.

Galinsky, E. 2010. *Mind in the Making: The Seven Essential Life Skills Every Child Needs.* New York: HarperCollins.

Gartrell, D. 2000. *What the Kids Said Today: Using Classroom Conversations to Become a Better Teacher.* St. Paul, MN: Redleaf Press.

Gartrell, D. 2011. *A Guidance Approach for the Encouraging Classroom.* 5th ed. Belmont, CA: Wadsworth/Cengage Learning.

Gartrell, D., & K. Sonsteng. 2008. "Guidance Matters, Promote Physical Activity—It's Proactive Guidance." *Young Children* 63 (2): 51–53.

Gilliam, W.S. 2005. "Prekindergarteners Left Behind: Expulsion Rates in State Prekindergarten Systems." New Haven, CT: Yale University Child Study Center.

Katz, P., & J.A. Kofkin. 1997. "Race, Gender, and Young Children." In *Developmental Perspectives on Risk and Pathology,* eds. S. Luthar, J. Burack, D. Cicchetti, & J. Wisz, 51–74. New York: Cambridge University Press.

King, M. 2004. "Guidance with Boys in Early Childhood Classrooms." In *The Power of Guidance: Teaching Social-Emotional Skills in Early Childhood Classrooms,* ed. D. Gartrell, 106–124. Clifton Park, NY: Delmar; Washington, DC: NAEYC.

Ladd, G.W. 2006. "Peer Rejection, Aggressive or Withdrawn Behavior, and Psychological Maladjustment from Ages 5 to 12: An Examination of Four Predictive Models." *Child Development* 77 (4): 822–846.

Mullins, A. 2009. "Single-Sex Schools Can Improve Education." In *Education: Opposing viewpoints,* eds. D. Haugen & S. Musser, 120–128. Detroit, MI: Greenhaven Press.

Nelson, B.G., & S.J. Shikwambi. 2010. "Men in Your Teacher Preparation Program: Five Strategies to Recruit and Retain Them." *Young Children* 65 (3): 36–40. www.naeyc.org/files/yc/file/201005/YCNelsonOnline0510.pdf.

York, S. 2003. *Roots and Wings: Affirming Culture in Early Childhood Classrooms.* Rev ed. St. Paul, MN: Redleaf Press.

## Chapter 16

Cozolino, L. 2006. *The Neuroscience of Human Relationships.* New York: W.W. Norton and Company.

Froebel, F. [1826] 1887. *Education of Man.* Trans.W.N. Hailmann. New York: D. Appleton and Company.

Galinsky, E. 2010. *Mind in the Making: The Seven Essential Life Skills Every Child Needs.* New York: HarperCollins.

Gartrell, D. 2008. "Guidance Matters. Comprehensive Guidance." *Young Children* 63 (1): 44–45.

Gartrell, D. 2011. *A Guidance Approach for the Encouraging Classroom.* 5th ed. Belmont, CA: Wadsworth/Cengage Learning.

Public Policy Forum. 2008. "Research on Early Childhood Education Outcomes." Accessed August 9, 2012. www.publicpolicyforum.org/Matrix.htm.

RAND Corporation. 2005. "Proven Benefits of Early Childhood Interventions: Labor and Population Research Brief." Excerpted from *Early Childhood Interventions: Proven Results, Future Promise*, L.A.Karoly, M.R.Kilburn, & J.S. Cannon. Santa Monica, CA: RAND Corporation. www.rand.org/content/dam/rand/pubs/research_briefs/2005/RAND_RB9145.pdf.

Sousa, D.A. 2012. *How the Brain Learns.* Thousand Oaks, CA: Corwin/SAGE Company.

York, S. 2003. *Roots and Wings: Affirming Culture in Early Childhood Classrooms.* Rev ed. St. Paul, MN: Redleaf Press.


## Chapter 17

Dodge, D., K. Burke, T. Bickart, D. Burts, L. Colker, J. Copley, J. Dighe, C. Heroman, & C. Jones. 2010. *The Creative Curriculum® for Preschool: Foundation.* 5th ed. Bethesda, MD: Teaching Strategies Inc.

Epstein, A.S., & M. Hohmann. 2012. *The HighScope Preschool Curriculum.* Ypsilanti, MI: HighScope Press.

Pianta, R.C., K.M. La Paro, & B.K. Hamre. 2008. *Classroom Assessment Scoring System (CLASS) Manual, Pre-K.* Baltimore, MD: Brookes Publishing.